CHARLOTTE HIGGINS

Charlotte Higgins's previous books include the acclaimed *Under Another Sky* which was shortlisted for awards including the Samuel Johnson (now Baillie Gifford) prize for non-fiction. She is chief culture writer of the *Guardian*, a past winner of the Classical Association prize, and a Fellow of the Society of Antiquaries. She lives in London.

ALSO BY CHARLOTTE HIGGINS

Latin Love Lessons

It's All Greek to Me

Under Another Sky: Journeys in Roman Britain

This New Noise

CHARLOTTE HIGGINS

Red Thread

On Mazes & Labyrinths

VINTAGE

1 3 5 7 9 10 8 6 4 2

Vintage is part of the Penguin Random House group of companies
whose addresses can be found at global.penguinrandomhouse.com

First published in Vintage in 2021
First published in hardback by Jonathan Cape in 2018

penguin.co.uk/vintage

A CIP catalogue record for this book is available
from the British Library

ISBN 9781784702649

Typeset in 10.8/15.7 pt Adobe Garamond
by Integra Software Services Pvt. Ltd, Pondicherry

Printed and bound in Great Britain by Clays Ltd, Elcograf S.p.A.

The authorised representative in the EEA is Penguin Random House
Ireland, Morrison Chambers, 32 Nassau Street, Dublin D02 YH68.

Penguin Random House is committed to a sustainable future for our
business, our readers and our planet. This book is made from Forest
Stewardship Council® certified paper.

For Richard Baker

Though of old a Palace, the 'Labyrinth', of which in spite of clearing and partial reconstitution we have only today a fragment of a fragment, is discontinuous in many directions and in places artificially linked. The visitor who wishes to explore its full circuit still needs the guidance that of old was provided by Ariadne's clew.

Arthur Evans, foreword to
A Handbook to the Palace of Minos at Knossos, by John Pendlebury

Europa

There was a girl who lived by the sea. She would often wander to a meadow near the water's edge to feel the grass beneath her bare feet, the rush of salt air in her mouth. One day she saw a white bull grazing there. How beautiful he was! His sharp horns gleamed as if some master of the Renaissance had carved and polished them. The girl came cautiously towards him: he took grass from her hand and ate, his brown eyes trusting. She grew bolder and reached out to touch the soft loose pelt on his neck and chest. He let her do it. She picked flowers, wove them into circlets, twined them around his horns. She stroked his shaggy neck and felt his warm whiskery breath on her cheek. She rubbed her face against the silky coat of his broad flank. Eventually he lowered his immense weight to the ground, tucking his front legs beneath him with a clumsy, grunting manoeuvre. She lay down next to him, and he nuzzled her with his soft, damp nose. After a while she wanted to adjust his crown of flowers and so, more and more confident, she straddled his muscled neck, his brawny back, reaching forward to neaten the garland. At that moment, he began to heave himself up. The girl felt herself move with him; she clung on as he jerked to his feet, and then all of a sudden there she was – what delight – actually riding her tame bull. He ambled through the meadow onto the beach. There, still placid, he lumbered into the softly lapping water. He trod deeper. The girl laughed, and her calves cooled in the chill of seawater.

That was when the bull made an ungainly plunge and shouldered himself right into the sea. The girl felt everything change as his hooves struck free from the sand and he began to swim. There seemed a new purpose in him, a new strength. In an instant they were in the open water. The girl screamed, but there was no one to hear her. She tried to twist off his back, but she was too late: they were so far from the shore, the bull moving with such uncanny speed, that to swim back would be beyond her strength. Instead, she clung on as he moved through the water. Her pink shawl ballooned out behind her like a sail. Bizarre marine creatures surfaced and formed a grinning escort: horse-headed hippocamps and fish-tailed nereids and tritons. A flock of cupids flew above and blew her mocking kisses. When she shrieked at them to help her, they only laughed. After a while she stopped screaming. She even stopped crying. Much, much later, the bull clambered up onto an unfamiliar shore. Exhausted, disoriented, almost paralysed with terror, she slumped off his back onto the sand. Then the bull was gone and in his place a blinding, terrible light, which resolved itself into something like – but not quite like – a man. He was a god, and she did what he wanted.

Nine months later, the girl, whose name was Europa, had a baby. She named him Minos. He grew up to become the ruler of the island, which was called Crete. Like his father, Zeus, the king of the gods, Minos was famous for his lawgiving and stern justice. His land was prosperous: ninety cities grew up there, which he ruled from a magnificent palace he built at Knossos. His power stretched from the island to the edges of the mainland, and the busy seaways between.

One day Minos's wife, Pasiphaë, was inspecting the great royal cattle herds. Usually it was a task that she endured rather than enjoyed, but on this occasion her eye was caught by a new beast: a great bull, splendid and handsome, with a glow about him, almost of intelligence, that set him apart from the other creatures. She took an interest in him: she began to go to him regularly, to feed him, groom him. At first her fascination seemed like a harmless diversion. But as the weeks passed, she found herself thinking about him all the time: his power, his animal beauty, his apparently inexhaustible understanding of her loneliness. It came to be that her nights were full of the bull: she'd dream about him, imagine doing extraordinary things with him. She was horrified with herself. She tried to put him out of her mind, tried to distract herself with spinning and singing. But the bull was all she could see: the creature had completely invaded her. It was as if she'd been possessed by some god; as if she were under a curse.

She went to Daedalus, the artist whom Minos employed at his court. In secret, and with the promise of much gold, she told him what was required. Daedalus responded with sketches, a maquette, a prototype: there was no moral scruple that he could not overcome with his joy in invention. In a hidden part of his workshop he fashioned a hollow simulacrum of a cow. It was so realistic that you would think it lived and breathed – it had a heifer's velvety fur, liquid eyes that really blinked, and trembling, sensitive nostrils. When Minos was off fighting one of his interminable wars, Pasiphaë summoned up her courage; she struggled into the cow machine and, carefully operating the mechanical legs as she had been taught by Daedalus, went to the bull.

Later, she had a baby, if you could call it that. Its lower half was boy-shaped, but the neck and shoulders were those of a little black calf. His name was Asterion, but mostly he was known as the Minotaur – meaning Minos's bull. He bellowed: all babies bellow. But he never formed words. He grew fast to maturity. After a year, he was a shaggy giant. He loved the wide meadows and the pastures, the cry of the hoopoe and the shadow of the hawk on the grass as it flew for its prey. He delighted to walk among the fields of orchid, of iris, of asphodel. They should have left him to roam the secret wilds, the mountains and the high valleys. He would have come to little harm – he might even have been happy – if he had found the centaurs in their remote woodland clearings, or the nymphs of the trees and springs, or the fauns and satyrs, the other biformed creatures of nature. But he was a shame and a disgrace to the king – a bestial reminder of Pasiphaë's unnatural desires. Which meant another job for Daedalus.

The king ordered him to construct an intricate building, full of crinkles and puzzles, the design of which would utterly confound all who entered. Imagine a hopelessly tangled ball of yarn that you are trying to unsnarl, patiently guiding the thread back through and through itself: Daedalus's building was as knotted and tortuous as that messy, mazy skein. The building was called the labyrinth, and Asterion was put to live in it.

Deprived of the sky, a prisoner of Daedalus's web of paths and tunnels, his mind misted over and he grew savage. His human nature began to cloud and overwhelm his bull nature. His solace in the dark was to feast on flesh.

One day, news arrived at the palace. Minos and Pasiphaë's son Androgeon – the apple of his father's eye – had been killed in Attica, over the sea in Greece. Minos, in his grief and fury, held the people of Athens collectively responsible, and demanded an unspeakable price from the city. Once every nine years, seven boys and seven girls were to be brought to Knossos. There, the young Athenians would be locked into the labyrinth. The Minotaur would hunt them down and feed on them.

The tribute was extracted twice – though who knows whether Minos's emptiness was eased by the Minotaur's satiety. But when an Athenian ship anchored at Knossos's harbour for the third time, something was different. Most of the lot-picked youths were as abject and terrified as ever. But this time, one boy disembarked free and proud. He was a volunteer.

Unbending and ferocious as he was, Minos was moved: the more so when it became clear that the young man was Theseus, the son of King Aegeus of Athens. And so he brought him into the palace, and lavished on him the hospitality due to a prince. Minos and Pasiphaë's daughter Ariadne was summoned to wait on him. The girl, who'd rarely seen a man from outside the island, let alone one so bold and handsome, was captivated as soon as she looked at him. She burned at the touch of his hand when she gave him wine to drink; she was pale and lost for speech; she felt as if her very marrow were melting. She sensed his arrogant belief that he was not here to die, but to defeat the Minotaur. But she knew better. Without help, the man would be meat.

She began to make plans. When the whole palace was asleep, she got up. First of all, she fished out of her work basket a ball of red thread. Not any red thread: it was as tough as the strongest rope and many miles long, miraculous stuff she had filched from Daedalus long ago. This she put in her pocket. Then, stealthily, she slipped into the artist's workshop, where she had often been as a child to play with his son, Icarus. This was the wondrous studio where he made golden bowls inscribed with stories of the gods; jewels in remarkable settings destined to adorn the queen; miraculous armour for the king from which arrows and spear tips flinched uselessly. Sometimes Daedalus had made trifles for the children: dolls with wings fashioned from real feathers and wax, for example, that could actually fly.

Ariadne had been the kind of small girl who'd learned to make herself inconspicuous. That way, she had found, people said more than they meant to in front of her. Hoarding scraps and ends of knowledge had given her a fleeting sense of power as she trod again and again the repetitive paths of a princess's life – a constricted life, a life in which she felt immured. She knew, for example, not only that Daedalus had secretly made a master key to all the rooms in the palace, but where he kept it. She now crept through his workshop, past the sheaves of designs, past the prototypes of self-playing musical instruments, past the never-missing bows and arrows, the engraved swords whose points always found their enemy, the automata that really snored and breathed and turned in their sleep, and that the princess feared to wake.

Right at the back of the workshop was a cracked old wine jar, half hidden beneath a pile of wood shavings and dusty offcuts. An arm's plunge into its spidery depths was the key. She took it and fled, pausing only to take a freshly forged sword, cold and heavy in her hand. Hiding the blade in the folds of her cloak, she made her way to the labyrinth and, hardly daring to breathe, used the master key to open its heavy bronze door. Summoning all her courage, she stepped into the enfolding gloom and, careful to wedge the door open behind her so that a tiny triangle of reassuring light remained, placed the sword and the ball of thread just inside. Then she left, closing and locking the door. The next morning, as she bent to serve food and wine to Theseus, she muttered her instructions – and her price.

It was the dead of night before Theseus returned from the labyrinth. When he did, he was spattered in blood, drained, barely functioning. A line of Athenian girls and boys followed, clutching each other's hands and looking exhausted and terrified. Ariadne was waiting. She hustled them to the Athenian ship, out of sight of the complacent, drowsing palace guards. The crew hurried about their tasks, and they were soon out on the open sea. Everything that Ariadne had grown up with was vanishing into the horizon. Everything that lay behind her, she had betrayed. And here she was, at last, with this beautiful boy, this boy admittedly still grey-faced and silent, this boy who was going to make her his wife. They set a course for Athens. They would break their journey on the island of Naxos.

The cedarwood box

Once upon a time, when I was a child, my parents took me to Crete. We went to Knossos, whose remains, discovered a little over a century ago, are not classical, but of the Bronze Age, traces of a civilisation a thousand years older than the busily literate Athens that grew up later. The little writing the people of Knossos left behind them, symbols scratched into clay using a script we know as 'Linear B', was deciphered in the early 1950s. It was found to consist mostly of lists of goods: the dull, unromantic stuff of bureaucracy. It did not unlock the hearts and imaginations of the people who had lived surrounded by an exuberant luxury of faience and glass and crystal, by dashingly elegant frescoes, by a swirling vigour of painted pottery.

I can recall moments of this trip with sharp clarity. I remember my father observing that the buildings had been heavily reconstructed, so that, he implied, our experience was a little compromised, less authentic than it might have been – though frescoes and rooms with ceilings were a good deal more persuasive to me than low rubble walls would have been. I remember a huddle of giant *pithoi*, terracotta storage jars, so tall that they loomed over me. I remember a guide pointing out pillars and saying that they were unlike later Greek columns in that they were narrow at the bottom and broadened out at the top. (This seemed immensely strange to me, brought up as I was on the Ionic and Doric of English municipal neoclassicism.) I remember walking down a stairway into the heart of the palace – to me it was definitely a palace, because that was what people called it, though looking back, the word seems to bring all kinds of notions with it from our own age that may hardly have been applicable three and a half millennia ago. Here was a bath to be filled with pure water where a queen might bathe, or so we were told. There was a stone throne with a narrow curving back that looked like something out of Narnia, standing in a room painted with gryphons and waving, coiling flower stems. Another room was painted with dolphins flipping through turquoise waters, a delight to the eye.

I can remember the guide saying that the myth of the labyrinth started here: the story that Minos, king of Crete, ordered the inventor Daedalus to build a labyrinth to house the half-bull, half-man Minotaur. That the Athenians were forced to pay the Cretans a regular tribute of seven boys and seven girls, who would be left in the labyrinth to be consumed by the monster. That one year Theseus, the son of the king of Athens, came to Crete as part of this tribute. That with the help of King Minos's daughter Ariadne, he killed the creature and found his way out of the perplexing building. That Theseus and Ariadne escaped over the sea, but instead of marrying her as he had promised, the Athenian prince left her behind as she slept on the island of Naxos. That when Theseus sailed within sight of Athens, he forgot to lower the ochre sail and hoist the white fabric that would signal to his father that he was alive, so the old king, in his grief, threw himself off the rocks and died. And that the god Bacchus came to Ariadne on Naxos, and fell in love with her.

The guide said that out there on the broad terrace, King Minos, or some Cretan king a shade more real, may have sat and watched acrobats twist and leap in the air, cascading over the horned heads of bulls, just like in the fresco of bull leapers here on the palace wall. (Though it turned out the fresco was a reproduction; the original was in the museum in the city.) Perhaps the bull acrobatics – if the frescoes showed us what really happened at Knossos – were the reason that stories began about the biformed Minotaur. The guide admitted that there was nothing you could *exactly* call a labyrinth at Knossos, but that the intricacy and complexity of the building, with its winding corridors and bewildering floor plan, may have been the basis of the legend, as memory dimmed into myth in the centuries after the palace was wiped out by earthquake, fire and war. I remember how much I wanted these narrow rooms and passages to be labyrinthine, to trap and contain me, to be magical, to be a code, to be something that could be unlocked. I wanted to lose myself in them. This was where it began, my longing for the labyrinth. Even here it seemed just out of reach: a rumour, a trace, a clue.

We also went to the museum at Heraklion, the city on whose outskirts Knossos lies. I remember the guide who showed us around. She must have been about the age I am now, neatly dressed in a formal brown suit, while we sweated in short sleeves and sandals. She showed us the fresco of the bull leapers, the real one (though we could see it was made up of fragments around which a magnificent modern completion had been painted). She showed us figurines of bare-breasted goddesses with snakes held in their outstretched hands. She showed us an intricately worked gold pendant, of two bees curving their bodies around a drop of honey, their wings furled behind them.

I remember her telling us that the techniques used to make this jewellery were lost. No one could make anything as fine as this now, she said. I had, and have, no idea whether this is true, but the notion that knowledge could disappear, that people of an impossibly distant era, fifteen hundred years before the birth of Christ, could do some things better than we can now, deeply impressed me. At the end of the tour she turned to me and gave me a little envelope containing three postcards – my reward for being an attentive and interested child. One was of the bull leapers' fresco. The second was of another fresco, this time of three beautiful women in blue dresses, with snaky hair, gesturing to each other with infinite delicacy. The last was of the bee pendant.

I never quite forgot about the woman in the Heraklion museum and her gift to me. The postcards were, together, a talisman, a key to a certain place that became harder to visit, in my imagination, as I became older. I tried to learn my way back there: I studied Latin and Greek at school. In my interview for university I talked about a long poem by the Roman writer Catullus in which the story of Theseus, Ariadne and the Minotaur is told. I described how the reader peels away the poem's outer layers to discover what lies inside its complex structure.

One day, some years after I left university, I found the postcards again, quite by accident. They were hidden away in my bureau, an oak desk that is as much part of me as any object, since my parents bought it for me soon after I was born. I had taken one of its drawers right out to hunt for an old letter, and put it on a table. That was when I saw a battered, forgotten cedarwood box – I didn't see it directly, in fact, but its reflection caught my eye in a mirror. I took it out, opened it, and there they were: the acrobats, the beautiful women, the bee pendant. In an envelope, too, a piece of paper bearing the name and address, in old, faded ink, of Sofia Grammatiki, who had guided us around the museum two decades before.

On a whim, I decided to send her a letter. I didn't really expect a reply. Some months later, though, I got one. It turned out that her son was living in her old flat in the city. She had moved away into the wilder reaches of the island, to the Amari valley. It pleased her that her tour, and her small gift, had meant something and that I had gone on to study classics. She herself, she wrote, had studied classical philology in Athens many years ago, before returning to Crete and becoming a high-school teacher of Latin and ancient Greek, often earning a little extra in the holidays touring visitors around.

By the time she wrote to me, she had left teaching, and was restoring an eighteenth-century wreck of a farmhouse she'd bought from a distant relative who'd moved away to Athens. Eventually she ran the place as a B&B she called Amalthea House, after the goat who'd nursed the young god Zeus on Mount Ida, which loomed over her part of Crete from the east. She took immense pride in her immersion in rural life, learning from the local shepherds when to gather the fragrant herbs from the mountainside, from the women how to cure the olives from her grove. Every summer, a German university brought students there to study Greek and tour the archaeological sites. In the winter months she continued her antiquarian studies; she kept, she wrote, a good library on Cretan history and archaeology.

Over the course of the long correspondence that followed, at first by letter and then by email, it turned out that we shared an obsession with labyrinths. Of course she knew all about the Knossian labyrinth of myth, but she was also knowledgeable about the labyrinths and mazes* of later literature and landscapes, for she had walked the maze at Hampton Court and the great thirteenth-century labyrinth picked out in the stone floor of Chartres Cathedral. She used to speculate on why they appealed to her so. 'The great Argentinian writer, Jorge Luis Borges, has compared the labyrinth to the boundless ocean, the desert wastes and the disorienting wilds of the forest,' she wrote. 'These are, yes, confounding and frightening places. And yet the labyrinth is never so terrifying. A maze or a labyrinth has always been designed by a person. This means that another person has always the possibility of breaking its code. To be

* The labyrinth and the maze are sometimes supposed to be conceptually different: some authorities say that the labyrinth has a single winding, convoluted route that often seems to turn away from the centre, whereas the maze has forking paths and choices, and thus contains the possibility of getting lost. In fact this strict distinction, though useful in its way, is a relatively modern one, apt to break down. For example, in early texts the labyrinth of Knossos is invariably described as a confusing and perplexing building in which one would certainly lose one's way, though it is illustrated, on ancient coins and in medieval manuscripts, as having a single coiling path, as if there is a gap between the thing itself and its means of being represented graphically. At any rate, until fairly recently, the terms were used interchangeably, with garden mazes referred to as 'labyrinths' well into the eighteenth century. However, whereas labyrinth is a Greek word, perhaps with its origins in the Near East, maze (and indeed the word 'amaze') derives from the Middle English 'mase', which meant a source of deception, confusion or fantasy. As if the maze itself were a kind of story, a fiction.

inside a maze or a labyrinth is to be bewildered, confused or afraid. But it is, nonetheless, also to be inside a structure. It is to be lost, but only up to a point. It is also to be held within a design and a pattern.' I wondered, though, if she were underestimating the infinite inscrutability of buildings: their darkness, their strangeness. I recalled how, as a little child, I spent years not daring to go to sleep facing the cupboards that lined the wall on one side of my bed, preferring always to have the comforting pale rectangle of the window, hung with blue-flowered curtains, in my sights when I opened my eyes. Perhaps I dreaded that the cupboards would fly open and unknown or appalling things emerge from their dark and shadowed spaces, which might contain depths unknown by mere daylight. Borges once told an interviewer about how, as a boy, he had been terribly afraid of an engraving belonging to his mother of the Seven Wonders of the World. He felt that if he looked too closely at the illustration of the Cretan labyrinth, he might be able to see the Minotaur moving around inside. In his terror, he refused his mother's offer to hang the picture in his room.[1]

In one email I asked Mrs Grammatiki whether she had ever had the kind of recurring dreams that I did – in which a door would spontaneously appear in an apparently familiar building, usually my flat in London, or my childhood home. In these dreams, which I still have, I push open the door and wander through room after room of ancient stacked-up furniture and cobwebbed bric-a-brac, exploring spaces that confound the known geometries of the building, that cannot possibly exist within the flat's footprint, and resemble the warehouse of some careless and untidy seller (or collector) of antiquities, one not too punctilious to amass mostly broken and useless junk. Sometimes I dream of whole wings and enfilades of rooms, each leading to the next; or of a single twining, corkscrewing passage that winds round into a centre. In these dreams, I feel a mixture of pleasant surprise (so much space I hadn't known about!) and dread. I tend, I told her, to understand them as representing the unknown regions of my unconscious, where many unexamined things lie awaiting my scrutiny. I was, therefore, less confident than her about the essentially benign nature of labyrinths. I think they have the capacity to terrify, just as does any man-made thing. The Minotaur lives there, after all.

After this, she wrote back: 'You are right to make this connection between the labyrinth and the world of dreams. For me it is very strong. Borges wrote that a library is a labyrinth. This is also true – the rows of bookshelves running on for miles, with paths and passageways between them, the classification of the texts working as a kind of cipher that the reader must decode in order to find what she wants. That is only the superficial idea, however. Borges meant that literature is itself a labyrinth, and that every library contains the possibility of infinite places and infinite existences. Open a book in a library and you can disappear into a world, its cities, and its landscapes. All books, in turn, are labyrinths that express the winding shapes of their writers' imaginations. Each writer builds the labyrinth, and then leads the readers through the myriad possibilities of their tale with a thread like that of Ariadne, guiding them down the paths of their story, wherever it might take them. You can put the book back and choose another, disappear into another world. If you choose a book like James Joyce's *Ulysses*, I think that you will really never get out, for you will enter the streets of his Dublin and find it hard to leave, for that is a labyrinth within a labyrinth.'

Lost in the midst

Perhaps because she seemed almost to be a figment of my imagination, so long was it since I had actually seen her and so miraculous was the manner of our reconnection, I developed a habit of confiding in Mrs Grammatiki. Once, in late 2013, when a friend of mine was dying too young, I expressed to her my bewilderment at life's cruelties, and my sense of the aimlessness of my own existence, my feeling of disorientation. She replied: 'We are always in the middle of the labyrinth. This is an inescapable part of our existence. We are in the story, but we cannot tell the end or see the shape of the labyrinth. This is one reason we like to tell stories – so as to impose order and pattern onto our existence, which otherwise seems chaotic.'

I have never been able to find my way. If I once possessed a sense of direction, I have long surrendered it to my smartphone. But I never had one, really: after one twist of the body, one turn of the head, I have always been confounded. Turn me loose in a city without a map and panic rises, as if I were a child who had lost the grip of a parent's hand in a crowd.

Conversely, I cannot even lose myself effectively. One night in Rome I set myself the task of trying to do it. I was living, for the month of February 2016, in a building in the Borghese gardens, and one evening, leaving behind my partner and his son, who were engaged in some task in which I played no role, I set forth with the express purpose of aimlessness. I would simply walk, I thought, taking random turnings when it felt right to do so. But all I did was wind round and around, covering no real ground, re-emerging frustratingly again and again on the straight and dreary spine of the Corso. Nothing was discovered. There were no revelations, only weariness. Having no destination in mind – no church, no gallery, no park or vista or bar, as we usually did on our wintry, twilit walks that month – I felt flat and dismal.

Eventually I turned a corner and came into a square in which stood a church, San Lorenzo in Lucina. Stepping inside, I came across the pale, restrained tomb of the painter Nicolas Poussin. On it was carved a likeness of his own painting, which hangs in the Louvre, of shepherds in some pastoral idyll stumbling upon a sarcophagus on which is inscribed '*Et in Arcadia ego*', meaning 'I, too, was in Arcadia'. The phrase is ambiguous. Who is this 'I'? The dead man, who once enjoyed all the pleasures of Arcadia? Or death itself, which haunts even the most beautiful landscapes? It felt, at least, that I had found an end to the walk.

On the path of my life, in the middle of my life, what do I know about where I have been, and where I might go? Everything is the woods, everything is the ocean, everything is the desert. I can see no shape. I am lost; in the middle of my life I am lost. I cannot find my way through the thicket. I cannot navigate. The path that lies ahead of me is a riddle. But the path that lies behind is indistinct, too: its myriad and confusing turns already half forgotten, the significance of the landmarks encountered along the way misunderstood, misinterpreted.

Mrs Grammatiki wrote, 'We follow the paths we are offered. We make choices and sometimes they lead only to dead ends. In order to reach the centre, we must take the counterintuitive decision to turn away from it. We circle round, apparently aimlessly, finding no pattern and no reason to our route. We are bound by blind walls – we cannot go where we like. It seems meaningless. Only if we were able to fly above the labyrinth and see it from a distance would we understand that it had a certain design and a pattern.'

That email was written in November 2015. It was her last to me: Sofia Grammatiki died early the following year, just as I was planning a trip to Crete for that same autumn. As I wrote this book, I thought of her. She had brought me so much of it, unasked for. It was as if I had dreamed it, or found it, as an archaeologist might stumble across a buried hoard. She was my guide through the maze, the sibyl who led me through the Underworld. She made me understand that to find my way I needed to make my own labyrinth – this book, this winding journey down my imagination's shaded byways.

I remembered her as I followed the tangled and multiple routes that she had indicated for me, digressing, delaying, following circuitous route after circuitous route. I walked labyrinths. I disappeared into the unmappable wilderness of the web, where Minotaurs lurk. I became biformed, half person, half machine, as I flitted through its dark and boundless territories. I tried to build a labyrinth of labyrinths.

THE EDGE

It had been hacked together from sheets of board and scraps of wood: stuff that looked like detritus dragged from ruins and derelict buildings, then screwed into a single surface. It was rough, unbalanced, and raw: but despite the improvisatory feel, there seemed to be a design at work. Here and there the structure had been painted, roughly but with a certain care, with daubs and dabs of various colours: black, liver brown, rust red, dark grey-blue, fleshy pink, even the odd streak of a lemony yellow. There was no graffiti on it, even though it looked as if it should have been covered in graffiti; in its own way, it was pristine. It was, I saw, a kind of fence or wall. It was much taller than head height and it was impossible to see what lay on the other side, if anything.

Curious, I began to follow it, this perimeter, if that was what it was. After a while it became clear that the wall was describing a curve, a shape that completely disregarded the surrounding topography. At one point, for example, it cut off the head of a flight of steps as if it didn't exist; it just went on going inexorably, consuming its surroundings. On the other hand, it seemed that the curve of the wall was not constant or regular: its outline sometimes bulged, or contracted, for no apparent reason. I was looking for an entrance: the wall had been built, I assumed, to keep something in, or indeed something out. Either way it stood to reason that there must be an opening of some kind. At one point it chinked sharply in on itself, creating a passageway so narrow as to be almost too thin for a human to squeeze into. I was sure that I would find a slim door at the end of this cleft, but there was none.

After some time I reached the point at which I had begun. So the fence was, as I had suspected, a stockade of sorts – but enclosing what? I became increasingly convinced that behind it, hidden within, there must be something wonderful, or strange; or perhaps dangerous. I wanted very much to find a way in. I began to walk the circumference again.

Immured between hedges

The first grand country-house maze I ever saw was in the grounds of Chatsworth in Derbyshire. But whenever I was taken there, on days out from my childhood home in the neighbouring county, Staffordshire, it was mockingly locked shut. The first maze I actually entered was the one in the 'wilderness' at Hampton Court Palace.[2] It is the oldest surviving proper maze – not just a knot garden of intricate topiary but a real puzzle, with hedges too tall to peer over, and dead ends and false trails. It was likely planted in the early 1690s, presumably because the Dutch king William III and his wife Mary liked the idea; they had a maze at their Huis Ten Bosch in the Netherlands. The Hampton Court maze was originally laid out in hornbeam, whose lime-green, crinkle-edged leaves fall in autumn, meaning the first maze-walkers would have been puzzled only in the spring and summer; now, however, it is an evergreen thicket.

Daniel Defoe, in his 1724 book *A Tour Thro' the Whole Island of Great Britain*, wrote approvingly that 'This labyrinth and wilderness is not only well design'd, and compleatly finished, but is perfectly well kept . . . so that nothing of the kind can be more beautiful.' But it did not stay long in fashion. Batty Langley, the wonderfully named English designer of gardens and Gothic follies, included sinuous and intricate labyrinth designs in his *New Principles of Gardening* of 1728, but even he strongly deprecated 'regular, stiff and stuft up' schemes of symmetrical parterres, and by the 1740s, when Capability Brown was starting out, the rigorous geometry of Dutch gardens was completely outmoded. In the 1762 edition of Defoe's *Tour*, the maze was dismissively referred to as being 'very far from affording any Pleasure' to 'every Person of Taste', for 'nothing can be more disagreeable than to be immured between Hedges, so as to have the Eye confined to a strait Walk'.[3] The maze survived an uprooting to prosper during the Victorian maze revival, when (the palace gardens having been opened to the public in 1838) it became famous again. It was emulated in commercial London pleasure gardens such as Vauxhall, Walworth and Cremorne, where its imitators starred alongside such attractions as 'Gypsy' tents, hermitages and marionette theatres.

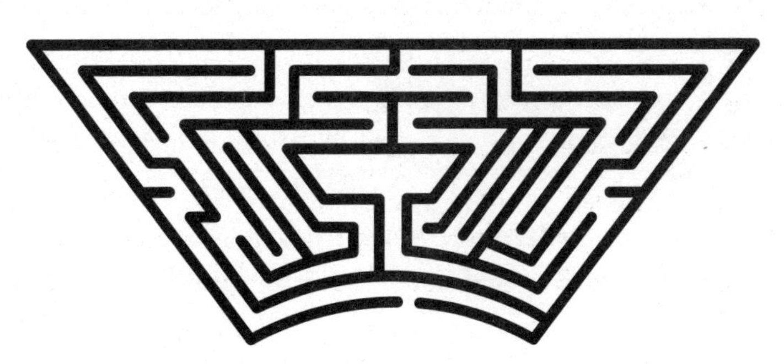

The design of the Hampton Court maze.

I visited the Hampton Court maze with friends in March 2017, when the wilderness was flooded yellow with daffodils. It was my first visit since childhood. I did not surrender myself to the maze's cunning and did not walk it alone – rather, I followed the whims of the children in our group and marvelled at their fearless curiosity, their lack of hesitation when paths divided, their carefree lack of calculation, their hurried, pounding footsteps and grinning sheepishness when we came up against the same dead ends.* For them, the sensation of being lost-not-lost brought not dread, but joy.

The biformed labyrinth

Like the creature that inhabits it, the labyrinth has two natures. On the one hand it conveys beauty, pattern and order; on the other, chaos, fear and bewilderment. To contemplate the shape of a labyrinth is to stand back and allow the eye to enjoy the intricacy of line and design, to feel a sense of mastery and comprehension. But to be inside the labyrinth is something else: the body, not just the mind, is implicated, and the experience

* As it happens, the Hampton Court maze can be solved by keeping one hand constantly in contact with the hedge: you will eventually reach the centre, if rather laboriously. However, this method cannot be relied upon in every maze, because it assumes that the hedges are planted in a continuous winding line. In the early nineteenth century, the Earl of Stanhope devised a maze whose centre was in an 'island' of hedges not connected to the perimeter.

is not cerebral and intellectual but physical. In that confined and controlled space, walking between high walls or upon a narrowly delineated pathway, comes an intense awareness of one's own heft and height, of one's way of moving. To feel trapped within the labyrinth's intestinal coils ushers in thoughts of entrails, of the strange unremembered red tunnels out of which we all, once, emerged. With thoughts of sex and birth come intimations of death: there is something crypt-like about its dark, catacombish twists. The labyrinth is, then, both a symbol of the body and its fragile mysteries, and a gesture of optimism that a corner of the universe can be mastered and given pattern and order by the human mind. And so, with its dual pleasures of detachment and immersion, it is the perfectly satisfying aesthetic object, the original feat of architecture, the great mythic symbol of human ingenuity.

The labyrinth appeals to our deepest and most basic desires – the longing to be held within a containing structure, just as the overwhelming red insides of our bodies are contained by their bones and sinews and skin. The labyrinth is about power and powerlessness, mastery and terror; it is also a coiled line, a thread, a narrative, a fabrication, a fiction.

The by-street

I think of Dickens's *Oliver Twist*, whose hero's name hints at the spiralling reversals in his story. He is a lost boy, whose penniless mother dies as she gives birth to him. Brought up in the workhouse, then apprenticed to an undertaker, he runs away to London, but is found by the Artful Dodger, an irrepressible con artist if ever there was one: the Odysseus of Dickens's London, who lies and invents his way around the city's confounding terrain. Oliver is primed for a life of petty thieving by the Artful's master Fagin, who gives him a roof and a grim kind of home in his den in Saffron Hill, a narrow alleyway in Clerkenwell.

By a series of chances, he finds himself pulled out of this dreadful life by a kind old gentleman called Mr Brownlow, who takes him home to Pentonville, where he is shown care and love for the first time in his life. One day Oliver offers to run an errand to Clerkenwell that involves returning some books, and a £5 note, to a bookseller. It is not a long journey: a mile or so. I know, because this is my part of London, where I live. But 'when he got into Clerkenwell, he accidentally turned down a by-street which was not exactly in his way; but not discovering his mistake until he had got half-way down it, and knowing it must lead in the right direction, he did not think it worthwhile to turn back, and so marched on, as quickly as he could, with the books under his arm'.

That was when he was accosted by Fagin's associates, Nancy and the brutal Bill Sikes. 'Darkness had set in; it was a low neighbourhood; no help was near; resistance was useless. In another moment he was dragged into a labyrinth of dark narrow courts, and was forced along them at a pace which rendered the few cries he dared to give utterance to, unintelligible.' Oliver is pitched back into his old life. We had thought him saved; now he is plunged once more into danger. Peace is replaced by terror, and language gives way to unintelligible cries. He is back where he was, no progress made, hope snatched away. One wrong turn and the story changes, life changes. He is lost. Until, that is, Dickens, kindly and despotic, pushes him onto another path, into another twist of his story, another turn of the screw.

What frightens me more than the wrong turns I have taken during my life are the right turns, the ones I so nearly didn't take. What if I hadn't gone to that place, on that day, and met that person, that person who now brings me happiness? Tug at a thread and everything could unravel.

THE VANISHING LABYRINTH

The labyrinth has something of the quality of a dream about it. We strain to make it real but it slips from view. It does not quite have a proper existence – paradoxically, given that it is the original magnificent *thing*, the first great ingenious building, an object that bears so much symbolic and metaphorical weight, a structure that we long to fill with significance.

To try to tease out the origin of the labyrinth, for example, is to tread slippery and indistinct paths. The word itself is obscure. Some have speculated that it derives from *labrys*, a (possibly) Lydian term for a double-headed axe, impressive examples of which were excavated at Knossos. The labyrinth thus could mean 'house of the double axe', a way of describing the palace that, because of its complex layout, because of the accretions of time and memory and myth, came to absorb the meaning of a trap and prison for the Minotaur. There is a Linear B inscription from Knossos that may be interpreted as 'the lady of the labyrinth', or 'lady of the double axe'; and another that may be interpreted as 'Daedalus'. But this evidence is fragmentary and hazy.

We might expect to find the story of the labyrinth in Greece's earliest surviving poems, the *Iliad* and the *Odyssey*, which between them are such generous repositories of myths and tales. And indeed, we find Minos and Ariadne and Theseus and Daedalus in Homer: but no labyrinth, and no Minotaur. In the *Odyssey* (which, like the *Iliad*, was probably composed between the late eighth and late seventh century BC, drawing on a long oral tradition), Ariadne is one of the shades of the dead whom Odysseus sees in the Underworld. Theseus had tried to take her from Crete to Athens, we are told. She can also be found in the *Iliad*, buried in a metaphor describing a work of divine craftsmanship. In the poem, the goddess Thetis, the mother of the hero Achilles, asks the god Hephaestus to forge her son a shield. He produces a masterpiece. It is marvellously decorated: there are scenes of the sun and the sky and the encircling ocean, of cities arming for war, of ploughmen tilling fields, of a harvest feast, of lustrous grapes ripening in a vineyard, of a lion hunt, of meadows in a shaded valley, and, finally, of a dancing floor, as broad, we are told, as Ariadne's at Knossos. On this dancing floor, which Daedalus made for her, boys and girls twirled and spun, and

> . . . they would run in rings on their skilled feet,
> Nimbly, quick as a crouching potter spins his wheel,
> palming it smoothly, giving it practice twirls

to see it run, and now they would run in rows,
in rows crisscrossing rows – rapturous dancing.[4]

The dance is full of mazy windings – and readers have often speculated that there could be hints of an unspoken labyrinth here, the paths of which the dance is meant to recall. But just as there is no 'real' labyrinth to be found at Knossos, but only a memory, a construction of the mind, this poetic dance is only a trace of a trace, footsteps that may or may not be following the design of an absent building. The labyrinth slips away again.

The most monstrous work of mankind

The first labyrinth mentioned in surviving Greek literature is, in fact, not on Crete and has nothing to do with the Minotaur. It is an elaborate Egyptian building described in the fifth century BC by Herodotus in his *Histories*. The work is ostensibly an account of wars between Persia and an alliance of Greek city-states, but is in fact a wonderfully digressive ragbag of a text that, in the course of a long backstory explaining the causes of the conflicts, presents an account of what was to Greek eyes the ancient and exotic land of Egypt.

The labyrinth, wrote Herodotus, was the tomb of twelve Egyptian kings and 'a wonder beyond description – and I speak as someone who has seen it with his own eyes. Certainly, there can be no doubting that the Labyrinth would have cost more in terms of sweat and gold than all the walls and public monuments built by the Greeks put together.'[5] The pyramids, to be sure, defied description, he wrote. But even they came second to the labyrinth. The stupendous structure contained twelve roofed courtyards and three thousand rooms, half of them below ground, where the bodies of the kings, as well as those of sacred crocodiles, were interred. These rooms alone – he saw only those on the ground floor – dwarfed any other work made by humankind. There were also colonnades, vestibules and chambers connected by passages, and the walls were decorated with innumerable figures.

No traces were found of this building until, in 1888, the Egyptologist William Flinders Petrie discovered what he believed to be its foundations, at Hawara near the city of Faiyum. Spread over a huge area was a deep layer of stone chips. Beneath these chips was a flattened-off zone that he took to be the foundations of the labyrinth building, which covered, he calculated, 304 by 244 metres. He was able to construct a partial floor plan, which showed the building as a sequence of pillared rectangular chambers and corridors – impressive, complex and massive if not actually bewildering in the vermicular, coiling fashion of a labyrinth that one might now imagine. 'The mere extent of it proved that it was far larger than any temple known in Egypt,' he wrote. 'All the temples of Karnak, of Luxor, and a few on the western side of Thebes, might be placed together within the vast space of these buildings at Hawara.'[6] The edifice, he wrote, had gradually fallen into desuetude and been used as a quarry, leaving, in time, nothing but an ocean of fragments. Indeed, the marble chips were spread so deep and wide that he recalled having difficulty in persuading anyone else that they were not simply a naturally occurring phenomenon.

Centuries later, in the first century AD, the Roman writer Pliny the Elder also described the Egyptian labyrinth, which he said was still standing in his lifetime. He included it in his compendious *Natural History*, a work that combined scholarship on biology with many avenues of human endeavour, from wall painting and sculpture to metallurgy and gardening. He made it sound alarming: bewildering mazelike passages, lofty upper storeys and raised porches, miles and miles of corridors. 'Some of the halls are laid out in such a way that when the doors open there is a terrifying rumble of thunder within; incidentally, most of the building has to be traversed in darkness,' he wrote.

Other prodigious labyrinths came later, he added. He claimed that these included the one on Crete built by Daedalus, another similar construction on the island of Lemnos, and the tomb of an ancient Etruscan king, Lars Porsena, in Clusium (perhaps modern Chiusi, in Tuscany). On the Etruscan labyrinth he quoted an earlier Roman author, Varro, who had claimed that to escape from its tortuous paths one would need to go in equipped with a ball of thread. None of these buildings, on Crete, Lemnos or in Clusium, are any more than hearsay; even Pliny acknowledged that those in Crete and Italy had left no trace, if they had even existed at all. For him these works of over-elaborate human craftsmanship, almost uncanny in their stupendousness, were '*portentosissimum humani opus*' – the most monstrous, or unnatural, or abnormal work of mankind.[7]

The visual arts may provide more clues. One piece of evidence is the decoration on the so-called François vase, an artefact that has had an eventful history. Its excavator, Alessandro François, found its pieces scattered widely around the entrance to a tomb near Chiusi in 1844; it was painstakingly remade and displayed in the Florence Archaeological Museum. Then, in 1900, it was smashed again into 638 pieces by a disgruntled museum employee. Despite all this, it remains a remarkable object. It is dated to around 570–560 BC and is, unusually, signed by both its potter and its painter, Ergotimos and Kleitias. It is painted with an array of scenes: the wedding of Peleus and Thetis, Ajax carrying the dead Achilles from the battlefield, the hunting of the Calydonian boar, and much more. A frieze on its wide neck shows Theseus and a troop of Athenian boys and girls, all given names by the painter – seemingly the Minotaur's intended victims. There is Ariadne, too, also neatly captioned. She is holding aloft some kind of round object. It could be a ball of thread. It is hard to tell, but distinguished scholars[8] have thought it to be so, and a ball of thread assumes the presence of the labyrinth.

On later vase paintings, things become less ambiguous. In the fifth century BC, Theseus was often depicted in combat with the Minotaur, sometimes with a dark red thread slung round his body; in the fourth century BC, labyrinth patterns began to be struck on Knossian coins, sometimes showing an image of a running Minotaur on the obverse. The kind of labyrinth found on Cretan coins can be drawn by anyone quite easily: you begin with a cross and four dots placed at the corners of the notional square. Then each arm of the cross is

How to draw a simple labyrinth.

connected in turn to its dot. You end up with a labyrinth of seven 'courses'.

After Herodotus, the first surviving literary mention of the word *labyrinthos* is by Plato, around the turn of the fifth and fourth centuries BC: he used it in his dialogue *Euthydemus* as a way to describe an argument that circles back on itself. (I think, too, of the philosophers in Milton's epic poem about Adam and Eve's temptation and fall, *Paradise Lost.* Lacking 'right reason', these misguided thinkers find themselves 'in wand'ring mazes lost'.) It is somehow appropriate, given the weight of symbolism that the labyrinth carries, that even before *labyrinthos* is unambiguously connected to the story of the Minotaur,* it should be found doing service as a metaphor. It is not until well over a century later that the first clear association with the Minotaur comes – in a hymn from the 270s or 260s BC by the Libyan-Greek writer Callimachus, who lived in the city of Alexandria in Egypt, where he worked at the great library established by the Ptolemies. The hymn is addressed to the island of Delos, birthplace of the god Apollo. On this island, recounts the poem, Theseus paused on his way back to Athens from Crete after killing the Minotaur and dedicated a statue of Aphrodite

> with the youths he had saved from the Labyrinth
> and the bellowing of Pasiphaë's monstrous son.
>
> Round your altar, lady, they raised the lute music
> and danced the ring dance with Theseus leading.[9]

This might remind us of the twirling steps performed on Ariadne's dancing floor in the *Iliad*, perhaps here meant as a ritual marking safe deliverance from the labyrinth.

---

* There may be at least one missing link. It is possible, for instance, that the playwright Euripides (writing in the second half of the fifth century BC) set a scene of his largely lost drama *Theseus* in the Cretan labyrinth.

Later, in the first century BC, Catullus elaborated the tale. A few decades afterwards Virgil alluded to it in his epic poem the *Aeneid*, then Ovid reworked it in his *Metamorphoses* and *Heroides*. In the streets of Pompeii, before it was destroyed by the eruption of Vesuvius in AD 79 (which also killed Pliny the Elder), someone scratched into a pillar graffiti in the form of a labyrinth and the words '*labyrinthus hic habitat minotaurus*' ('the labyrinth: the Minotaur lives here'). A fine mosaic of a labyrinth was also set into the floor of one of the houses of the town, in its centre the fight between Theseus and the Minotaur; there are also lovely labyrinth patterns in black-and-white tesserae set into the floor of the House of the Geometric Mosaics. Another building, the Villa Imperiale, contains a fine sequence of wall paintings depicting Cretan stories: Ariadne mourning for the departing Theseus, Daedalus escaping from the island on wings of feather and wax. The story as we know it had been woven, but was ready to be unravelled and remade.

PELIACO QUONDAM

The first poem I truly loved was Catullus 64 – a work that Mrs Grammatiki once described, in an email she wrote in 2010, as 'the perfect poem about a labyrinth in the form of a labyrinth'. It is the sixty-fourth poem in the corpus of a hundred or so that were rediscovered and copied in some dusty corner of a library in northern Italy in the Middle Ages. It is sometimes called *The Marriage of Peleus and Thetis*, but that is like the title of an Old Master: merely a name adopted in later ages for convenience's sake. I think of it as its first two words: '*Peliaco quondam*' (once upon a time, on Pelion's . . .). Or just as Catullus 64. Formally, it is an epyllion, that is, a mini-epic. It has 408 lines. Very long by comparison with Catullus's lyrics and epigrams; very short for an epic.

Catullus was born in about 84 BC and died in about 54 BC, at the age of thirty or so. That year, Caesar made his second unsuccessful attempt to invade Britain, Virgil was in his mid-teens and Ovid's birth was still a decade away. Catullus was (probably) from a well-off family of Verona, then part of provincial Gaul, but his poems are written in the voice of a metropolitan, sophisticated Roman – they speak of dinner parties and liaisons with girls and boys, a bohemian mix of high life and low life. In tone they range from heartfelt and tortured, through playful and allusive, to filthy and furious. A whole cycle of love poems is addressed to a woman he calls Lesbia, a pseudonym that pays homage to Sappho, the poet who wrote bittersweet love lyrics on the island of Lesbos in the sixth century BC. Some scholars have speculated that the real subject of these 'Lesbia' poems was an aristocratic woman, Clodia Metelli, who would have been slumming it if she really had had an affair with Catullus. Still others have argued that 'Lesbia' was simply a literary construct, a name to hang poems from, which seems oddly bloodless as an idea. The sheer directness of his voice – by turns love-drunk, despairing, elated, lustful, angry – makes me want to imagine that there really was someone; that he might have said, like the poet Eileen Myles, 'My dirty secret has always been that it's of course about me.'[10] The poems are so visceral, so sexy, that they collapse the millennia between his writing and our reading them.

I fell in love with Catullus, a little, as a teenager. My description of him is, I admit, largely projection: this is the Catullus I imagined for myself through his poems, as a young provincial with a romantic notion of what the artistic life might consist of. At school I studied him from a bowdlerised edition, which simply omitted poems deemed unsuitable for teenage eyes. I was one of many schoolchildren over the generations who found their curiosity piqued by such a prohibition; I searched out and puzzled through the Latin of the sexy, scurrilous missing poems – such as number 32, in which the libidinous narrator, erection pushing through his cloak, addresses a girl called Ipsitilla, suggesting that they get together that afternoon for '*novem continuas fututiones*' (nine fucks in a row). You didn't get that sort of stuff across the corridor in English literature. Not in north Staffordshire in the 1980s.

Peliaco quondam seems on first reading very different from Catullus's other work. It is elaborate, decorated, shimmering and extremely self-conscious; a game-playing poem. It starts with a rollingly rich description, full of baroque detail, of the very first ship made by humankind – 'when pine trees are said to have swum through the clear waters of Neptune'. That description of a boat is not mere playful eccentricity: it imagines a time when no one yet had a word for 'ship'. So the vessel is a swimming pine tree, and its oars are hands that brush the waves. That boat, the *Argo*, was built to take a band of Greek heroes, led by Jason, to Colchis on the Black Sea to capture the Golden Fleece. Athena herself – or in this Roman context, Minerva – fitted the pinewood structure, the '*texta*', to the curving keel.

('*Texta*' is from the same root as the words text and textile; it means, literally, something woven. Minerva presides over these areas – the shape of something written, the weave of a fabric, the structure of an object.) At this moment, the poem feels as if it is going to be about Jason and the Argonauts.

Abruptly, though, it changes tack. It tells how the Argonauts catch sight of nymphs swimming naked in the sea, their breasts exposed in the surf. Thetis, one of these divine creatures, looks up from the waves and her eyes lock onto the hero, Peleus. At first sight, the two fall in love, man succumbing to sea goddess and vice versa. The poem now leaps ahead in time and space to Thessaly in Greece and starts to describe the couple's wedding feast, completely abandoning the Argonauts' story. It starts to look like another kind of tale altogether, for the couple will become the parents of Achilles, the greatest hero of the *Iliad*, and the reader might wonder whether the story is nudging itself towards, say, the narrative of Achilles' childhood and youth, perhaps a prequel to Homer's epic.

Catullus starts to give an extravagant description of the wedding feast: the whole of Thessaly comes, leaving the countryside deserted; the vineyards become overgrown, the trees are left unpruned, the oxen lie idle, the ploughs become rusty. In contrast to this scene of rural neglect, Peleus's palace is luxuriousness itself: as far as it stretches back, room after room, it shimmers with gold and silver. Gleaming are the cups on the tables, gleaming is the ivory inlay on the couches, the whole house rejoices in the splendid royal treasure. In the very centre of the palace the marriage bed is being made ready, draped with a precious coverlet dyed Tyrian purple.

This coverlet, continues the poem, was embroidered with images; with wonderful skill it depicted stories, heroic deeds from long ago. In the centre there was a scene of Ariadne, wild fury in her heart, looking seawards from the shore of Naxos. It is another abrupt shift. All at once we are leaving the world of Peleus and Thetis and being sucked, via this textile, into Ariadne's. The Cretan princess has just woken up on the water's edge, the poem tells us, and finds herself alone. Theseus, whom she had helped to kill her half-brother, the Minotaur, has left her there, stealing away from her in the night, even though he had promised to marry her. His ship is now a speck on the horizon.

Intricate descriptions of artworks – descriptions so vivid and dynamic that they challenge the capacity of the dumb, static objects under scrutiny to contain them – go right back to the first Greek literature. In the famous description of Achilles' shield in the *Iliad*, the scenes picked out on the armour – including the dancing floor that resembles that of Ariadne at Knossos – bristle with movement and sound. Any mental image of a mere cold, metallic shield dissolves as one reads. So it is with this textual description of a miraculously beautiful textile. What Catullus does differently is to extend the description so that Ariadne takes over most of the poem – so that the 'digression' more or less becomes the poem itself. Soon it will feel as if the stories that got us here – the whole matter of the *Argo*, and of Peleus and Thetis – have been dead ends, or false turnings, or elaborate edgings or framings; we followed each of these tales only to be brought up sharp against poetic walls, with the story going so far and no further.

The fact that Ariadne's story is embroidery on a textile is something that we both know and don't know as we read: our imagination allows her to wriggle out of her carapace of stitches. And yet the poem will occasionally nudge us back into awareness. At one point, just as we are entirely caught up in Ariadne's story, just as we have forgotten that she is made of coloured threads, the narrating voice starts a line, 'In another part of the textile ...' Except of course that we are not exactly looking at an embroidery at all; we are reading a poem that contains a description of one. Story in textile in text. It is a '*texta*' (structure) sufficiently cunning to have been contrived by Minerva herself.

In this other part of the embroidery then, we are shown a further scene in the story, flipping back in time to learn how Ariadne came to be abandoned. The Athenians, forced to pay the penalty for the murder on Attic soil of Ariadne's brother Androgeon, were obliged to send a regular tribute of young men and women to be consumed by the Minotaur. When the Athenian king's son Theseus grew up, he volunteered to join that year's victims, and sailed to Crete. As soon as Ariadne saw him, her eyes and her heart began to burn with passion. And so she helped him: she gave him the means to kill her half-brother and find his way out of the labyrinth.

After the poem tells us Ariadne's story, and what happened afterwards to Theseus too, it switches back out of the description of the coverlet and returns to the wedding of Peleus and Thetis. There, new guests arrive: among them, most significantly, the Fates, three extravagantly described old women who spin out the destinies of humans, making the threads that are the very material of people's lives. The Fates start to sing a joyful wedding song, but it soon becomes strange and dark: they prophesy the dreadful things to come to Achilles, the child of Peleus and Thetis: the Trojan War, his bloody deeds.

The poem is intensely artful and allusive; it is strongly influenced by the elaborate poetics of figures such as Callimachus, and other Greek-speaking writers who lived in Alexandria in the third and second centuries BC. Since I was a teenager I have been drawn to its aesthetic brilliance and oddness: its self-conscious artistry and its curious, enchanting slips in tone. But it quivers with movement and sound, too. It is entirely alive. It contains passages of heart-rending, plangent loss and bitter anger. When my heart has been broken, I have turned to this poem and recognised Ariadne's grief and fury as my own, for hers is the original poetic lover's lament that sets the tone for all lovers' laments, influencing Virgil's Dido in the *Aeneid* and, directly or indirectly, all those myriad that have come after.* The poem plunges us deep through

---

* The best-known opera based on Ariadne's story is Richard Strauss and Hugo von Hofmannsthal's playful *Ariadne auf Naxos*, where she is as self-consciously framed as she is in Catullus's poem, a character in an opera-in-an-opera. As in *The Mousetrap*, the play-in-a-play in *Hamlet*, the performance does not go quite as planned: the action is merrily interrupted (to the irritation of the composer) by a *commedia dell'arte* troupe, who cause pleasurable genre disruption to the solemn and tragic proceedings. Handel also wrote an 'Arianna' opera set on Crete, with extra romantic knots and complications thrown in. Martinů wrote a one-act opera called *Ariadne* with a coloratura aria for a Callas-like voice. Harrison Birtwistle's *The Minotaur* (2008), set on Crete rather than Naxos, is the fullest recent treatment of the story in opera, with David Harsent's libretto set to a labyrinthine, spiralling score by the composer. In this version, Ariadne is liberated from her role as tragic heroine and becomes something darker; and the Minotaur is given a voice, if only in his own dreams.

a temporal labyrinth: first to the 'once upon a time' of Peleus and Thetis, then to their 'once upon a time' of Ariadne and Theseus, then to the 'future' of Peleus and Thetis's child. All this is punctuated by moments of direct address from the narrative voice – bringing us not exactly into the 'now' of the twenty-first century, nor the 'now' of the poem's composition in the first century BC, but the magical, impossible 'now' that sparks into being when two points in history are suddenly and briefly fused by one person's reading words that another once wrote. Sometimes I think of the poem as full of zigzags, crinkles and dead ends. Sometimes I think of it as resembling the rooms in Pompeii (dating from some decades after its composition) painted with fantastical architecture, with *trompe l'oeil* colonnades and porticoes whose perspectives don't work at all. In these schemes, images of panels painted with beautiful views are sometimes placed within the picture, and these landscapes-within-landscapes suck you into a different place altogether. Sometimes I feel that reading its interlocking stories is like passing through a succession of rooms like those in the palace of Peleus. It is a seemingly endless enfilade, in which light glints off the precious treasures held inside them, but the geometry of the rooms feels odd, out of proportion; they shouldn't, somehow, fit together, and they stretch and shrink bewilderingly. This poem is part of me: my labyrinth within.

Dictys of Crete

Mrs Grammatiki argued that Crete, that island that had colonised my mind as a child, was the original home of yarns and tall tales, of fiction, of lies, of pretended truths miraculously dug up from the earth. 'Daedalus was the first great liar,' she wrote. 'It was he who built the deceptive labyrinth, and he who invented the sham cow for Pasiphaë.' To my mind it went back even further, since all stories of Crete begin with a fraud: Zeus's disguise as a bull; his tricking and rape of Europa.

In support of her theory, Mrs Grammatiki introduced me to a figure called Dictys of Crete, author of *Diary of the Trojan War*, a Latin prose work purporting to be just that – a diary of a soldier's experiences fighting on the Greek side at the siege of Troy. I'd not heard of him before; he hadn't been taught or even mentioned, as far as I could remember, when I studied classics at university. In fact the *Diary* has been subject to a momentous cultural reversal. Now Dictys is barely heard of outside academia (where, in actual fact, interest has revived). In the Middle Ages, though, the work was famous and popular, one of the most important storehouses of tales from ancient Greece. That was because Greek was unknown to – and therefore Homer unread by – the vast majority of Western European readers, even such learned figures as Petrarch and Dante. Chaucer so admired the *Diary*, for example, that he placed Dictys among the figures lining the approach to his goddess's throne in the poem *The House of Fame*.

Dictys was, claimed the *Diary*, a native of Knossos, who fought alongside King Idomeneus of Crete, the grandson of Minos. The work is prefaced with an account of the text's survival from that misty era, apparently written by a later, Roman editor of the work, one Lucius Septimius, probably in the early fourth century AD. This account is in the form of a letter from

Septimius to a friend, describing how, by chance, he had come across some 'little books' containing the diary. They were in Greek, so he had decided to translate them into Latin.

Elaborating, he cast back several centuries to AD 66, when, he said, the 'little books' had first come to light. That year, he wrote, the thirteenth of the emperor Nero's reign, an earthquake caused the ancient tomb of Dictys at Knossos to collapse. Afterwards, shepherds wandering nearby spotted a box in the rubble that the tremors had exposed. Thinking it might be full of treasure, they broke it open; but discovering that it contained limewood tablets inscribed with writing, the proto-archaeologists took the find to their master. He recognised the script as Phoenician. The language, though, was Greek, and so he had the text transliterated. He presented the work to Nero, and was richly rewarded for his trouble. A second preface, seemingly written long before Septimius's letter, closer to AD 66, gave similar details of the work's emergence from the unquiet soil of Knossos, with a slightly more elaborate account of its arrival in Rome. (In this version, the antiquarian-minded emperor himself recognised the script as Phoenician, and had his staff philologists transliterate it.)*

---

* The presence of this 'double preface' is strange. If the discovery of the text in a destroyed tomb seems too good to be true, so does the claim that Septimius discovered 'little books' in Greek and decided to translate them. However, there is evidence that he was telling the truth. In the winter of 1899–1900, the Oxford scholars Bernard Grenfell and Arthur Hunt were excavating at Umm el Baragat in Egypt, the ancient city of Tebtunis. They were searching, specifically, for ancient papyrus. Only a decade previously, Flinders Petrie had found that 'cartonnage',

When the study of Greek began to be revived by humanist scholars, and, from the mid-sixteenth century, the *Iliad* and *Odyssey* translated into modern European languages, the popularity of Dictys waned. The *Diary* also began to be looked upon as a 'fake' as the Homeric epics themselves came to be understood as poetic inventions rather than accounts of actual historical events. Castigating Dictys on the grounds of fraudulence,

---

the papier-mâché-like material used to wrap mummies, was sometimes made from recycled papyrus sheets, some of which contained writing. With care, the sheets could be separated, and thus read. This observation opened up the exciting possibility of discovering hitherto lost classical texts. Over the past century many intriguing fragments have been found, by poets and playwrights including Sappho, Euripides, Pindar and Menander, and tremendous quantities of ordinary, but revealing, non-literary material such as legal documents, religious texts, letters and receipts.

In their search for lost ancient texts, Grenfell and Hunt (later immortalised in Tony Harrison's play *The Trackers of Oxyrhyncus*) dismembered a thousand crocodile mummies. They found quantities of written material including passages of the *Iliad*, magical charms, astrological calculations, a summons for an arrest, the accounts of a beer-seller, and a medical tract on how to treat severe thirst during a fever. They also found a note of tax returns on a certain corn harvest, and, on the other side of the sheet, a fragment of the *Diary of the Trojan War* – in Greek. The sheet could be dated to AD 206, a century or so before the probable date of Septimius. It seems that the Roman had, as he claimed, been working from a Greek original. But what of the truth of the rest of his account? Did he really think it was an authentic text written as the Trojan War unfolded? Or was Septimius slyly adding to the game by way of his preface? Scholarly opinion now tends to the view that the original Greek work was written within a generation or two of AD 66. Perhaps, in that year, there really was an earthquake on Crete, providing a memorable context for the 'find'. As for Septimius, I like to hope that he was in on the joke.

however, is not a fruitful approach. What we would now think of as metafictional playfulness courses through ancient literature. For example, *Wonders Beyond Thule*, Antonius Diogenes' prose fiction work perhaps dating from the second century AD, was filled with extravagant fantasies about space travel and magical potions, contained within a framing device that absolutely insisted that it was a true story. Its source, the text claimed, was another manuscript discovered in a tomb, this time in Tyre, by Alexander the Great himself.* The literary culture of classical antiquity was one in which farming manuals might be composed in verse, philosophy was frequently cast in dialogue form, and historical writing, notwithstanding sober claims to eyewitness veracity, might contain lengthy speeches that very often must have been authorial inventions, since there were no bilingual Roman reporters lurking behind enemy lines, ready to jot down pre-battle pep talks delivered by foreign generals. In the classical world, there was no clear division between purely factual and purely invented literary genres. The great library at Alexandria did not contain separate sections for fiction and non-fiction.[11] The border between the two, so fundamental to English-

* The text of *Wonders Beyond Thule* no longer exists, except in four brief fragments, and it is known largely from a lengthy, and possibly inaccurate, synopsis written by the ninth-century patriarch of Constantinople, Photius, so that the whole work exists in another kind of metafictional limbo. It is a scenario that could have been dreamed up by Borges, who wrote in the introduction to his short-story collection, *Fictions* (translated by Anthony Kerrigan): 'The composition of vast books is a laborious and impoverishing extravagance . . . A better course of procedure is to pretend that these books already exist, and then to offer a résumé, a commentary.'

language reading and publishing culture, is a modern one that exists largely for convenience's sake, despite numerous books that have breached or undermined it, and despite the fact that other cultures place their own boundaries along different lines, delineating books by, for example, literary style rather than factual or fictional content. Dictys, as Mrs Grammatiki understood well, is best understood neither as 'authentic' nor as a 'fraud', but as a tease, a knowing Cretan fabrication.

As a literary trope, the motif of happening upon a story in an obscure, lost source went on to have enormous traction. It would be used by authors from the twelfth-century Geoffrey of Monmouth, who claimed to have translated his *History of the Kings of Britain* into Latin from a 'most ancient book' in the 'British language', to Henry James, whose *Turn of the Screw* purports to derive from a manuscript in 'old, faded ink' kept for years 'in a locked drawer'. A scary story is made scarier by the hint that it is true: the great writer of ghostly tales, M. R. James,* knew this. Arthur Conan Doyle used similar devices repeatedly in his short fiction – the tale told to a friend of a friend, for example, written down in a letter, discovered many years later. The Sherlock Holmes stories, too, purport to be 'authentic' accounts by Dr Watson of his friend's exploits.

In fact, such claims are as old as books. In *Gilgamesh* – the Babylonian epic that pre-dates Homer – the deeds of the long-ago titular hero are said to have been set down in his

---

* A story by M. R. James, *Mr Humphreys and His Inheritance*, explores the uncanny properties of a garden hedge maze, kept locked for many years.

lifetime. The narrative voice enjoins the reader to open the cedarwood casket, release its bronze clasp and find the text set down on the precious lapis lazuli tablets. It is not so far from here to Homer's appeal to the Muses to sing him the story of the *Iliad* and the *Odyssey*. Nor to Muriel Spark's character Fleur, the novelist heroine of her *Loitering with Intent*, who feels she has a 'daemon' inside her. Nor to the scriptures. I have on my desk a postcard of Caravaggio's work known as *The Inspiration of St Matthew*, from the church of San Luigi dei Francesi in Rome. The saint, who is at his table, pen and paper in hand, leaps up in amazement, knocking his stool half out of the frame of the picture, as a rather grubby angel nose-dives from the ceiling, presumably requiring him to take dictation. (If only writing were so simple, so dramatic and so exciting.) The first Greek prose writer known to have used such a device was the very early-fifth-century writer Acusilaus, whose stories of the gods and heroes he transcribed from mysterious bronze tablets excavated by his father, or so he claimed.[12]

A text excavated from the earth, found in a drawer, discovered in the pages of some mildewed book or received from a god, guide, daemon, angel or dream: there may be different stratagems afoot in these claims, but underlying all of them is a distancing between the work and the writer, almost a superstitious (or, perhaps, ironic) denial that the impious act of godlike creation is being undertaken at all. But there is also, paradoxically, a bold claim that the work created must contain some deep authenticity, some profound truth – the kind of truth given weight by its derivation from a higher, external source; or the kind of truth that can be told only obliquely, in story or metaphor.

Odysseus the Source

Towards the beginning of *Diary of the Trojan War*, Dictys of Crete tells his readers that, when describing events he has been unable to verify personally, he will use the Greek warrior Odysseus as his source.

Odysseus the Liar

Odysseus is the first great literary fabulist, the teller of tales within a tale. His stories in the *Odyssey* are not like those told by characters in the *Iliad*, where memories are unlocked as evidence of past glories or old sorrows. Like Scheherazade's never-ending stories in the *Arabian Nights*, his tales, his fabrications, are a survival strategy. They keep him alive, better than any weapon would do. He likes to lie, above all, about Crete.

The *Odyssey* is the story of the hero's ten-year struggle to return home after the siege of Troy. He is tossed and whirled around the Mediterranean, encountering monsters, witches and sirens; he descends to the Underworld, where he meets the ghosts of many heroes and sees Ariadne, daughter of Minos; he enjoys sexy sojourns with various semi-supernatural women. Along the way he loses his men to monstrous storms and divine retribution. Odysseus, the long-enduring, ends up alone, a survivor by virtue of his caution, his inventiveness and his mind of twists and turns. (The word for this is *polytropos*, which means both 'much travelled' and 'much turned', as if the notions of journeying, mental shrewdness and a complicated, involuted shape are all coiled together.) The looping, winding, reversing journey he undertakes is like the path of a labyrinth. It corkscrews through time, too, for unlike the linear story of the *Iliad*, the *Odyssey* is a poem of flashbacks and elaborately nested stories. At times, it has the quality of a fairy tale about it. When I was young, I read over and over again a book of tales from the epic, retold for children. I imagined myself Odysseus: resourceful, wily, bold, tossed on the ocean waves.

The hero's most marvellous adventures – his tangles with the Cyclops and the Lotus Eaters and Scylla and Charybdis and the rest – are narrated by Odysseus himself at the court of the final kingdom he encounters, the strange and rich country of the Phaeacians. The king and queen, moved by his story, offer to convey him home. Loaded with gifts, he sets forth on a miraculously swift ship, which cuts the sea faster than any hawk could fly. He falls into a deep sleep on deck, and when he wakes, he finds himself on yet another beach: the crew have put him ashore and disappeared. Believing himself cheated, he cries out: 'Man of misery, whose land have I lit on now? What are they here – violent, savage, lawless?'

At that moment, the goddess Athena* appears: she is his celestial patron, her clever, calculating mind the divine counterpart of his own. Like Odysseus, she is not one to do things straightforwardly: she has disguised herself as a shepherd boy. Odysseus, ignorant of whom he is really addressing, asks where he is. The goddess begins teasingly (I paraphrase, but not much). 'Well, it's a famous land, though it's too cramped for driving

* Minerva is Athena's Roman equivalent.

horses; but it's got plenty of grapes, and grain, and it's good for goats, and cattle ... It's Ithaca, you might have heard of it.'

Odysseus doesn't miss a beat. He disguises his delight and replies: 'Yes, I might have heard of it. Though I myself am from Crete – I have been exiled from there, because I killed the son of the king, Idomeneus.' And he spins out an elaborate, entirely invented tale of murder and seaborne adventures. He is too wily to arrive home openly in pomp and arrogance like the Greek leader Agamemnon, who, oblivious to the risks of a vainglorious return, was slaughtered the minute he crossed his own threshold by his wife's lover. Athena – 'beautiful, tall, and skilled at weaving lovely things' – sees right through him, of course. But she is delighted by his adroit fabrications. Revealing her identity, she says:

> ... We're both old hands
> at the arts of intrigue. Here among mortal men
> you're far the best at tactics, spinning yarns,
> and I am famous among the gods for wisdom,
> cunning wiles, too ...[13]

The goddess disguises Odysseus as a ragged old man: to regain his kingdom, he will have to proceed by stealth and deception, she advises. Arriving at his own lands, he repeats his Cretan cover story, with entertaining variations, to his old swineherd Eumaeus, and to his own wife, Penelope. For Eumaeus, he constructs a complex tale, threaded through with the occasional truth: he fought at Troy, returned to Crete, headed off to Egypt, lived there for seven years; he endured storms at sea, outsmarted treacherous crews, devised daring escapes. For Penelope, he makes himself the grandson of Minos, Idomeneus's brother. He hosted Odysseus at Knossos before the war, he says. I will tell you the whole truth and hide nothing, he continues, shamelessly. Odysseus is coming. He's on his way back; his men ate the Cattle of the Sun and perished, but he didn't: he ended up in the land of the Phaeacians, and he'll be here soon. He has gone now to the oracle of Zeus at Dodona, there to seek advice on whether to return to Ithaca openly, or in secret. (Now there's a clue, if she's got ears to hear it.)

For the reader, these invented tales are part of the joy of the story. We know, with Odysseus, that he didn't really go to Egypt, he didn't really narrowly avoid being sold into slavery in Libya, he didn't really wash up on the shore of Thesprotia, he didn't really enact a bold escape from a ship's betraying crew, who'd lashed him to the mast of their vessel. But the stories are good. There is pleasure, great pleasure, in watching Odysseus spinning his tales, and we feel his pleasure, too, in a job of lying well done.

Epimenides of Crete

In St Paul's letter to Titus in the New Testament, he wrote of the inhabitants of Crete (in the King James translation): 'One of themselves, even a prophet of their own, said, "The Cretians [*sic*] are always liars, evil beasts, slow bellies." This witness is true.' St Paul might have paused over that statement, for if a Cretan tells you that all Cretans are liars, then he must be lying about Cretans being liars and so what he says must be true ... but Cretans are liars, and he's a Cretan, so what he says cannot be true. And if a Cretan tells you that all Cretans are liars, then he must be lying about Cretans being liars and so what he says must be true ... but Cretans are liars, and he's a Cretan, so what he says cannot be true. And on and on ...

What Paul was quoting is known by philosophers as the 'paradox of Epimenides'. Epimenides may or may not have been a real person, living in Knossos around 600 BC. Diogenes Laertius, the (possibly) third-century AD biographer of philosophers, related that he wrote works about, among other things, King Minos, the building of the *Argo*, and the voyage of Jason. And that one day, while out looking for a lost sheep, he took a nap in a cave – and woke up fifty-seven years later to find his home occupied by strangers and his brother an old man. During this sleep he conversed with Aletheia herself, the divine personification of Truth.

Cretan Lies

The Greek verb *kretizo*, used by authors such as Plutarch, means 'to speak like a Cretan', that is 'to lie'.

Pendlebury of Crete

Dilys Powell's book *The Villa Ariadne* tells of the bold actions on Crete during the Second World War of the British archaeologist

John Pendlebury, who had been appointed curator of the Palace of Minos. Before the German invasion, he had spent months criss-crossing the island, often on foot, plotting and organising with Cretan guerrilla fighters; he knew the terrain and the people from years of excavating and, a prodigious athlete, he was used to climbing the island's mountains and sleeping in its wildest, most secret places. When the invaders arrived, he fought hand-to-hand with a parachutist and was wounded. He managed to make it to a nearby house, where he was cared for – but later died, perhaps as the result of an execution-style shooting.

The circumstances were only gradually pieced together, painfully and imperfectly, in the years after the war. 'The web of myth and fact, hearsay and official testimony was still further complicated by the later accumulation of witnesses and by the element of personal drama with which those inheritors of saga the Cretans would decorate the tale,' wrote Powell. All who had known Pendlebury had a story to tell, and accounts of the end of his life took on the flavour of legend.

Arthur Evans and the Minoans

For Mrs Grammatiki, Sir Arthur Evans was a fabulist in the Cretan tradition. 'He did not find a labyrinth when he discovered the ruins of Knossos,' she wrote, 'but in a way he built one, for he pieced together from the scattered objects he found lying in the earth a wonderful and inventive story of a whole people. And of course he really did piece it together too, for he reconstructed so much of the palace and restored many of the beautiful things in the museum at Iraklion that would otherwise be in shattered fragments and incomplete. There are those who say that he took great liberties both with what he wrote about Crete and in the way that he reconstructed the artefacts and remains of Knossos. But for me there is something beautiful about this: he shows us that the act of excavation and the act of creation are not so different. Excavators make stories from the objects that they discover, and poets and artists also excavate the work of their forebears, bringing it up from the earth, remaking it for themselves and for us. Arthur Evans was all these things: excavator, storyteller, creator, labyrinth-maker.'

Evans, who died a few days after his ninetieth birthday in 1941, transformed knowledge of Europe's past when he excavated Knossos on Crete in 1900. In so doing he not only discovered the remains of a hitherto unknown people; he also changed the course of the future, for the implications of his discoveries rippled into the wider culture, influencing figures from Freud to Picasso. Digging up the past, in his case, also involved shoring up the foundations of modernism.

He dug in search of an ancient writing system pre-dating the Phoenician and Greek alphabets. He discovered three: an early pictographic script; the still undeciphered Linear A; and Linear B, the syllabic script that was finally decrypted in the 1950s. He also unearthed the remnants of a prosperous, cosmopolitan-seeming people, who had lived in lavish buildings decorated with frescoes and filled with exuberantly painted ceramics and sculptures. In his mind, these inhabitants of Crete were a powerful, peace-loving people who had built a maritime empire that had dominated parts of the Greek mainland. He believed he had found the first European civilisation.

When he wrote up his findings, publishing four gloriously illustrated volumes between 1921 and 1935, he called the work *The Palace of Minos.* There was absolutely no evidence to suggest that the Minos of Greek legend had been a historical figure who had walked the corridors and colonnades of Knossos, still less built a labyrinth. Nor, indeed, did Evans argue for the historicity of the mythical character. Rather, he speculated that 'Minos' was the title given to Cretan rulers, like Caesar or Kaiser. But clearly he found that the resonance of the myth was so great that he could not do without it, and 'Minoan' was a suitably elegant word to adopt for the civilisation as a whole. In this appropriation of the power of legend, Evans was following in the footsteps of Heinrich Schliemann, the nineteenth-century German archaeologist who claimed to have found the Troy of Homer, and the 'real' golden death mask of Agamemnon. But no one was better than Evans at breathing texture, life and narrative into the shattered fragments of an impossibly ancient civilisation. He was a natural storyteller – indeed, he was an erstwhile reporter for the *Manchester Guardian.*

Evans and his collaborators found that this 'Minoan' culture collapsed in around 1400 BC. There was some great calamity – perhaps an invasion from mainland Greece, or perhaps an earthquake or tsunami caused by a volcanic eruption on the Aegean island of Thera. In his 1930s guidebook to Knossos, John Pendlebury, then the site's curator, wrote in elegiac style of that collapse: 'Something went out of the world which the world will never see again; something grotesque perhaps, something fantastic and cruel but something also very lovely.' To these Englishmen the Minoan civilisation seemed to exhale both beauty and brutality, elegance and savagery: something more magnetic and more ominous than the rationality and balance that might be found in the remains of classical Greece; something that seemed even to echo the hidden and untamed desires of the unconscious, whose subterranean layers Freud was so busily bringing to light. The novelist, travel writer and biographer Rose Macaulay,* in her 1953 book *Pleasure of Ruins*, wrote eloquently about how the Minoan civilisation contained 'that monstrous strangeness which lends to pre-Hellenic ages something of the dissolving, uneven quality of dreams'.[14] She found that the old, frightening gods of Crete 'still brood unexorcised over the pillared lanes and courts of the restored palace of King Minos'.

Evans was born in 1851. His father John Evans, a wealthy owner of paper mills, was a voracious antiquary, an expert in coins and flints, writer of numerous papers for learned societies. When Arthur was six, his mother Harriet died from an infection shortly after giving birth, leaving her husband with five children, Arthur the eldest. He would end up outliving all of his siblings except Joan, his half-sister, who was born in 1893, to the then septuagenarian John's third wife. A prolific and respected art historian, Dame Joan Evans also put together the

---

* If you have not read her novel *The Towers of Trebizond*, you have a pleasure in store.

book-length index for *The Palace of Minos*, and wrote her half-brother's biography.* In that work, *Time and Chance*, she described how John Evans observed in his diary after Harriet's death that Arthur and his siblings did not seem to feel their mother's loss. She noted: 'More than seventy years later Arthur Evans was to write an indignant NO in the margin.'

Evans was small and slight, and from a young age had terribly short sight and poor night vision. He was happy examining the minutest artefacts, and in the pages of his notebooks one can stumble across tiny sketches of wild flowers, made with a miniaturist's care for detail. Alongside this love of the small and the close was a taste for adventure and distant landscapes: in one vacation from Oxford, where he studied history, he made an ambitious overland trip to Constantinople via Croatia and Bosnia; and the following year went to Bulgaria and Romania, where, in true English public-schoolboy fashion, he made himself understood 'by speaking a kind of Italian Latin'. The next summer it was Sweden and Finland and Inari in the Arctic Circle, where a local pastor told him about a grotto on an island that was still paganishly venerated. After he got his first, he headed to Göttingen to continue his studies; from there he travelled again to the Balkans and was briefly imprisoned by the Austrian police, suspected of being a Russian spy. On this trip he came for the first time to the old Venetian port of Ragusa, now Dubrovnik in Croatia, and fell in love with the place: he

* She died in my lifetime, in 1977. Her paternal grandfather, born in 1781, would have remembered reports of the French Revolution.

adored its blue sea and distant mountains, its handsome architecture and terracotta-red roofs.

His first book, *Through Bosnia and Herzegovina on Foot*, established him, though precociously young at twenty-six, as an expert on the Balkans. The region was of vivid interest in Britain, as news spread of atrocities against Christians by rogue troops operating unchecked by the weak regional Ottoman rulers. The editor of the *Manchester Guardian*, C. P. Scott, whose uncle was a friend of John Evans's, agreed to give Arthur a job as a correspondent. Travelling again to Ragusa, he met Edward Freeman, the Regius professor of modern history at Oxford, and his daughters. The elder, Margaret, was her father's secretary: she was fluent in French and German, and had reasonable Latin, Greek and Italian. According to Joan Evans, she had been brought up to strenuous foreign travel and, in particular, 'had acquired the art of going on without grumbling when she was tired'. This was a quality that was to stand her in good stead when, later, she became engaged to Arthur Evans, on the occasion of which Edward Freeman wrote to his future son-in-law, using his daughter's pet name: 'I do think my Gretchen rather a precious thing to give away, but I can give her to you with a hearty good will as I am sure you will know what to do with her.' Arthur and Margaret's betrothal treat in London was to visit a display of finds made in Troy by Heinrich Schliemann.

After their marriage, they moved back to Ragusa, from where Arthur made many expeditions in search of ancient remains. The politics in the region was unstable, though: the old Slavic territories of the Ottomans were being annexed by Austria, and

Evans railed in the *Manchester Guardian* at examples of the new rulers' repressive policies towards the Bosnians. In 1882, his inflammatory articles got him imprisoned for seven weeks. It was entirely typical of him that at one point during this unpleasant period he should smuggle a letter out of the prison via the gaoler's wife – written in his own blood. He had a taste for the dramatic.

After that, Ragusa was over for the Evanses. They came home to England, and Arthur became keeper of the Ashmolean Museum in Oxford, beginning a long struggle to modernise and unify the university collections (then straggling around the city in a number of locations). He did not like to stay still: he took Margaret on a tour of Greece. Poor Margaret. An operation to enable her to become pregnant had been unsuccessful, and her health was delicate. This splendidly unromantic West Country girl wrote to her sister from Delphi that the place had 'disappointed me a little, and I still think that Wookey Hole and its basin beats the Castalian fount out and out in grandeur'. Over the years she became increasingly dogged by illness, and in 1893 she died at the Ligurian resort of Alassio. 'I do not think anyone can ever know what Margaret has been to me … All seems very dark, and without consolation,' wrote Arthur to his father.*

---

* Quoted in Evans, *Time and Chance*, p.304. There was clearly more to his sexuality than this early marriage. At seventy-three, he was convicted of an act of public indecency in Hyde Park with a seventeen-year-old boy. Cathy Gere, in her book *Knossos and the Prophets of Modernism*, p.12, calls the Minoan civilisation he summoned up through his scholarly books and articles 'an inverts' paradise of female deities, cross-dressing priests, and girl athletes'.

By that time he had already started to become intrigued by Crete. 'It is hard to say what chance had first drawn his attention to the unknown island; it seems as if a thousand tiny facts and things had drifted like dust and settled to weigh down the scales of his decision,' wrote Joan Evans. He had a hunch that he might find evidence of an ancient script there. Examining seal stones from Mycenae, he had discerned tiny markings he thought might be writing, and he found similar examples in the dealers' shops in Athens that were said to have come from Crete.

He finally arrived at the island's capital, Candia (now Heraklion), on 15 March 1894, and headed straight for the bazaar for some antiquities shopping. His diary recorded: 'I bought 22 early Cretan stones at about 1½ piastres apiece, 2 small Greek heads from Gortyna, some coins, one silver from and of Phaestos, and a small marble image from Phaestos ...' He was determined to excavate at Knossos, a place rich with mythical associations. He was by no means the first to think of so doing. A French archaeologist had scoped out the site, and made an agreement with one of the co-owners of the land. Schliemann himself, before his death in 1890, had wanted to tackle it. More pertinently, perhaps, a Cretan dragoman (an interpreter working with the ruling Turks), with the propitious name of Minos Kalokairinos, had already done some digging, finding pottery of the Mycenaean type. Evans met him on 16 March, and three days later visited the site. He found meadows 'brilliant with purple white and pinkish anemones and blue iris', empty of visible traces of habitation but for what the British traveller Robert Pashley had described, several decades earlier, as 'some rude masses of Roman brickwork' and a 'miserable hamlet'.[15]

It was six years before Evans could start to excavate. There were endless, dragging negotiations to be conducted with the various owners of the land, all of whom had to be persuaded to sell. The Heraklion *syllogos* – the association that protected the island's antiquities and looked after the town's museum – was reluctant to grant its blessing, fearing that any significant finds would be taken to the museum in Constantinople. At the same time, the political situation on the island became extremely volatile: insurgencies were rising against Ottoman rule, Greece weighed in in support, and appalling violence erupted between Crete's Christian and Muslim inhabitants. The unrest made Evans a journalist again: for the *Manchester Guardian* of 25 May 1898 he turned in a harrowing account of Christian massacres of Muslim villagers. He visited one Muslim village, Etea, the entire population of which had been killed except for one girl who had fainted and was thought dead. The men had been 'cut to pieces' and the women and children shot. '[The] old walls have never looked forth on more atrocious deeds than those so recently perpetrated here,' he wrote.

Although the Turks successfully suppressed the Christian uprisings, the European powers forced the Ottomans, who had ruled the island since capturing it from the Venetians in 1669, to allow Crete to become autonomous. Late in 1898, Prince George of Greece was inserted by the Great Powers as high commissioner, before formal unification with Greece in 1913. It was the island's extraction from the Ottoman Empire that created the conditions for Evans to begin his excavation: as the nineteenth century ended, he came rapidly to an agreement with the newly independent local authorities, undertaking not to remove any finds from the island, except in the case of 'duplicates'. His argument that Knossos was 'at once the starting point and the earliest stage in the highway of European civilisation'[16] helps explain why it is such an important anchor of Cretan identity to this day, establishing the island at the origin of a specifically European cultural tradition (albeit one that Evans argued drew its most important influences from Egypt, Libya and sub-Saharan Africa). There was that – and there was Evans's skill at publicising, romanticising and reconstructing the splendid finds.

He began digging in March 1900. His deputy was a Scot called Duncan Mackenzie, of whom he wrote in his unreflecting patrician manner, in the fourth volume of *The Palace of Minos*: 'His Highland loyalty never failed, and the simple surroundings of his earlier years gave him an inner understanding of the native workmen.' Mackenzie was also a much more experienced digger than Evans, up to date on the latest 'scientific' archaeological techniques and punctilious in measuring and recording as he went. Reading Evans's diaries of the excavation is to feel him speculating and synthesising on the spot. He thinks aloud and leaps ahead. His handwriting loosens and sprawls. He sketches particularly intriguing objects. He records the reactions of the workmen. Mackenzie's day books, on the other hand, keep a solid account of fact; they are as sober as Evans's are exuberant. He records how many labourers are employed each day (always a mixed crew of Christians and Muslims, at Evans's insistence). He fills out each line of his notebook exactly to the end. He marks the left-hand margin with a summary of what the body of the text describes. He makes clear scale drawings. He does not indulge in swooning descriptions of objects or rooms, or speculate very often on their purpose. Occasionally he remarks that a find is 'capital', the outer limit of his lexicon of excitement.

The excavation advanced with tremendous speed and success. On 26 March 1900, three days after they began work, they found an 'earthenware hand-polished and incised figurine of a female without the legs but with the broken surface, where they joined to the body, traceable'. So Mackenzie wrote. Evans called it 'Aphrodite of Knossos!' and recorded that the workmen, thinking it a male figure, had christened it 'Stavros'. On 5 April, Evans recorded a 'great day': two large pieces of fresco. 'One represented the head and forehead, the other the waist and part of the skirt of a female figure holding in her hand a long Mycenaean "rhyton", or high funnel shaped cup … The profile of the face was a noble type: full lips. The eye was dark and somewhat almond shaped … In front of the ear is a kind of ornament & a necklace & bracelet are visible. The arms are beautifully modelled. The waist is of the smallest … It is far and away the most remarkable human figure of Mycenaean age that has yet come to light.' He also noted that one of the boys employed on the dig, Manoli, thought of it as a 'Saint with halo' and had said of it, '*phantazei*' – it's spooky.

Mackenzie was less susceptible to the full lips, the almond eyes, the beautifully shaped arms and waist. 'Some fresco in a large piece appeared in a horizontal position with the surface up. It turned out to be the hand, life size, of a human figure (youth) with the right hand holding the handle of some vase. A little later part of the body including the left arm and hand came into view. The left hand held the lower part of the vase the handle of which was held by the right hand. The vase scaled downwards to a point like the typical Mycenaean pillar. The figure was in profile left.' Mackenzie's account was a good deal less speculative than his chief's; Evans's almost certainly the version one would prefer to read. All three of the recorded observers of the fresco (including Manoli) interpreted it in the light of their own prejudices, temperament, education and experience.[17] A few days later, on 10 April, Evans was calling the figure 'Ariadne', in inverted commas. Later it became known as the Cup-bearer Fresco (and established as a male figure, as Mackenzie had thought all along) – one of the most famous images that can now be seen in the museum at Heraklion.

By 13 April, the excavators had moved on to a room that Evans called the 'Bath chamber', which contained a bench and a seat and what appeared to be some kind of impluvium or basin. The throne, he felt, was too delicate for manly buttocks, so he decided that it had belonged to a woman. The basin was, he thought, 'the Queen's – Ariadne's bath'. His earlier inverted commas around the name had disappeared.* (Later, he had reproductions of the chair made for his house Youlbury,

---

* This basin, or whatever it was, continued to perplex the excavators: if a bath, it was a bath without drainage. Not a happy thought in the heat of summer, as Evans wrote. My partner recalls being taken to Knossos in the 1970s, when a guide solemnly introduced it as 'a lustral basin of purification', whatever that really meant (it was Evans, in fact, who grandly called it a 'lustral basin'). In reality, no one understands its purpose with any certainty.

on Boar's Hill near Oxford, which also contained a mosaic of the Cretan labyrinth, with the Minotaur at its centre. The house was pulled down many years ago.) By 18 April, the layout of rooms and passages was coming into focus. 'The whole plan very labyrinthine,' he wrote. On 8 May, he was giving the rooms of the building wonderful romantic names on a sketch map. 'Steatite Vase Room' was crossed out in favour of 'Flower Gatherer Room'. He also marked a 'Room of Lotus Lamp' and a 'Room of Spiral Cornice'. His notebook proposed Ariadne as the chatelaine of these remains, I think only half seriously; but even in the pages of *The Palace of Minos*, the perfume of legend lingers in the air. 'The palace traditionally built for Minos by his great craftsman Daedalus has proved to be no baseless fabric of the imagination,' he wrote in the introduction.

In Knossos, Evans found, or constructed, an imaginative home. He had formed it, in Joan Evans's words, from an 'inchoate mass of pottery and stone, metal and faience, clay tablets and seals, walls and pavements'. It was 'exactly to his taste: set in beautiful Mediterranean country, aristocratic and human in feeling; creating an art brilliant in colour and unusual in form, that drew inspiration from the flowers and birds, and creatures that he loved. It provided him with enigmas to solve and oracles to interpret, and opened a new world for eye and mind to dwell in: a world which served to isolate him from a present in which he had found no real place.'[18] It is a curious thing to have written about a brother, one who had so much success and found so much fame: Joan hints at a sense of disorientation and displacement in this stray sentence that is absent from the rest of her narrative. Perhaps Arthur was lost, too, and trying to build a structure that he hoped would contain and satisfy him. The Knossos he made for his 'mind to dwell in' was an escape, a holt, a haven, a realm over which he presided as its benign and loving god, a place over which he could exert control: and in making it, he allowed others to step inside and wander about its finely built halls, its endless, labyrinthine passages.

The Ring of Nestor

In *The Palace of Minos* Evans described how one of his most beloved possessions, his 'Ring of Nestor', had many years earlier come to light. The story went like this: it had been found by a farmer searching for building material in an ancient beehive tomb in Kakovatos, in the Peloponnese in mainland Greece. Some time later, in 1907, a group of German archaeologists excavated there. The Germans' investigations convinced them that they had found the location of Homer's 'sandy Pylos', the home of the hero Nestor.

But, wrote Evans, the existence of the gold ring had been 'kept dark' from the Germans, and on the death of the original finder it was bequeathed to the owner of a neighbouring vineyard. On a trip to Athens, Evans saw 'an imperfect impression of the signet' – perhaps made by a fellow archaeologist, perhaps by a dealer or another intermediary. Convinced of its importance, he 'at once ... undertook a journey to the West Coast of the Morea [the Peloponnese], resulting in the acquisition of this remarkable object, which … is conveniently described as the "Ring of Nestor"'.

Evans wrote as if some other person had named it thus: it was he, though, who had the knack for inventing or borrowing evocative tags to attach to his finds and theories, tags that, it turns out, are ineradicable even if the sober scholarship of later generations finds them to be fanciful. *The Palace of Minos* abounds with such phrases: the 'Horns of Consecration'; the 'tomb of the Double Axes'; the 'Queen's Megaron'; the 'Snake Goddess'; the 'Halls of the Just'; and, an allusion to Homer, 'Ariadne's Dancing Floor'. Perhaps he half believed that his ring did once belong to Homer's voluble veteran warrior. At any rate it was, he said, an early Minoan artefact, dating from the sixteenth century BC.

Evans wrote of the ring's intaglio decoration[19] with wild enthusiasm. 'The composition of the whole,' he decided, 'gives us the first glimpse into the Elysian fields of Minoan and Mycenaean religion.' The design, as he described it, was divided into four by the trunk and two spreading horizontal branches of a tree, which brought to his mind, at least, 'the four rivers of Paradise or the triple-branched water-course of the Fields of Ialû in the Egyptian "Isles of the Blest"'. Under and upon the branches of the tree were figures, sixteen of them. In one quarter of the decorated field, he identified the 'Minoan Goddess seated in animated conversation with her wonted companion, while above head there flutter two butterflies'. Two tiny objects, mere scratches in the gold, he decided were chrysalises. He continued: 'It is difficult to explain them otherwise than as an allusion to the resurgence of the human spirit after death.' Two human figures standing close to them, it could 'hardly be doubted', represented these 'resurgent souls'. (Earlier, in an article of 1924, Evans had argued that the story of Cupid and Psyche, recounted in the Roman prose-fiction work *The Golden Ass*, represented a fragmentary survival of this idea, for '*psyche*' is the ancient Greek word for both soul and butterfly.) They were, he wrote, 'a young couple whom Death had parted'. He identified, too, 'the lion-guardian, tended by the handmaidens of the divinity; and "the Griffin's Court", representing a ceremony of initiation'.

As a whole, he wrote, the ring provided a glimpse into the 'World Beyond as conceived by the Minoans'. It is a realm to which he was clearly strongly attracted. There is no gloom about the picture he conjured up: 'Surprise, joy, affection and encouragement are alternately suggested,' he wrote. Evans's imagination seemed to slip him into some charming and elegant room in his own London or Paris. 'All alike wear fashionable raiment, reflecting indeed the latest modes, and the imagination is left free to fill in the bright colouring.'

The ring can be seen in a case in the Ashmolean in Oxford, alongside other artefacts from the Aegean that Evans acquired* and bequeathed, on his death, to the museum. It is tiny: a plain gold signet ring for the most delicate of ancient fingers.

---

* The finds excavated at Knossos were very largely kept on Crete, in accordance with Evans's agreement with the Cretan *syllogos*. But he took a pretty relaxed view of the antiquities trade and, a rich man after the death of his paper-mill-owning father, acquired many ancient artefacts on the open market.

The incised decoration is hard to pick out with the naked eye, even under museum lighting. It seems incredible that from these faint marks and signs Evans constructed a whole world. In a study room at the museum, I read the notebook from 1923 in which he jotted down his first rough thoughts on the ring, alongside an ink sketch of the object itself – perhaps he did this very soon after he had managed to buy it, or perhaps after he had seen that 'imperfect impression' of it in Athens. Here one can begin to observe how he built his ideas, thinking while looking, changing his mind. 'Both butterflies rather than bees,' he noted of the barely visible twitches in the gold surface of the ring. 'Short skirts … Attitude of "Court Ladies" of Min. fresco … Enchanted ~~wood~~ bower of sacred lion or griffin … Lion on couch. Tended by handmaidens under leafy canopy. Griffin on throne adored by griff women.' At first, he took the squiggles and flicks at the bottom of the scene, below the image of the tree, to represent a ship carrying the souls of the dead across the ocean. But the words 'boat' and 'sea of fishes' are scored through – he decided that the boat was, in fact, a dog, which changed his understanding of the whole image. Other scribbles, for example, look like this: 'The Elysian Fields beyond the ~~Great Water. Fourfold division by streams. The boat that carried over the departed.~~' There will be no 'Great Water' in his published text, no sea beyond which the souls of the dead live, but rather a tree, even if its trunk and branches did bring to mind 'the four rivers of Paradise'.

Evans's interpretation of the ring drew on the rich vein of stories and myths he had absorbed through a lifetime's reading, and the intellectual preoccupations of his peers (including, surely, James Frazer, the anthropologist author of the great compendium of world mythologies, *The Golden Bough*, first published in 1890). His reflections are not terribly sober: but there again, who would want a mere 'wood' when one could have a 'bower'? Cathy Gere, who has analysed Evans's interpretation of the ring in her book *Knossos and the Prophets of Modernism*, has written of him, waspishly but probably accurately, 'He always knew what he was looking for – and he made sure that he found it.'[20]

Over time, Evans's imagination was not to be the only supplier of the 'bright colouring' he imagined when he gazed upon the tiny engraved scene. During the excavations at Knossos, he worked with a father-and-son team of Swiss artists, Emile Gilliéron the elder and younger, whom he commissioned to restore the fragmentary frescoes – though many of their reconstructions were and are considered to be highly imaginative and tendentious. The Gilliérons also produced many fine reproductions of Minoan artefacts that were eagerly acquired at the time by museums. Evans asked Gilliéron the younger to work up the scene on Nestor's ring as a painting, for publication in *The Palace of Minos.* In the book one can see the tiny ring's design enlarged into a magnificent full-page colour illustration, with the griffin, lion goddess, butterflies and fashionably dressed women all rendered in sumptuous blues, golds and scarlets.

Many scholars are now sure that the Ring of Nestor is fake. The iconography is all wrong, argue its detractors, and the provenance dubious, to say the least: the raid of the beehive tomb, the discovery kept secret from the Germans, the original finder lost from history. The label in the Ashmolean acknowledges the possibilities. There is a school of thought that the Gilliérons may also have had a shady sideline in manufacturing fakes. It is possible, though far from certain, that Evans, in asking the younger Gilliéron to rework the ring's decoration as a painting, may have been commissioning him to reproduce a design that he himself had had a hand in creating. There is a stranger possibility yet: the ring has recently been defended by some scholars as genuine after all, by way of iconographical comparison with objects discovered after Evans's death. What if it were so good a fake that its imagery actually foreshadowed authentic objects that in the 1920s had yet to be discovered?[21] Whatever the Ring of Nestor's precise status, which may never be quite proven, one thing is certain: the Gilliérons were, par excellence, blurrers of the boundaries between authentic object, elaboration, restoration, reproduction and, perhaps, forgery; between fact and fiction.

Heraklion, 2016

In September of 2016, I returned to Knossos and Heraklion for the first time since that childhood visit. I had hoped to visit the museum with Mrs Grammatiki, to have her lead me once again around its galleries. Instead I was left with fleeting memories and vague recollections of that earlier time, as if she had been a dream, as if she had never existed.

I had first come here as an innocent. Now I was a cynic, alert to semi-inventions and reconstructions. The museum at Heraklion showed the treasures of Knossos off to marvellous advantage. How could one not fall in love with these richly painted ceramics, tendrilling with lilies, or narcissi, or papyrus flowers, or crocuses? I had not remembered these lively, spiralling things: these painted octopuses, these partridges and water birds, this aquatic profusion of weed and frond and sea creature: an abundance that seemed entirely in tune with Evans's own generative, teeming brain. And of course the first thing I caught myself thinking was how modern it all was. I could drink out of that cup over there, put my own bunch of lilies in that jug.

I gazed into the case of famous 'snake goddess' figurines – one ivory, one faience, both topless, wasp-waisted, flounce-skirted, holding snakes aloft, the taller of the two just over thirty centimetres high. For Evans these female figures had formed the basis of Cretan religion, a matriarchal earth-goddess cult in which the snakes (whose bodies ever hug the ground) symbolised her female chthonic powers. For this he had only the evidence of the figures themselves, as well as images of similarly clad women depicted on objects such as rings. His interpretation was much influenced by the contemporary theory that there had been an early matriarchal period in prehistoric religions, an idea propounded in *Das Mutterrecht* (*The Mother Right*, 1861) by the Swiss antiquary Johann Josef Bachofen.

For a moment I succumbed to the figurines' powerful allure. But not for long. I knew that my fascination was contingent, in part at least, on the narratives woven around these objects by Evans. What the uninitiated would struggle to know by merely looking into the glass case was that the slightly smaller of the two figurines was discovered lacking her head and one of her arms, which were later constructed by Halvor Bagge, a Danish artist. The larger had lacked her skirts – nearly everything from the waist down was a 'reconstitution', as Evans called the restorations.

Kenneth Lapatin's book *Mysteries of the Snake Goddess* tells the story of another, similar figurine, known as the Boston snake goddess, which was fashioned from gold and ivory. It was bought for the Boston Museum of Fine Arts in 1914 for the then stupendous price of $950, supposedly having been transported in pieces to America by a Cretan emigrant in a cigar box, or possibly a cigarette tin. Evans described it in volume three of *The Palace of Minos*: he speculated that it must have been stolen from Knossos during the excavations,[22] but took a relaxed view of this supposed depredation. 'None need regret,' he wrote, 'that the Knossian Goddess – so admirably reconstituted – should have found such a worthy resting-place and that she stands to-day as a Minoan "Ambassadress" to the New World.' Of the figure's 'remarkable' physiognomy, he wrote, 'It is a curiously modern type.' Indeed, more than he knew: as Lapatin has shown, it was probably forged, quite possibly by the Gilliérons, and came to Boston not in the hands of some mysterious emigrant, but rather via two American archaeologists, Richard Seager and Burt Hodge Hill.

There are other 'Minoan' figurines that, despite shaky provenances, found their way onto the market and into major collections in, for example, Toronto and Cambridge. One of them, called by Evans 'Our Lady of the Sports', appears as the gilded frontispiece to the fourth volume of *The Palace of Minos*.

She has the splendid breasts of the 'snake goddesses' but the kind of lower half typically associated with male figures in Minoan iconography. A 'matronly corset ... combined with male lion clothing and masculine "cod-piece"', as Evans put it. The sculpture inspired a whole section of *The Palace of Minos*, entitled 'The Minoan Goddess as Patroness of the Palace Bull-ring'. But it is another probable fake, 'the most absurd figurine ... like a magnificently perverse bit of 1930s pornography', as Gere has written.[23] It seems that the forgers knew exactly how to fuel and tempt Evans's desires: more Cretan lies.

Upstairs in the museum were the frescoes. Old friends, almost. They had been in my mind for years, and they were everywhere on Crete. The standard plastic carrier bag for tourist purchases on the island ('HAPPY HOLIDAYS IN GREECE', it proclaims) reproduces images of the most celebrated examples: the bull leapers, the Ladies in Blue, the Prince of the Lilies. The first two were among the three images that Mrs Grammatiki had sent me away with all those years ago. The last shows a youth, in half-profile, wearing a feathered headdress that arcs from his head like a rainbow. One arm is raised to his chest and to the long ringlet of hair that falls down his torso; the other is stretched behind him. His body is posed awkwardly: his legs and head are in profile but his chest faces us. Around him, growing as high as his wasp-thin waist, are gorgeous stylised lily blooms, their petals curling into tight little spirals. Above them a butterfly flits. The Prince of the Lilies is another reconstruction, by the Gilliérons, of shattered fragments. Later observers have proposed that the various shards of the figure – which were found scattered on the ground – may in fact have come from several bodies, and a number of different solutions to the jigsaw have been proposed,[24] some radically different from the Gilliérons'. But the 'Priest-king', as Evans also called him, is now ineradicably associated with Knossos: in stylised form he is even the logo of the Cretan ferry company Minoan Lines.

The Ladies in Blue, a famous trio of elegant women with snaking, elaborate hairstyles, had always been a favourite with me as a child: they had seemed to represent the epitome of an unreachable adult femininity. When I saw them again in the museum, I realised how meagre the original parts were – a mere scrap of a necklace, a shred of a wrist, the tip of a raised finger. Those beautiful profiles, those almond eyes, those seductive curls of hair: all invention. The fresco had been restored by the elder Gilliéron; though perhaps restored is too weak a word for what he did, since he made a whole image from mere fragments, just as you might conjecture or invent the design of a large, immensely complicated jigsaw from three or four pieces. This 'restoration' was in fact damaged in an earthquake in 1926, and then re-restored by the younger Gilliéron, so that what one actually sees in the museum has been called 'the restoration of a re-creation – or a re-creation of a restoration'.[25] When Evelyn Waugh visited the Heraklion museum while on a Mediterranean cruise in 1929, he commented, with characteristic tartness: 'Only a few square inches of the vast area exposed to our consideration are earlier than the last twenty years, and it is impossible to disregard the suspicion that their painters have tempered their zeal for accurate reconstructions with a somewhat inappropriate predilection for covers of

Vogue.'[26] Perhaps: but I suspect the traffic of influence travelled both ways.

Evans found the female figures depicted in Knossian frescoes fascinating, and wove some of his most arresting narratives from them. Another fragment, of 'seated ladies' – foregathered to watch, he thought, the famous Knossian bull-fighting – were 'scenes of feminine confidence, of tittle-tattle and society scandal' that 'take us far from the production of Classical Art in any age'. He wrote: 'A curiously artificial atmosphere of social life pervades these highly polite groups of Court ladies with their puffed sleeves, their wasp waists and elaborate hair-dressing.'[27] A famous image of a single female figure in profile was dubbed 'La Parisienne'. 'Her elaborate coiffure and suspiciously scarlet lips are certainly marks of a highly artificial social life,'[28] he decided, somewhat disapprovingly, as if she were a high-class courtesan, no better than she should be. The French archaeologist Edmond Pottier wrote, soon after her discovery, of her 'mixture of naive archaism and spicy modernism … this Pasiphaë who looks like an habitué of Parisian bars'.[29] So easily, so unreflectingly was the image eroticised by its male viewers.

Evans's 'court ladies' needed only a change of outfit to become 'bull leapers' like the ones depicted on the famous fresco, he decided: 'Slim, lithe, vivacious, many of them were no doubt ready, according to the practice of Minoan girls – seemingly even in a good position in life – to exchange their gay jackets and flounced skirts for boys' loincloths and to step down into the Bull Ring to take part in the athletic and acrobatic performances.'[30] When in 1903 or 1904 Isadora Duncan, the

Nietzsche-obsessed pioneer of modern dance, visited the site, she 'threw herself into one of her impromptu dances ... Up and down the steps she danced, her dress flowing around her', according to an account by Evans's ward James Candy.[31] Her antics shocked the conservative Duncan Mackenzie and aroused Evans's disapproval. He found it 'quite out of keeping'. But surely it was precisely 'in keeping' – certainly with Evans's less sober writings. Rose Macaulay wrote of Evans: 'A brilliant showman, having conjured a civilisation out of the earth he enjoyed it so much, and made everyone else enjoy it so much, that there was never a dull moment.'[32]

Knossos, 2016

The dusty hamlet and open fields that Evans first encountered at Knossos are things of the past: now a whole village has grown up around the site, and its car and coach parks. Tourist shops line the main road, and new streets almost surround the Villa Ariadne, the substantial, handsome house Evans built for himself, where he dined on supplies from Fortnum's 'under the olives, while wine flowed and mandolins played and Cretans danced', according to Macaulay.[33] As my partner and I entered, prompt at 8.30 a.m., the guards were at their stations, outnumbering visitors, each with a whistle round his or her neck, primed to chastise the disobedient if they strayed from the approved paths. For now, however, before the rush of coach parties, they were chatting on their phones or drinking coffee from Styrofoam cups. The signboards and labels around the site had been subject to a certain post-Evans revisionism, his lovely names for the rooms placed in distancing, ironising inverted commas – the 'Queen's Megaron', the 'Lapidary's Workshop', the 'Hall of the Double Axes'. But you can't entirely eradicate Evans, quotation marks or not. He is still there, setting the intellectual agenda, feeding imaginations, as solid as his bronze portrait-bust standing in the courtyard as you enter the site.

After his first season of digging, it became clear to Evans that rainfall and poor weather were likely to do great damage to the recently uncovered remains, and so over the years he employed architects to shore up roofs and build concrete structures that in some cases could be only speculatively connected with any original building forms. One of the architects was Piet de Jong, who worked for most of his career with archaeologists in the Mediterranean, and started his long association with Knossos in the 1920s. His only built work in Britain was a Christian Scientist church in his home town of Leeds, which he designed in an Egyptian-classical-art-deco style that actually somewhat resembles his reconstruction work at Knossos. His are the tapering pillars that I remembered so well from my childhood. He gave some of his concrete beams a grain as if they were wood, and uneven edges as if they were the shattered remains of larger structures. He built ruins; or perhaps a better way of putting it is that he constructed neat, complete buildings that contained the suggestion of ruin.

Knossos has teasingly been called the best art deco in Greece; de Jong's modernist 'reconstitutions' have not been to everybody's taste. In 1932, Robin Collingwood, the archaeologist and philosopher who wrote *The Idea of History*, was taken round the site by John Pendlebury. 'The first impression on the mind of a visitor is that Knossian architecture consists of garages and public lavatories,' he noted grimly. 'This impression is partly due to matters of detail – open-fronted flat-roofed shed-like buildings, and cubicle box-shaped structures with small high windows: partly it is due to concrete restoration, which may in this respect give it a false idea of the original.'[34]

On closer inspection, though, he decided that the modern reconstructions probably *did* give a reasonable idea of the original structures; in fact, they were perfectly in tune with each other. Proportion, which was key to classical Athenian architecture, was utterly lacking in both ancient Knossos and the work of the moderns, he wrote. 'Modern architecture has lost this ideal [of proportion] and ... in the main is an architecture of comfort and convenience ... This is the secret of the Knossian "modernity". The Cretan artists were modern in the sense of being barbarously utilitarian, not Hellenistically classical ...' He thought it all, both modern and Minoan, 'undignified and mean'. Collingwood seems to imply that it was mere chance that ancient remnants and new buildings should be so neatly aligned, as if architectural fashion had predicted the aesthetics of the Minoan civilisation before it had been discovered.

The concrete interventions now require their own upkeep: they are almost archaeological relics in themselves, a century on. When I visited, part of the site, the base of the grand staircase, was blocked off from visitors and occupied by builders with their scaffolding and ladders and banter and roll-up cigarettes; ducts snaked through the old spaces and under the frescoes. Knossos was not precisely a let-down. I didn't feel disappointed, as I might have expected to do, by the fact that rooms into which I could remember wandering freely as a child were now cordoned off behind Plexiglas barriers. But it was curious to revisit a place that had sparked so much in me – whose halls and corridors I had walked so often in my imagination – and to find myself, while intrigued, so unmoved. The Knossos of my mind, the Knossos I had populated with my own dreamlike Ariadne and Daedalus, the Knossos that Catullus called 'the lofty palace / of great-souled Minos', had taken on its own life, far away from its source, this half-remembered, oddly prosaic ruin.

Later on that trip to Crete, we visited another Minoan site. It took two attempts to find it, winding frustratingly round narrow, steep roads in our hire car and at length asking directions in terrible Greek from a woman driving one of the ubiquitous pickup trucks that Cretans use in the countryside. Once we found it, a kilometre or so outside a silent mountain village, we were the only visitors. Peaks lightly veiled with cloud stretched out on all sides. Fragments of masonry crumbled, visible beneath fronds of end-of-summer vegetation: etiolated fennel, papery mallow, dry thistle. The dilapidation, the solitude and the dramatic situation appealed greatly to me, though the stones and low walls were, more or less, unreadable by my untutored eyes. There was no labelling, and no reconstruction. A makeshift cover, rattling alarmingly in the wind, fretted with rust, had been built over the most delicate remains.

At the end of the visit we were ushered into the attendant's hut and asked to sign the visitors' book, then smilingly rewarded with a couple of boiled sweets. Ours were the only names in the book for a week: I had a suspicion that our signatures were going to end up as (feeble) ammunition in a battle to keep the place open, since so many archaeological sites on the island, particularly after the financial crisis of 2008, stood closed and locked. As the mountains loomed up in the distance, and the breeze ruffled the carpet of desiccated grass and columbine, it seemed that the contrast with Knossos was complete. For a moment I imagined what it would be like here if the ancient tumbled walls were built up, if information boards were dotted around, if there were a car park and a coach park and gift shops. It seemed that I had become a romantic in my forties, more attracted to this wild and lonely spot than to Knossos's curious modern mixture of pragmatism and wild fantasy. And yet it was Evans's concrete 'reconstitutions' that had provided me with the materials to build my own Knossos, the Knossos of my imagination.

ARIADNE'S CLEWE

For Sigmund Freud, the unconscious resembled the dark corridors and hidden places of a labyrinth. Navigating the chaos of that maze – achieving mastery over it, mapping it, finding one's way out of it – was the work of psychoanalysis, he told an interviewer[35] in 1927. 'Psychoanalysis simplifies life. We achieve a new synthesis after analysis. Psychoanalysis reassorts the maze of stray impulses, and tries to wind them around the spool to which they belong. Or, to change the metaphor, it supplies the thread that leads a man out of the labyrinth of his own unconscious.'

The Minotaur's lair in Chaucer's *The Legend of Good Women* is 'crinkled to and fro', and 'shapen as the mase is wroght'. To find his way through it, Theseus must use the 'clewe of twyne' that Ariadne gives him. The word 'clewe' derives from Old English *cliwen* or *cleowen*, meaning a rounded mass, or a ball of thread. Eventually it became our word 'clue'. It lost its material significance, and retained only its metaphorical meaning. But still, there it is, hidden but present: the clewe is in the clue (and the clue is in the clewe). Every step towards solving a mystery, or a crime, or a puzzle, or the riddle of the self, is a length of yarn tossed us by the helping hand of Ariadne.

TIME'S LABYRINTH

In a letter he sent in 1931 to his friend the writer Stefan Zweig, Sigmund Freud confessed that he had 'read more archaeology than psychology'. Evans's *The Palace of Minos* and works by Schliemann stood on his bookshelves; he was an avid collector of antiquities and his study was (and is, having been preserved *in situ* at the Freud Museum in London) filled with Greek, Roman and Egyptian artefacts, a veritable museum. Louise Bourgeois, the artist, once wrote of him that 'he was so in tune with the misery of people and with the misery of their fantasies and superstitions that he needed to look at the comforting spectacle of civilisations that have died and yet still live today'.[36] Each figurine, positioned with such care and delicacy, reassured him that he would have a place in history, she theorised.

Over the course of his career, Freud used archaeology repeatedly as a metaphor for his digging into human minds, his reconstruction of damaged, fragmentary selves. In *Studies on Hysteria* (1895), he wrote of developing a procedure that involved 'clearing away the pathogenic psychical material layer by layer', as if the self were an accumulation of buried, stratified detritus. He added: 'We liked to compare it with the technique of excavating a buried city.' In *Constructions in Analysis* (1937), he likened his approach when confronted by gaps in a patient's memory to an archaeologist's technique of inferring a whole structure from scattered fragments. 'Just as the archaeologist builds up the walls of a building from the foundations that have remained standing, determines the number and position of the columns from depressions in the floor, and reconstructs the mural decorations and paintings from the remains found in the debris, so does the analyst proceed when he draws his inferences from fragments of memories,' he wrote. The newly discovered Bronze Age Minoan and Mycenaean cultures represented, he argued, a kind of pre-Oedipal state for humanity. Influenced by Bachofen's theories about a prehistoric matriarchal period, he speculated that the transition to patriarchy was somehow laid down or embedded in the life stages of modern individuals as they swapped strong babyhood allegiance to their mothers for close attachment to their fathers.

The idea of Rome, city of stupendous ruins and boundless archaeology, was powerfully attractive to Freud. It is the subject of one of his most memorable descriptions of the nature of the mind: in *Civilisation and Its Discontents* (1930), he summoned up a vision of the city in which all of its multiple pasts – from the earliest settlements on the Palatine Hill onwards – are simultaneously present. According to this impossible vision, Nero's lavish palace, the Domus Aurea, would coexist with the later Colosseum; the footprint of the church of Maria sopra Minerva would be occupied by both the church and the temple over which it was built; the renaissance Palazzo Caffarelli (which is now part of the Capitoline museums) would share its space with the temple of Jupiter Capitolinus, which would 'be seen not only in its later form, which it assumed during the imperial age, but also in its earlier, when it still had Etruscan elements and was decorated with terracotta antefixes'.[37] It would be an impossible collage of the ages. This city, this fantastical city containing all former versions of itself, would be like the mind, Freud suggested, in which 'everything is somehow preserved and can be retrieved under the right circumstances'.[38] If a city is a labyrinth in space, Freud invented a city that was a labyrinth in both time and space, truly an 'eternal city'. This universal and impossible Rome reminds me of Borges's story 'Funes the Memorious', in which the character remembers absolutely everything he has ever experienced, so that he can relive, for example, the complete and precise details of a long-ago day, in real time – his mind an infinite palimpsest.*

---

* As the Argentinian novelist Carlos Gamerro points out in his essay of 2009, 'The Aleph and the Labyrinth', this is 'a very Joycean feat'. One might think also of Proust, or Knausgård.

It took Freud years actually to visit Rome, despite his fairly extensive travels around the rest of Italy, despite planning trips to the city, despite the fact that it haunted his sleeping life. (In one dream he arrived by train only for it to pull out of the station again without his having alighted.) On one occasion he travelled as far as Lake Trasimeno in Umbria, only to turn round again. He decided that he was like Hannibal, his childhood hero. The Carthaginian leader had won a great battle at the lake in 217 BC but inexplicably failed to push home his advantage by marching on Rome. Finally, on 2 September 1901, Freud arrived in the city; he would visit a further six times before 1923. While he was admiring the grandeur that was Rome, Arthur Evans was digging out Knossos.

THE RIDDLE OF THE KNOT IN THE BEARD

On that first visit, and regularly on subsequent occasions, Freud went to look at the monumental statue of Moses that Michelangelo had sculpted for the tomb of Pope Julius II. 'No piece of statuary has ever made a stronger impression on me than this,' he wrote. The reason for this deep impression, though, was a mystery to him. 'Some of the grandest and most overwhelming works of art are still unsolved riddles to our understanding,' he noted. 'We admire them, we feel overawed by them, but we are unable to say what they represent to us.' Freud disliked an unsolved problem: this was a challenge to his intellect, and solutions were more satisfying than mere rapturous acceptance. 'Some rationalistic, or perhaps analytic, turn of mind in me rebels against being moved by a thing without knowing why I am thus affected and what it is that affects me.' He needed a solution to the conundrum. He needed Ariadne's clewe.

'The Moses of Michelangelo', the essay in which Freud analysed his reaction to the sculpture, was itself a riddle, since he published it without a byline. When it came out in 1914 in the art-history journal *Imago*, a teasing footnote stated only that the author moved 'in psycho-analytic circles' and that his mode of thought had 'in point of fact a certain resemblance to the methodology of psycho-analysis'. Thus cloaked in anonymity, he began (one can perceive the temptation) by heaping praise on his own earlier interpretation of *Hamlet*, set forth in 1900 in *The Interpretation of Dreams*, which had attributed the hero's hesitation in avenging his dead father to feelings of displaced guilt based on his own repressed longings for his mother. 'It was not until the material of the tragedy had been traced back by psycho-analysis to the Oedipus theme that the mystery of its effect was at last explained,' wrote anonymous-Freud, admiringly, of Freud. Just as Oedipus had solved the Sphinx's riddle,* so psychoanalysis had cracked the riddle of Hamlet. And now it was going to get to work on Moses.

The sculptural group that Moses dominates is of almost excessive size, crowding into a transept of San Pietro in Vincoli,

* Freud's bookplates showed an image of Oedipus and the Sphinx and a verse from Sophocles' *Oedipus Tyrannos* that translates as 'who knew the famous riddle and was a most powerful man'. See Armstrong, p.54.

a church with an unassuming facade off the Via Cavour in Rome, not far from the Forum. The tomb has two levels and is adorned with sculpted figures – seven of them, or eight if you include the baby Jesus; more, even, if you count the various decorative heads and telamones. Julius himself is the least of it: he reclines on the upper deck, a slightly silly-looking figure in papal robes and tiara, supporting himself on his elbow, as if an awkward guest at some ancient Roman feast. He commissioned the tomb in 1505, but Michelangelo's work on it was slow and frequently interrupted by other pressing commissions – not least the reluctantly undertaken frescoes of the Sistine Chapel.

The monument was conceived, at first, as a much bigger assemblage – free-standing, with three levels, forty sculptures, and bronze panels depicting the pope's achievements. It was meant to stand in glory in the new basilica of St Peter's. But Julius died in 1513, and it was not until 1547 that his executors settled on the less glamorous location of San Pietro in Vincoli, much of the sculptural work having been subcontracted to other artists and the monument reduced in scale to a wall tomb. (In fact, Julius was actually interred in St Peter's basilica, so it is not, strictly speaking, a tomb at all.)

The figure of Moses, though, is a masterpiece of the hand of Michelangelo. Sitting at the centre of the lower rank of the tomb, he inexorably draws the eye, overwhelming the other sculpted figures in both scale and impact. Ascanio Condivi, Michelangelo's early biographer, described him as seated 'in the attitude of a wise and pensive man, holding the tables of the law under his right arm and supporting his chin with his left hand like a person who is weary and full of cares; and long strands of beard pass through the fingers of this hand, which is something very beautiful to see. The face is full of animation and spirit, apt to inspire both love and terror, which was perhaps the truth.'[39]

Deeply drawn as he was to the sculpture of Moses, Freud also found it inscrutable and disturbing. What did the odd pose of the prophet signify? Why was he sitting with his head turned to the left, but at the same time diverting the downward flow of his long beard towards the other side with his right finger? There was immense power and energy in the prophet's physique, and he seemed caught in the act of some dramatic movement – but what, and why? Surveying recent criticism on the sculpture, Freud found a consensus: Michelangelo had depicted the moment when the prophet, having received the Ten Commandments from God and descended from Mount Sinai, caught sight of his people dancing around the Golden Calf. Appalled by their idolatry, he was about to leap to his feet, letting drop the tables, which would smash to pieces.

Freud rejected this view of the sculpture. For him, it showed not anger about to burst forth, but anger in the act of being restrained. 'What we see before us is not the inception of a violent action but the remains of a movement that has already taken place. In his first transport of fury, Moses desired to act, to spring up and take vengeance and forget the Tables, but he has overcome the temptation, and he will now remain seated and still, in his frozen wrath and in his pain mingled with contempt.' For Freud, Moses had 'renounced an indulgence of his feelings'.

Freud extracted this meaning through a conjectural reconstruction of the actions leading up to the position in which Moses had been sculpted. He used a series of drawings, almost a storyboard, starting with Moses sitting straight and facing forward, then moving through a sequence of gestures, finally arriving at Michelangelo's chosen pose. He was especially interested in Moses's beard, describing it in a long and dense paragraph. There is something, to me, almost queasy in the way he summons up how the prophet is touching it: 'At the place where the right index finger is pressed in, a kind of whorl of hairs is formed; strands of hair coming from the left lie over strands coming from the right, both caught in by that despotic finger. It is only beyond this place that the masses of hair, deflected from their course, flow freely once more, and now they fall vertically until their ends are gathered up in Moses's left hand as it lies open on his lap.' He has fixated on the great fleecy beard, rendering it almost abstract: finger shape on whorl shape.

The route by which Freud arrived at his interpretation was, he noted, influenced by the techniques of an Italian called Giovanni Morelli, who wrote under the pseudonym of Ivan Lermolieff (Ivan is the Russian equivalent of Giovanni, and Lermolieff a near-anagram of Morelli). Trained in medicine and anatomy, Morelli advanced the idea that correct attribution of Old Masters could most accurately be achieved not through an expert's 'general impression, or intuition', but rather through the diligent examination of what most people would regard as insignificant anatomical details. (His essays are scattered with sketches of body parts as depicted by Renaissance painters, so

(above) The three postcards given as a gift in the museum at Heraklion.

(right) The Cup-Bearer Fresco, one of Evans's early finds at Knossos.

(below) An enlarged photograph of 'the Ring of Nestor'.

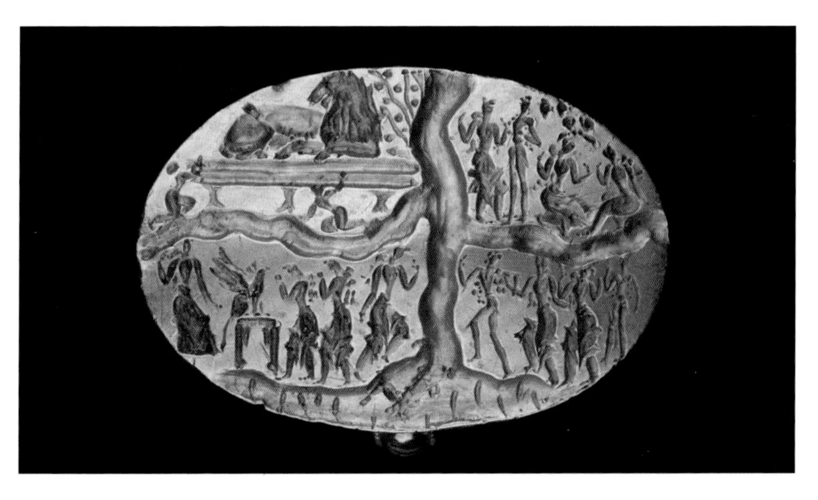

(*above left*) One of the 'snake goddess' figurines, heavily restored.

(*above right*) 'Our Lady of the Sports', almost certainly a fake.

(*right*) The Moses of Michelangelo. 'No piece of statuary has ever made a stronger impression on me,' wrote Freud.

The labyrinth at Chartres Cathedral – thirteen metres in diameter.

(*above*) *Laocoön*. The ancient sculpture was discovered in a vineyard in 1506.

(*right*) Crete on the *mappa mundi*. The labyrinth is called, in Latin, 'the house of Daedalus'.

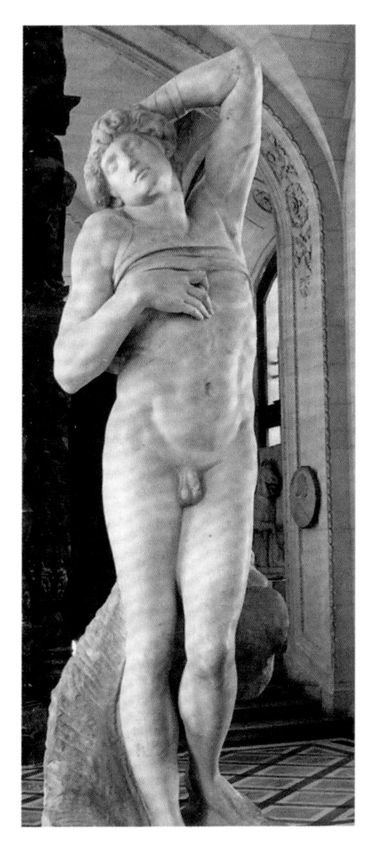

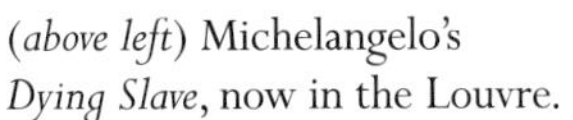

(*above left*) Michelangelo's *Dying Slave*, now in the Louvre.

(*above right*) Michelangelo's *Rebellious Slave*.

(*right*) A detail of Titian's *Bacchus and Ariadne*, 1522–23.

The Creto di Burri – a town whose ruins are encased in concrete.

Laocoön in an earlier restoration: the priest's right arm points skywards.

Robert Smithson's *Spiral Jetty*, seen from the air.

Constantin Brâncuși's *Portrait of James Joyce*.

Anatomical drawings of the inner ear. Engraving by Thomas Milton, 1808.

(*left*) The Vatican Ariadne, once known as Cleopatra.

(*below*) Giorgione's (or Titian's) *Sleeping Venus*, c. 1510.

that they almost resemble medical texts.) The particular and personal way an artist depicted a hand, an ear, even a fingernail, could act like a signature; they 'gave away' the painter, as a clue gives away a crime, a symptom gives away a disease or a stray detail from a dream gives away the self. And Morelli was right: many false attributions were corrected through this new methodology, which, though disliked in some quarters for its mechanical pragmatism, would prove influential to later generations of art historians such as the great expert on Greek pottery John Beazley. Perhaps most sensationally, Morelli identified a reclining Venus in Dresden, which had been thought a copy by Sassoferrato of a work by Titian, as likely to be one of the very few surviving canvases by Giorgione.

Morelli's essays were first published in a German journal in 1874–6, translated from the Russian by one Johannes Schwartze (another pseudonym, this time a German play on Morelli's name, since *moro* can mean dark-haired or dark-skinned, like *schwarz*). In a preface to a collected volume of his essays he claimed that he had derived his methods from conversing with 'an elderly gentleman, apparently an Italian of the better class' whom he had met by chance in the Pitti Palace in Florence. The volume records a dialogue with this nameless stranger, described as 'a former student of medicine', in which the stranger encourages 'Lermolieff' to examine a work by Raphael in the Uffizi in Florence, taking note of 'the hand of the Madonna with the broad metacarpus and somewhat stiff fingers, the nails extending to the tips only' – an arrangement, he points out, that is typical of the artist. Such instructions cause 'Lermolieff', who at this point in the conversation is expressing scepticism of his new friend's methods, to muse that 'this matter of fact way of identifying works of art ... savoured more of an anatomist ... than of a student of art'.

One might be advised to be suspicious of the writer who claims that his or her ideas derive from a figure encountered by chance in a museum. It seems clear that there was no such person as 'Lermolieff's' intriguing interlocutor – or, rather, that the elderly Italian gentleman with his medical training was simply a version of Morelli himself. Not that one ought to mistrust Morelli, exactly: his scholarship was honourable, and he later published his work under his own name. Sometimes a writer might have a reason for a small piece of subterfuge.

Freud wrote in 'The Moses of Michelangelo' that Morelli's 'method of inquiry is closely related to the technique of psycho-analysis. It, too, is accustomed to divine secret and concealed things from despised or unnoticed features, from the rubbish-heap, as it were, of our observations.' The psychiatrist and the art critic, then, are like the archaeologist, who must search the discarded ephemera, sift through the refuse, pick out the broken and obscure fragments. Then reconstruct, and build.

A great deal of analysis has been visited on Freud's interpretation of the sculpture: the extent to which he, the bearded harbinger of the new discipline of psychoanalysis, identified with this lavishly hirsute Jewish prophet; the unconscious projection of his own restrained anger onto the sculpture; his fascination with this stupendous depiction of an Old Testament figure, as muscled and physically beautiful as the classical statues he so admired. He saw the sculpture as a conundrum: he wanted to solve 'the riddle of that knot in the beard' – a phrase that could almost serve as the title of a Sherlock Holmes story. He did so by treating the sculpture as a single image around which he constructed a narrative of his own devising. In the end, the whole analysis rested on a presumption: that Michelangelo was depicting a moment caught in time like a still from a film, rather than (say) creating a symbolic synthesis of idea and mood. And, as Freud himself acknowledged: what if we had 'strayed on to a wrong path? What if we have taken too serious and profound a view of details which were nothing to the artist, details which he had introduced quite arbitrarily or for some purely formal reasons with no hidden intention behind?' Clues can deceive. Paths can turn out to be dead ends.

Over a quarter of a century later, in his book *Moses and Monotheism* (1939), Freud reflected on his period of obsession with the sculpture – offering an elaboration, if not an explanation, of his decision to publish the essay, his 'lovechild' as he called it, without using his own name. 'For three lonely September weeks in 1913 I stood every day in the church in front of the statue, studied it, measured it, sketched it until I captured the understanding for it which I ventured to express in the essay only anonymously. Only much later did I legitimise this non-analytical child.' In the essay itself, he wrote about the sculpture as if it contained some immanent life force: 'I used to sit down in front of the statue in the expectation that I should now see how it would start up on its raised foot ...' He was almost afraid of it, there, alone, in the murky dark of the silent church: 'How often have I mounted the steep steps from the unlovely Corso Cavour to the lonely piazza where the deserted church stands, and have essayed to support the angry scorn of the hero's glance! Sometimes I have crept cautiously out of the half-gloom of the interior as though I myself belonged to the mob upon whom his eye is turned ...' Stone might, it seemed, turn flesh.

Freud's Moses was paternal and godlike and frightening. The one I encountered first was erotic, at least by proxy. Half a lifetime ago I also came to this church. It was my first time in Rome, and I turned twenty-one the day I arrived (for years I kept the train ticket from Poppi, in Tuscany, to Termini station, as a commemoration of this significant passage). Mobile phones were a rarity, and so plans had been made far in advance that I would meet a friend by Gian Lorenzo Bernini's stupendous Fountain of the Four Rivers, in Piazza Navona, at a certain time on that day of arrival, 6 September 1993. One day he and I visited San Pietro in Vincoli: not ascending, like Freud, the little covered stair that rises from the Via Cavour, but descending from the Oppian Hill, where we had visited the Domus Aurea, the 'golden house' of Nero. As I remember it, the church was empty but for us. We stood by the rail that ran around the sculptural group, and spent a long time looking at Moses. For my friend, the prophet was not forbidding and scornful, as he was for Freud, but handsome and powerful: he lavished attention on the well-developed shoulders, the strong arms with defined muscles, their veins and sinews. His Moses was bound up with a new sense of sexual freedom and masculinity, and I looked at the sculpture with his eyes, and tried to understand.

When I returned after the passage of another twenty-one years, walking Freud's route from the Via Cavour, the church was no longer deserted, nor was the square outside: a busker played tangos on the accordion, and Giorgio's Souvenir, a kiosk, sold T-shirts and fridge magnets. Within, a crowd flocked around the tomb, and another, larger one, around the chains after which the church is named: the very chains, so the faithful believe, that bound St Peter when he was imprisoned in Rome, which are displayed below the altar in a golden reliquary. The 'half-gloom' that Freud described was banished; the frescoes in the apse were brightly lit, and a sign, handwritten in round, curlicued letters, informed visitors that '*per illuminare Mosè*' – to light up Moses – one could insert a one-euro coin. It was not possible, as it had been on my first trip, to approach the sculpture at close quarters. A red rope stopped visitors about three metres short of the tomb. Every so often, between coins, it would sink into shadow. My head was filled with memories of the first encounter with the statue, but I felt both a great distance from it and a great longing: I wanted to touch and caress those splendid limbs, which I would never do.

After a while, having photographed the sculpture, like everyone else, on my smartphone, I went to the back room in the church and bought four postcards. The first was of the tomb as a whole, both storeys; the second showed just the lower deck, with Moses flanked by the smaller statues of the Active Life and the Contemplative Life; the third showed Moses at full length; the fourth was a detail of his head and shoulders. Taken together, these postcards formed a kind of procession, each taking one nearer the figure than the last. In buying them,

I understood that I was indulging a nostalgic feeling: one can google images of Moses and find him at every angle, rank upon rank of him, to be scrutinised and consumed at will.

Standing near the doorway of the church, I pulled that last postcard out of its paper bag and looked at it. I realised that it was only by studying the image that I could pick out, for example, the small fold of skin at the base of Moses's right little finger, the veins on the backs of his hands, and the creases on his knuckles; even the large veins coursing through his forearms. From the red-rope barrier all these things had been invisible to me, even the sinews that had so attracted my friend half a lifetime before. Then I realised that the procession of postcards was not leading me towards the sculpture, but away from it. It was receding.

Turning away

Only a rookie maze-walker, wrote Mrs Grammatiki, would try to approach the centre directly. 'Somewhere towards the beginning of the journey,' she wrote, 'it is necessary to turn away from the middle. In a labyrinth with its single path this happens without the walker choosing to do so: one must simply surrender. In a maze, on the other hand, we choose our path, and turning away from our destination is a question of tactics, since in my experience, the designer will very often try to show his power over the walker by tricking him with a promising-seeming path just at the start, which will promptly turn out to be a dead end, whereas the least obvious path often turns out to be the right one. But even the dead ends are there to be savoured, and they are part of the beauty and intricacy of the design. In a maze or a labyrinth, then, one must enjoy travelling by a circuitous path, abandoning rational impulses.'

Umberto Eco's labyrinth

In a celebrated essay, the great Italian historian Carlo Ginzburg, who is perhaps most famous for his work *The Cheese and the Worms*, about the life and beliefs of a sixteenth-century heretic in northern Italy, noted Freud's enthusiasm for Morelli. He even suggested a direct line of influence between Morelli's work and Freud's development of psychoanalysis. He likened both their methodologies to the deductive skill of another exceptional collector of unremarked details and 'giveaway' signs: Sherlock Holmes. In his essay, first published in Italian in 1979 and titled in English 'Clues: Morelli, Freud and Sherlock Holmes', he pointed out that the art historian, the analyst and the author of detective stories were all medics by training: anatomists and diagnosticians. All three built up pictures of the world from the analysis of signs. And this analysis of signs must go very deep into human history, he suggested, into the remote past of hunter-gatherers.

To support this notion, he mentioned a folk tale told in the Middle East 'among Khirgiz, Tartars, Jews, Turks and so on'. The story is about three brothers who meet a man who has lost a camel (or in some versions, a horse). They immediately describe it to him. It's white, and blind in one eye; it carries two skins, one of oil, the other of wine. And yet they haven't seen it. The man accuses them of stealing it and brings them to be judged. At which point the brothers show precisely how, from the tiniest traces, they were able to reconstruct the appearance of the missing animal. Elementary, my dear Watson.

The story of the three brothers and the camel was, via a variety of retellings and translations, adapted for use centuries later by Voltaire in his philosophical novel *Zadig*. The hero is accused of stealing, this time, a bitch and a camel; again Zadig is able to prove his innocence by showing the steps he had taken to deduce and describe things he had not seen. In this story 'lies the embryo of the detective story', argued Ginzburg, for the episode directly influenced Edgar Allan Poe and the French pioneer of detective fiction Emile Gaboriau. And, indirectly, perhaps Arthur Conan Doyle himself.

Ginzburg's essay was collected in 1980 in a volume called *The Sign of Three*, edited by Umberto Eco, his colleague at the University of Bologna. Of all his work as a semiotician and a writer of fiction, Eco's most famous book is his novel *The Name of the Rose*. Published in English in 1983, it is a postmodern detective story that starts with a highly elaborate preface, full of intricate bibliographical, academic and personal detail, in which Eco claims that the ensuing tale is a transcription, by him, of a nineteenth-century edition of a lost medieval manuscript. The story that follows is set in a wealthy northern Italian abbey in 1327 and is laced with sly literary references (the old blind monk Jorge de Burgos, for example, recalls Jorge Luis Borges, who also went blind towards the end of his life). At the start of the novel, a disillusioned English inquisitor, William of Baskerville, is making his way to the abbey on delicate diplomatic business. He and his young assistant, Adso, witness a kerfuffle of worried monks and servants outside the abbey's gates. William proves his credentials as a man of great sagacity by deducing not only what has so disturbed them (the loss of the abbot's horse) but what the creature looks like and where it is to be found, despite not having seen it. Like Zadig, like the three brothers of the folk tale, William of Baskerville is a reader of signs. Indeed, as his name suggests, he is a very Holmesian figure, and Adso, the narrator of the tale, the faithful and frequently baffled Dr Watson.

The abbey's calm will be disturbed by more serious events: a series of murders, which, it quickly transpires, are connected in some mysterious way to the enormous, and forbidden, library of the monastery. William and Adso eventually gain access to it, but become hopelessly lost and bewildered inside it: for it is a spiritual and a terrestrial labyrinth, as the abbot has indeed explained to them. It is only when they are outside the building that William can deduce its precise layout. How come, asks Adso, you were able to solve the mystery of the library looking at it from outside, when you were unable to solve it from the inside? 'Thus God knows the world, because He conceived it in his mind, as if from the outside, before it was created, and we do not know its rule, because we live inside it, having found it already made,' replies William. He can unpick the rules of the labyrinth because it was conceived by a human, and because he is human, he explains. Any labyrinth, or maze, is a clear and beautiful thing, full of pattern and sense when contemplated in the mind, or seen from above. When experienced from the inside, it may be confounding and even frightening, especially when its coils are hemmed in by walls or confused further with mirrors. The world too is a kind of labyrinth – it can be understood only by God, for He made it, and so sees its whole design clearly. The library is like a little world – made by humans, not God, and containing human history, stories, thinking, fantasies.

A maze or a labyrinth is also like a book, most obviously a detective story. The reader may find it confusing and impenetrable, but simultaneously take comfort in the knowledge that it will have been constructed according to a pattern and certain generic rules. As William tells Adso of his penchant for solving mysteries: 'When as a philosopher I am in doubt the world has an order, I am consoled to discover, if not an order at least a series of connections in small areas of the world's affairs.' G. K. Chesterton, the writer of detective stories solved by a sleuth who is also a Roman Catholic priest, once wrote that 'what we all dread most is a maze with no centre'. For him that meant a universe with no God, but it also reminds me of Dante's *Inferno* – his Hell is a series of concentric circles that contains some of the features of a labyrinth (confusion, disorientation) but lacks the possibility, for its inhabitants, of progression to the middle, or a route out. A maze with no edges would, perhaps, be just as terrifying.

Perhaps this is why there are labyrinths set into the pavements of some churches, particularly certain Gothic cathedrals in France: to hint at the notion that the universe is subject to design, however impenetrable its patterns might appear to a mere human sinner. At Reims, an octagonal labyrinth destroyed in the eighteenth century contained images of the cathedral's architects – its Daedaluses – holding compasses, an angle iron and dividers. It was perhaps a clue that on one level, at least, the labyrinth stood in for the cathedral itself, a building as complex and loaded with significance as the pattern on its floor. At Chartres, the cathedral – built at the turn of the twelfth and thirteenth centuries – has a pavement labyrinth that occupies the full width of its nave, nearly thirteen metres in diameter, precisely matching the scale of the mighty rose window set into the west wall. It is thought by some that such labyrinths symbolised the coiling path towards Christ that sometimes seems to advance to, sometimes drift away from, its goal. Walking the path might thus be an aid to meditation, or a kind of stage set for rituals. (At Auxerre, for example, the cathedral labyrinth was the scene of an Easter dance performed by the dean and the canons, who would throw a ball between them and move in a formation resembling a garland.)[40] The labyrinth at Chartres has eleven 'courses' or layers in its winding progress towards its centre; and is bounded, at its edge, by a scalloped pattern that, to me, seems to recall the crenellations of a city wall.

I visited it in the summer of 2016, on what was, at that time at least, the hottest day of the century. I was amazed by the scale of it. It was as if some vast serpent had coiled itself there in the wide cathedral nave. It was not only the labyrinth that bewitched me. The whole building seemed to tremble with meaning. The thirteenth-century stained-glass windows overflowed with life. Huntsmen, fishermen, masons

The design of the Chartres labyrinth, its scalloped edges recalling a crenellated city wall.

toiled. Abbesses expired on deathbeds. Holy men cast out demons. Peasants worked the fields and merchants trundled goods along roads in wagons. A man murdered his parents, then rowed Christ across a river. A demon upset a cart. Someone was tortured on a wheel. Brigands attacked hermits in their caves; queens prayed for the conversion of their husbands. Kings feasted and kegs were miraculously refilled with wine. A man choked on a fishbone and pagans worshipped golden idols.

It was cool inside the cathedral and the beating, impossible sun illuminated the panes as if they were gems. At a certain point, someone started playing the organ: an explosive, torrid improvisation. Beneath the music – a dissonant undertow to the frenetic runs and arpeggios – came the basso profondo of some vast and unseen piece of machinery that was being used in a part of the cathedral under restoration. The labyrinth, the windows, the music, the low, dull roar – all of it seemed of a piece. It was as if the building itself, the labyrinth at its heart, were a giant, obscure mechanism for understanding the universe.

The Figure in the Carpet

In Stanley Kubrick's 1980 film *The Shining*, Jack Torrance, his wife Wendy and their son Danny move to an isolated hotel, the Overlook, so that Jack can take up a job as its caretaker when it closes to guests for the winter season. There is an enormous hedge maze in the hotel's grounds, and a model showing its complex design on display inside. There's a moment in the film when Kubrick will, through a single, spine-tingling sequence, transport the viewer from watching Wendy and Danny rushing joyfully towards the maze, to an image of Jack, back inside the hotel, glowering balefully over the tabletop model, in which his wife and child can be seen as curious miniaturised figures. Watching these few seconds of the film, one has the destabilising sensation of being simultaneously above and within the structure. There's a third labyrinth: the Overlook Hotel itself. It is 'such an enormous maze', says

Wendy anxiously, when the couple first arrive, 'I feel like I'll have to leave a trail of breadcrumbs every time I come in'. Breadcrumbs, as we learn from the story of Hansel and Gretel, are not the most effective signs to leave in the confusing expanses of a maze or forest.

Young Danny, however, is a true labyrinth-walker. There are tracking shots of him riding his trike in loops through the various floors of the hotel, the wheels smooth on the rich rugs of the palatial halls and then bumping and rasping on the parquet. He explores the building's every inch. He discerns its hiding places – as well as, it turns out, its bitter memories and hauntings. The Overlook is a place of mirrors and disturbing reflections, a very Borgesian labyrinth. Ariadne-like, Danny will be alert to the dangers of the place, and at a crucial moment give his mother a knife, just as the Cretan princess gives Theseus a sword. They will need it, because Jack has become a monster. He has already been filmed by Kubrick with a downturned gaze like a furious bull's, an antlered stag head pointedly hanging on the wall behind him. Danny will finally outwit his murderous father in the snow-filled hedge maze by faking his own footprints, walking backwards into them, allowing them apparently simply to stop, then darting into a side alley and covering his tracks. His deranged father, by now a wild Minotaur, is deceived by these false clues. In his last moments, trapped and defeated in the maze, he simply bellows bestially. He has lost language.

The film itself is a labyrinth, for it attracts interpreters who wish to decipher its apparently arcane and secret meanings. There are those who believe that it is an allegory of the Holocaust, others who contend it is really about the genocide of the Native Americans, others who believe it is an occluded confession by Kubrick that he faked footage of the moon landings, others still who say that it contains references to the precise date of the Mayan apocalypse. There is a documentary[41] that has collected some of these interpretations; the internet heaves with many more. It is not hard to see why. Kubrick loads his scenes with details, with 'clues': there are significant-seeming objects and numbers; and curious visual anomalies (disappearing pieces of furniture, changing props). I myself find it striking how similar the Overlook appears in its decor, its stately halls and long enfilades of rooms, to Knossos as reimagined by Arthur Evans and the Gilliérons: all those geometric friezes and lofty pillars; all those deep-red chambers.

The Middle of The Turn of the Screw

In Henry James's story 'The Figure in the Carpet', a critic for a literary journal called *The Middle* becomes convinced that a novelist, Hugh Vereker, has buried an 'exquisite scheme', a 'little trick', into all his works, which, if only he tries hard enough, can surely be decoded. In an encounter between the novelist and the critic at a country-house party, Vereker teasingly tells the young man: 'To me it's exactly as palpable as the marble of this chimney.' The critic asks: 'Is it a kind of esoteric message?' to which Vereker replies, 'Ah my dear fellow, it can't be described in cheap journalese!'

His expression reminds me of an exchange at the start of James's novella *The Turn of the Screw*, which begins, like *The Name of the Rose* and *Diary of the Trojan War*, with a prologue that claims the story has been transcribed from an old manuscript. In this case, the narrator remembers an occasion, many years earlier, when friends of his at a country-house party were in the mood for telling chilling stories. One of their number, Douglas, recalls that at his home in London is a manuscript, written by a governess he used to know, detailing certain disturbing events that occurred while she was caring for two children on behalf of their absent guardian. It is this story, written 'in old, faded ink', that will form the main narrative of the novella. One of the friends asks whether the governess had been in love with the guardian. 'The story will tell,' the narrator says. But he is sharply contradicted. '"The story *won't* tell," says Douglas, "not in any literal, vulgar way."'

The scheme can't be described in cheap journalese. The story won't tell – not in any literal, vulgar way. The warning, in both cases, is against a reading of a story that attempts to smooth out mystery or ambiguity. You can appreciate the design of James's subtle spirals, his lovely labyrinths, but don't expect them to translate into some glib, crude meaning, to be delivering 'an esoteric message'. As Borges remarked of the ambiguities of meaning in *The Turn of the Screw*, 'People shouldn't know [the explanation], and perhaps he didn't know himself!'[42]

In 'The Figure in the Carpet', the narrator and his friends become consumed by the project of discovering the 'secret' of

Vereker's books. One of them claims to have cracked the code, and is about to write an article that will 'trace the figure in the carpet through every convolution', but he dies before he is able to do so. The narrator finds himself trapped in Vereker's puzzle, 'shut up in my obsession for ever – my gaolers had gone off with the key'. Vereker's last novel is called *The Right of Way*: the artist forges ahead, leaving the interpreters flailing around in the labyrinth, lost in the midst.

PASSE AVAUNT

The *mappa mundi* of Hereford Cathedral was made around 1300, probably in Lincoln. It shows the world as it was known at the time, from St Andrews to Samarkand, from Armagh to Alexandria. There are a few, a very few such objects that survive from the medieval period. This one, at 1.6 by 1.3 metres, is the largest.

This *mappa mundi*, this 'cloth of the world', would be very little use, however, as any kind of guide for travellers, with its outrageously swollen landmasses and oceans reduced to canal-like channels; rather it is a mine of knowledge earthly and cosmic, a pile-up of allegory and metaphor and myth. It throbs with images and text, with the accumulated wisdom of the Bible and of classical and medieval works such as Pliny the Elder's *Natural History* and Isidore of Seville's *Etymologies*. Here is Noah's ark, Alexander's camp, Sodom and Gomorrah; here are the Amyctyrae who shade themselves from the sun with their huge bottom lips; the Blemmyes with eyes in their chests;

and the Gangines, whose only sustenance is the perfume of apples. Snake-wreathed Minos is here, ready to judge the souls of the dead; Charybdis is like a giant whorled seashell; the Golden Fleece waits to be plucked by Jason. Jerusalem stands triumphantly at the centre of all this, depicted as a series of concentric crenellated circles around which the great orb of the world, fringed by ocean, is gathered. The single compass hole used to draw both Jerusalem and the world's outline is clearly visible. The *mappa mundi* is not just a diagram of space, it is a map of time and destiny, for we see Adam and Eve expelled from the Garden of Eden, and at the apex of the whole scheme, the Last Judgement: thus the world is completely described from its creation to its dissolution.

For all the *mappa*'s age – meaning that the once bottle-green brightness of its oceans and sparkling blue of its rivers is dulled to a leathery, yellowy brown – it's not hard to imagine its vellum as having once been part of a living creature, a calf perhaps raised on the Lincolnshire wolds. The skin is itself now a landscape in its own right, duned and hillocked, a terrain of ridges and valleys. When I first caught sight of it in the little museum at the side of Hereford's quiet and gentle cathedral, the *mappa* looked rather colourless and unappealing. The joy of it is in the detail, in imagining oneself inside it. Standing close before it, I wanted to make myself small, to put to sea and explore among its fabulous beasts, its phoenix, its marsok and its manticore; its sphinx, its mandrake and its salamander.

Just down from the image of Jerusalem – or rather, west, according to the *mappa*'s orientation – is Crete, grown to enormous scale and prominence by the mapmaker. On the island is drawn an eleven-course labyrinth, itself oriented west–east. (In this it is like a French cathedral labyrinth, which is entered from the west, like the building itself.) As with the image of Jerusalem, you can see the pinprick used by the illustrator to draw its perfect circle. The labyrinth is, of course, marking the position of the Minotaur's lair (it is captioned '*laborintus id est domus dedali*' – 'the labyrinth, that is, the house of Daedalus'). But it also summons up a rich store of labyrinthine associations that one can find in medieval texts: the labyrinth as the world, the labyrinth as the difficult path from ignorance to knowledge, the labyrinth as a symbolic marker of Jesus's descent to the Underworld for the Harrowing of Hell. Since this labyrinth figures on a map, it's hard not to think of it as a metaphor of God's skill in designing the world – and in turn of the artistry of the *mappa* itself, this world-in-miniature, and of the Daedalian talents of its maker. The *mappa mundi* labyrinth is a world within a world within a world.

In the bottom right-hand corner of the *mappa* is a man on horseback riding out of the picture, but facing backwards into the image, his hand raised. Behind him comes a huntsman on foot, leading a greyhound. '*Passe avaunt*' is the Norman French text that hovers between the figures – 'go ahead', or 'pass beyond'. What can it mean? Perhaps the lifted hand is not raised in farewell, but in a gesture of wonderment at the map itself – an acknowledgement that a new way of seeing has been found. Or perhaps this '*Passe avaunt*' is the map itself bidding farewell to the viewer, showing us a route out of the beautifully ordered world-in-miniature to the great (and confusing) world of reality beyond the frame. Here, perhaps, is a right of way.

Laocoön

When I lived for a month in Rome, when I was in the middle of my life, I fell in love with a statue. Not Michelangelo's Moses, the subject of Freud's obsession, but a statue that has bewitched innumerable others since it was pulled out of the soil of a vineyard on the Esquiline Hill on 14 January 1506. It is the famous ancient sculpture known as *Laocoön*, which shows a Trojan priest and his sons struggling to overcome the attack of two great serpents. They will fail. One of the boys looks already on the point of death. It is a study in writhing agony and also, perversely given the subject matter, a thing of great beauty, as the straining muscled limbs of the humans intertwine with the coiling bodies of the snakes. Every time I passed it, in the Belvedere of the Vatican Museums, it would stop me in my tracks with its erotic tangle of naked bodies, its sheer fame (the shock of seeing 'the original' of a much-reproduced work of art).

Laocoön relates to a scene in Virgil's *Aeneid*, the great epic the poet left unfinished on his death in 19 BC.* Whether the poem or the sculpture came first, no one can say for sure. The poem tells the story of the Trojan hero Aeneas: his flight from Troy after its destruction by the Greeks, his adventures with the monsters and maidens of the Mediterranean, his eventual

* The relative capabilities of poetry and the visual arts – what the words can convey with their ability to track change over time, what art can represent with its one-moment-only capture of an event – are drawn out in one of the most important early texts on aesthetics, which uses this sculpture as its case study: Gotthold Ephraim Lessing's '*Laocoön*: An Essay on the Limits of Painting and Poetry' (1766).

arrival in Italy and his wars there, and his establishing of a dynasty that will, generations later, found the city of Rome. The *Aeneid* is a national epic. It takes the heroic stories of Homer – combining the perilous seaborne adventures of the *Odyssey* with the war narrative of the *Iliad* – and builds out of them something political, purposeful and Roman. It is a poem that someone, somewhere, has probably been reading every day since its manuscript was saved from burning, according to Pliny the Elder, by the emperor Augustus, contrary to Virgil's own wishes.*

I didn't realise, when I started reading the *Aeneid* as a fourteen-year-old schoolgirl, that I was stepping into such a vigorously rushing river, such a torrent of readers stretching back two millennia. It is the poem that, more than anything else I read when I was young, taught me how to read. I recall, for example, disagreeing with my teacher about Aeneas: I contended passionately that he was hesitant and irresolute, while she argued with complete certainty that he was heroic and dutiful. It was a revelation to me that we had each seen such contrary qualities in the poem's hero – and that what was really being expressed was the difference between our own characters. Later I realised that the point of a poem like this, one so densely read, one that seems to echo with the voices of the millions of readers who have trodden its paths before, is that it can

* Although I cannot think of this melodramatic anecdote now without recalling Borges's wise observation, in his *Paris Review* interview, that if a writer really wants to destroy their own work they will pick it up and throw it onto the fire rather than leaving instructions for some friend to do it instead.

offer both these interpretations simultaneously. The *Aeneid* is a magnificent city of a poem, like Freud's impossible Rome containing all previous versions of itself. Every reader who visits it experiences it differently, losing himself in it, picking out different landmarks here and there, admiring different viewpoints, stopping to examine different details of its lofty, ambitious architecture.

We meet Laocoön towards the start of the poem. The Trojan War has not yet ended. After ten protracted years of siege, the Greeks have, without warning or reason, launched their ships and sailed away. Have they given up, gone back to Greece? Is it a trick? They have left behind them a giant horse woven from fir branches – '*intexunt … contexus … textis*' – a structure that reminds us of a text, a textile. The words are reminiscent of Catullus's description, at the start of *Peliaco quondam*, of the *Argo*, another human invention woven from pinewood using Minerva's arts of fabrication. Laocoön, a priest, alone identifies it as a trap and a lie, a fiction. He reads it in a flash: it has Greek soldiers hidden inside, he says. He asks his fellow citizens: Do you really believe that the Greeks have left? Do you really, honestly think that Ulysses* is a man of his word?

He casts a spear into its side and it seems to roar like a bull (we might be reminded here of the Minotaur, another roaring creature kept inside an elaborate human invention). But still no one believes him. Instead they believe Sinon, a sinuously named Greek spy posing as a defector, who spins them a tale:

* The Roman name for Odysseus. He keeps up his Homeric reputation for duplicity and cunning in the *Aeneid*.

if the Trojans take the horse into their city, they will prosper in war and rise higher than the Greeks, he says.

Meantime, the doubting Laocoön is sacrificing a bull in the temple of Neptune. But as he does so, two monstrous serpents are swimming towards the shoreline and making straight for him. They are enormous, ferocious, their bodies as heavy and strong as chains. With horrifying speed they swarm up the temple steps and wrap his two young sons in a lethal embrace. Then they turn to the priest, spiralling him in their coils while he struggles, vainly, to burst the knots pulled tight around his neck ... All three of them die, and the snakes slink back into the sea. The Trojans are sure this portent is punishment: Laocoön should not have flung his spear into the horse. They drag it into the city. But they have been terribly deceived, by Sinon and the snakes: at night the horse disgorges what's lurking in its belly: Ulysses, Neoptolemus, Menelaus and the rest of the Greek leaders. Troy is breached; Troy is lost.

The snakes are a kind of living labyrinth: a trapping, coiling, deadly device. John Milton, one of Virgil's most perceptive readers, understood this passage well – saw that deceiving poetic snakes can also be deceptive poetic labyrinths – when he wrote of Eve's temptation by Satan in *Paradise Lost.* Satan finds a sleeping serpent 'in labyrinth of many a round self-rolled'. He borrows its form, hides himself inside it; he becomes a 'surging maze'. He begins by beguiling Eve with his lovely shape: he 'curled many a wanton wreath in sight of Eve' with his 'tortuous train'. There's sensuality here, a sensuality that is never very far away from the maze, which, when it is not hiding a monster (and perhaps sometimes when it is), might be providing concealment for all kinds of erotic games and licentious pursuits. Satan then seduces her with his serpentine, confounding rhetoric. 'Not unmazed' (that is, in a state of bewilderment), she answers him; eventually he leads her towards the tree of the forbidden fruit, his tangled but sinuous movements making the 'intricate seem straight'. His form, his words and even the motion of his serpentine body all become fused into a quintessence of error, of 'wand'ring'. In the *Aeneid*, the Latin word *error* recurs over and over again: it conveys both the act of erring from the right path, from the destined journey to Italy; and the notion of a mistake that can shade into moral error. Milton's use of the word 'wand'ring' has a similar force. Eve takes the fruit and launches humankind on its epic adventure of love and pain and loss. To err is human. So is to wander (and to wonder).

Recounting the story to Dido, the queen of Carthage upon whose shore he finds himself washed up after a terrible storm, Aeneas points out that what happened to Laocoön marked a great fork in the path of Troy's story. If he and his countrymen had listened to the priest, Troy would still be standing. By ignoring him, and then interpreting his death in the way that they did, they took a road that was, at least in the short term, destructive and painful: it meant the loss of a home and a nation, the terrible death of their comrades and children. But this was the laborious path that fate had in mind for Aeneas. Without the slaughter of Laocoön and his sons; without the acceptance of the horse into Troy; without its spewing out of Greek troops; without the destruction of the city – without all these apparently pointless and bloody events there would be no journey to Italy for Aeneas and his band of Trojan refugees, and no Rome. Just as in *Paradise Lost* there would be no humankind and no redemption without Eve's sin. Though readers for millennia have wondered why Aeneas's journey to Italy across the trackless wastes of the sea is loaded with so many frustrations and involutions, so many false trails and doublings-back, so much error and hardship and delay.

Michelangelo and Laocoön

The miraculous moment of the rediscovery of *Laocoön* was described in detail by the artist Francesco da Sangallo. In a letter written in 1567, he recalled how, on his first trip to Rome as a boy, there came word that certain very beautiful statues had been found in a vineyard near the church of Santa Maria Maggiore. The pope, Julius II, had requested that Francesco's father, Giuliano* – one of the architects working on Rome's fine new buildings – should immediately go and examine them.

Michelangelo was always in and out of the Sangallo house, and so he joined his friend, with young Francesco in tow, on the Esquiline Hill (now hard to imagine as a semi-rural zone of vineyards, since it is near the great railway station of Termini). There they saw it, in a cavity that had been opened up in the earth: a bearded, mature figure flanked by two boys, all three

* Giuliano da Sangallo is the subject of a great portrait by Piero di Cosimo, now in the Rijksmuseum in Amsterdam, in which his gaze seems quite as sharp as the nib of his quill and the points of his compass, emblems of his profession depicted by the artist.

of them caught in the coils of winding snakes, their faces full of agony, their limbs contorted. While young Francesco jumped down into the hole to get up close to the figures, his father – light-bulb moment! – recognised the group as the very work described in a famous classical text: 'That is Laocoön – the one that Pliny mentioned,' he declared. Pliny the Elder had indeed mentioned a statue of Laocoön and his sons that was 'superior to any other artwork in painting or sculpture'. It had been made, he wrote, by the Rhodian team of Hagesander, Polydorus and Athenodorus, sculptors (probably) working around the turn of the first centuries BC and AD. News of the find spread quickly: ten days later, the 'supremely beautiful ancient sculpture of marble' was already the subject of an excited letter home to Florence from a Rome-based Medici legate.

The farmer and his vineyard; the chance archaeology; the stumbling across, of all possible sculptures, one of which an admiring description had survived from antiquity; the instant identification by the informed eye of Sangallo ... The story of the discovery seems almost too good to be true. The history of Renaissance Rome is full of such 'chance' discoveries of antique sculptures. They never seem to arise from systematic searches, odd given how prized and important such finds were, and how transforming for the artists who encountered them.[43] But randomness is a deeply embedded motif in archaeological narratives of discovery. Joan Evans's biography of her half-brother insisted that 'Time and Chance had made him the discoverer of a new civilisation'. But chance had nothing to do with it: he had planned relentlessly for his Knossian adventure, and he knew precisely where he wanted to excavate because Minos

Kalokairinos's exploratory dig had already proved promising. But something in us cleaves to the notion that the earth must offer up its gifts to us spontaneously.

Michelangelo had a reputation as an expert forger of ancient objects. In truth, the notion that an artist's work was so good that it could be mistaken for a classical 'original' was something of a Renaissance trope. But still: it was by imitating antique artefacts that he learned how to be an artist. Condivi's biography tells us that as an adolescent in Florence, Michelangelo haunted Lorenzo de' Medici's garden of classical sculptures, regarding it as the 'best school' for his studies, and made such a good copy of a Roman faun's head that Lorenzo, impressed and amused, invited him to live in his own household. In fact, recounted Condivi, he improved the original, since he supplied 'from his imagination all that was lacking in the ancient work', reconstructing its missing and damaged parts. On another occasion, one of the Medici cousins was shown a sculpture of a sleeping Cupid that Michelangelo had made. 'If you would fix it so that it looked as if it had been buried, I would send it to Rome and it would pass for an ancient work, and you would sell it much better,' said the cousin. Michelangelo did precisely that and a cardinal bought it for 200 ducats – a fraud that was, in the event, rumbled, though it served to bolster rather than crush his reputation. In Rome, his first important commission was for a (sexy, louche) sculpture of Bacchus, closely based on antique models, for Cardinal Raffaele Riario della Rovere's new palace, the Palazzo della Cancelleria.

To go to Rome is to encounter a city that is a great and chaotic collage. Cardinals' palaces are supported on Roman columns, and churches have gorgeous walls lined with marble stripped from antique ruins. Frescoes – both ancient and Renaissance – baffle the eye with *trompe l'oeil* porticoes and landscapes; walls are swagged with drapery that turns out to be a painted sham. In the Palazzo Spada, there is a seventeenth-century colonnade by the architect Francesco Borromini at whose terminus stands a heroic statue that, though it looks much larger, is only ninety centimetres tall – the result of sleight-of-hand perspectival tricks. In the Palazzo Altemps, there is a Roman sculpture of the god Mars whose missing parts were supplied by Bernini. Looking at it, it's hard to know whether to take more pleasure in the antiquity of the body of the marble god or the beauty of its elegantly extended right foot (and protruding second toe), the work of the greatest sculptor of the seventeenth century. The Roman sculptures themselves are very often copies of the masterpieces of ancient Greece. All is illusion. All is knowing, artful make-believe. Rome is fabrication, fiction, glorious, shameless made-uppery.

RANSACKING THE CITY

During my time in Rome, I lived in the same place as a painter who was spending three months in the city. She would often go out into the museums and draw. I was visiting museums, too, and sometimes I could track her by recognising the original of something she had sketched in her notebook. My eye would be caught by a certain relief in a loggia of the Palazzo Altemps, say, which seemed familiar, though I had never been there before, and then I would realise that it was her drawing that I knew. She drew as casually as another might take a snap on her phone, but with infinitely more attention, her eye fixed, her pencil busy. Most often she'd draw from a sculpture or an antique pot, but sometimes she'd be attracted by a book cover, or a photograph on an entrance ticket someone had left lying around. She ransacked it all, greedy and indiscriminate; and then she began transforming, transforming, transforming.

When she made an exhibition, a year later, it was as if she were displaying her spoils and captives. Cupid and Psyche embraced. A boxer wrapped his wrists in cloth. A Gaul died. Medusa petrified anyone who cared to look at her. A monk grabbed at a woman's breast. Apollo raped Daphne. St Theresa thrilled in her ecstasy. A Neapolitan tart wiggled her hips. Dancers stood on their hands. Horses started and reared. Everything was colour: pale marble made pink and fleshy, and touched with green and turquoise and scarlet. Everything collided in a kicking, swirling, orgiastic tumble of tangled limbs and flesh.

Laocoöns

Soon after *Laocoön* was discovered, Pope Julius II bought and put it on display where it still stands, in the statue court in the Vatican Belvedere. The work seemed to colonise Michelangelo's imagination: the deathly coils of the serpent are in his frescoes for the Sistine Chapel, encircling the grotesque figure of Minos of Crete in his guise as judge of the dead; and they are in the unfinished sculptures of slaves, once intended for Julius's tomb, that now belong to the Louvre.

Michelangelo began these works in 1513, but abandoned work on them before they were ready; they ended up, in his lifetime, in the possession of the French king. The slaves are bound and lashed, the cords cutting hard into their skin. One of them is young and beautiful. His right arm cups the back of his head, his left gently skims his chest. His lips are sensuous and his eyes closed. Perhaps he's dying: the sculpture is, indeed, usually called the *Dying Slave.* But he looks instead as if he's experiencing a moment of great bliss. The other figure, known as the *Rebellious Slave,* writhes and wrings out his body. His left arm is yanked back, revealing the landscape of muscles on the side of his body; his head, too, is twisted to face up and behind him.

Looking at these two sculptures in the Louvre's Michelangelo gallery, as I did one summer day, resting on the seat beside them while the crowds rushed by, it was impossible not to be reminded of *Laocoön*'s pose, his limbs contorted and wrenched by the whipcord strength of the serpent, his left arm straining back, his face a howl of pain as it tilts back and up. Months later, in Rome, I was even reminded of *Laocoön* one day as I contemplated Michelangelo's *Pietà* in St Peter's basilica (while French nuns crowded around me gently harmonising a hymn, venerating the sculpture for its proximity to God, rather than for its godlike artistry). It seemed to me that there was something of the form of *Laocöon* in the *Pietà*'s broadness, in the wide spread of the Madonna's thighs as she steadies the corpse of her son across her knees – while everything about him pulls down, droops, his body's armature disabled by death, and you think about how Michelangelo has convinced you that of these two figures, both carved from inanimate stone, one is dead and one is alive.* But that doesn't work at all, for Michelangelo had already made his *Pietà* by the time *Laocoön* was pulled from the soil – and he couldn't (could he?) echo the form of something that he hadn't yet seen.

His younger Venetian contemporary, Titian, seemed equally incapable of escape from the inextricable twinings of *Laocoön.* His *Bacchus and Ariadne*, in the National Gallery in London, depicts the moment when the god finds – and falls in love with – the abandoned Ariadne on the shore of Naxos. Still a young man when he undertook this commission in the early 1520s for Alfonso d'Este, the duke of Ferrara, Titian had not yet travelled to Rome, had not yet seen *Laocoön*, but he had consumed the sculpture's image through the copies and drawings that quickly began to circulate via the humanist cognoscenti.

I have always loved this painting, not least because one of its most important sources is *Peliaco quondam.* In fact it was reproduced on the cover of the paperback translation of Catullus I bought when I was at school, so that I associated it with the poem long before I saw the painting itself in London. That bright shock of blue sky, that urgent leaping god bounding down from his chariot to hurl himself towards Ariadne – the vividness of it all made me feel I could step into the poem. In the foreground there is a muscular, bearded figure wreathed in snakes and with a body twisted not in pain but in the swerving choreography of the god's wild dance. It's a translation of the

* Matthew Fox made this observation as we stepped from the gloom of the basilica into the light of Piazza San Pietro on 10 February 2017.

poem's description of Bacchus's rowdy entourage in *Peliaco quondam*: '*pars sese tortis serpentibus incingebant*' – 'some were twining themselves with twisting snakes'. And it is, at the same time, *Laocoön* transformed again.

VIRGIL'S TROY

After the death of Laocoön, the Trojans pull the wooden horse into their city. Darkness falls. Sleep slinks over the city. '*Serpit*' is the verb Virgil uses, a word too closely related to the slithering of those fatal serpents for comfort. In the middle of the night the ghost of the hero Hector comes to Aeneas in a dream and warns him to leave the city at once: the siege is broken, the city is overrun by Greeks, it cannot be saved, the war is lost. And you, Aeneas: you have a destiny to fulfil. You must find a new home for your people, in a new country, which you will do in time, though first you must wander over the sea. (Virgil's word for 'wander' is '*pererrato*', with overtones of paths lost and mistakes made.)

Aeneas wakes up and climbs to the roof of his father's house, from where he looks down over the calamity-struck city. Even with this clear view of what is happening, this complete, bird's-eye picture of the marauding Greeks, he refuses to obey Hector's instructions. He rushes back down into the streets, mindlessly grabbing his sword and armour. The phrase is '*arma amens capio*' ('mindless, I grab my arms'), which echoes, in its words and rhythm, the opening line of the epic '*Arma virumque cano*' ('I sing of arms and a man'). But '*arma amens capio*' is like a parody of that heroic overture: Aeneas has lost his head. He and his comrades fight without hope in the city streets, like wolves in a black mist, driven blindly on. Night hovers around them, casting them into concealing, deceiving shadow.

At last, after a crescendo of urgent portents and signs from the gods, Aeneas is persuaded to leave the burning city. He gathers his family: his son Ascanius, his old father Anchises and his wife Creusa. But in the dark and the rush and the chaos, he strays from the paths he knows and plunges down side streets and alleyways. Suddenly he realises that Creusa is nowhere to be found. She is lost in the confusion and '*error*' of Troy.

He rushes back to look for her, tries to retrace his steps, searches madly through the burning streets. But she is already dead, or as good as dead, and he will only ever see her ghost now. When he tries to embrace it, it will flee from his arms like a breeze, like a winged dream.

This story, which I painfully unlocked from its Latin hexameters at school in the 1980s, old pipes clanking and sighing as they overheated the classroom, knots my stomach with fear now in a way it never did then. I cannot bear the thought of those tight-clinging hands cut loose in the crowd, the refugees separated in the chaos of the besieged city, the family unravelled, never to be made whole again.

TROY TOWN

This story of the end of Troy is recounted by Aeneas to Dido. They are already falling in love, but their passion will sour. He will leave her when he receives god-sent signs that his time in Africa is wasted, a dead end. He must forge on towards his real destiny: Italy. The whole of the first half of the epic is, in a way, a story of delay and wandering and waste, of a failure to arrive. Dido is one of the casualties of this circuitousness: she will commit suicide out of anger and grief after Aeneas leaves her, after he slinks away in the night without a farewell or explanation, just as Theseus leaves Ariadne in *Peliaco quondam*.

This great looping and indirect journey takes Aeneas and his fellow exiles to Sicily – twice. The poem begins on Sicily, before a storm sends the Trojans to Carthage. It will take us nearly half the poem to find them on the island again, within reach of Italy once more, by which time they will have covered enormous quantities of poetic and geographical ground but got themselves precisely nowhere. Odysseus's colourful journey around the Mediterranean seems picaresque and joyful compared with Aeneas's tortuous meanderings. But then he does not carry the fateful burden of Rome's future.

On Sicily for the second time, then, the Trojans decide to hold funeral games in honour of Anchises, Aeneas's father, who died before the exiles reached Carthage. There are boat races, foot races; there is boxing and archery. Then come the equestrian events. Ascanius, Aeneas's son, and other young boys appear on horseback. First they wheel and charge in mock battle. Then they perform manoeuvres and patterns, the woven intricacy of which are like the coils of the Cretan labyrinth.

So complex the labyrinth once in hilly Crete, they say,
Where the passage wove between blind walls and wavered on

> In numberless cunning paths that broke down every clue,
> With nothing to trace and no way back – a baffling maze.
> Complex as the course the sons of Troy now follow, weaving
> Their way through mock escapes and clashes all in sport.[44]

This game became the basis, the poem continues, of a Roman cavalry display – the '*lusus Troiae*', or Trojan game – that was performed in Virgil's day. Virgil is bestowing a venerable origin story – it goes all the way back to Troy! – on a Roman ritual of uncertain vintage that had been 'revived' by Julius Caesar and augmented by Virgil's patron, the emperor Augustus, into a glamorous and impressive spectacle, featuring young horsemen of noble family. There is in existence, dating from the seventh century BC, an Etruscan wine jug that is decorated with figures of horsemen and a diagram of a labyrinth, in which the word '*Truia*' is written – which may have a connection to this '*lusus Troiae*'. According to some scholars, the poem may have been using creative etymology to historicise a ritual that actually meant 'weaving game', for in one ancient lexicographical source, *troa* is said to be a Greek word meaning the weft thread.[45] It may be that the riders, on some level, were 'weaving' a defensive ritual for their city, invoking the labyrinth's powers of control and containment. (On the Etruscan jug there are also images of copulating couples, which may make a further hint at the inherent licentiousness of the maze.) At any rate, Virgil's imagery conflates the idea of the labyrinth with the notion of weaving and thread, already first cousins among metaphors. It also contains an echo of the dance performed on Ariadne's dancing floor in the *Iliad*, and the dance that Callimachus had

Theseus and his band of Athenian survivors dance after their escape from the labyrinth in his *Hymn to Delos*.

This mingling of the idea of the city and the labyrinth; of weaving, dance, games and display, carries a curious resonance in parts of northern Europe, especially Britain and Scandinavia, where certain labyrinths can, by those who know where to look, be found in the landscape: cut into turf on village greens or commons, or laid out in boulders near the sea. In England, where the labyrinths tend to be cut from turf (as opposed to the stone labyrinths of Scandinavia), they often carry the name Troy Town, or the Walls of Troy. One lost labyrinth (for only a handful survive) was called Tarrytown, presumably a corruption of Troy Town but nicely expressive of the time one might once have wasted in walking its curves and loops in Temple Cowley, Oxfordshire. Those that remain include a labyrinth called the Walls of Troy in Dalby, North Yorkshire, and another called Troy Town in Oxfordshire, in the grounds of Troy Farm. In Wales, they are called *caerdroia*, which means 'city of Troy' – but there's a double meaning to be found there, for *caer y troiae* can mean 'city of turnings'. In fact, *caer* is more commonly translated as a fort or encampment – Caer, for example, is the Welsh name for the city of Chester, and both words are derived from the Latin *castrum*, meaning military camp. I like the idea that in Welsh all these ideas might be knotted together: the city of Troy, a sinuous, coiling path, and a defended fortress protected from the outside world.

Over the centuries there has been much speculation about what Troy Towns were actually for. William Stukeley, the great, and greatly eccentric, English antiquary, recorded his theories in his work on the ancient monuments of Britain, *Itinerarium Curiosum* (1724). He linked them directly with the '*lusus Troiae*' passage in the *Aeneid*, taking them to be direct survivals from the Roman occupation of Britain, which had ended some 1,300 years earlier. ('It is admirable that both name and thing should have continued through such a diversity of people,' he wrote, optimistically.) 'They are generally upon open green places, by the side of roads or rivers, upon meadows and the like near a town ... The lovers of antiquity, especially of the inferior class, always speak of them with great pleasure, and as if there were something extraordinary in the thing, though they cannot tell what ... The boys to this day divert themselves with running in it one after another, which leads them by many windings quite through and back again.' Other antiquaries noted that Troy Towns sometimes became the stage for summertime lovers' trysts, or dancing, or chasing games. Those coiling pathways are the perfect place for flirtation, the perfect container for performance.

In reality, for all that these turf mazes carry an air of mystery, or even, for some, a breath of the occult, they cannot be direct survivals from the Roman period. Turf labyrinths require regular re-cutting and maintenance if they are not to fold and fade back into the landscape, and Britain has been through too many vicissitudes to allow us to take seriously the notion that there has been regular and continuous upkeep of these enigmatic, fragile monuments over two millennia. The great late-twentieth-century compiler of the physical traces of mazes and labyrinths, Hermann Kern, speculated that the earliest Troy Towns in Britain may have derived from medieval cathedral labyrinths.

In medieval England there were no labyrinths like those set into the floors of the cathedrals at Chartres or Auxerre, but there was, for example, the 'house of Daedalus' drawn on the Hereford *mappa mundi* in around 1300, and a lovely ceiling boss, decorated with a labyrinth, was made in about 1390 for the great parish church of St Mary Redcliffe in Bristol (which also has a wonderful stone-carved Green Man). There are labyrinths depicted in English medieval manuscripts too, including an eleventh-century codex containing Boethius's *Consolations of Philosophy*, now in the Cambridge University Library. A poem about the Virgin Mary is written within the seven winding courses of this labyrinth, while a text hopes that the dedicatee Siweard – probably the abbot of Abingdon – be accepted into the 'hall of the sevenfold heaven'.[46] Later, there are also hints of mazes and labyrinths as part of elaborate medieval garden designs, though their precise nature is hard to divine: in around 1450, an anonymous English poet wrote a work called *The Assembly of Ladies* in which a group of women enter a labyrinth, becoming 'mased in theyr minde'.

Whatever the origin of these Troy Towns – and the existence of none of them is recorded in surviving texts until the early-modern period – they are irresistible. They simply demand that you enter them. Such is the nature of all mazes and labyrinths – they seduce you into contending with them, dallying with them, wasting time in them. There is a turf labyrinth, for example, simply known as the Maze, in the town of Saffron Walden, in Essex. It is first attested in town records in 1699, when it was re-cut, but is thought to be much older (though it is not mentioned by William Camden in his

Britannia, an antiquarian account of British monuments first published in 1586). It is forty metres across, with seventeen looping circuits and four swollen protuberances at equal distances around its edge.

One February day, sick with a cough and frozen to the bone, I walked this maze, feeling self-conscious, almost as if I were on a stage. I could not shake the feeling that I was locked into a kind of contract with the ground, a contract that forbade me

The design of the Maze at Saffron Walden. Its looping path covers almost a mile.

from cheating by stepping across the low turf ridges that delineated its path. I felt a requirement to dance its dance, to follow its tortuous, repetitive relationship with the land around it, which I necessarily saw from every possible angle, learning the gentle curves of the town common and the buildings around it. The route was intestinal, switching back and back on itself in claustrophobic, dizzying frequency but then – moments of odd relief – coursing in bold, wide swoops for a while. The tightly wound path covers almost a mile. It was odd to be walking without covering any significant ground, moving without really moving. The American writer and activist Rebecca Solnit once wrote of a labyrinth's effect of compression, how it 'winds up a path like thread on a spool'.[47] Walking the maze felt like walking around a huge diagram. Solnit has written, too, that 'a labyrinth is a symbolic journey ... but it is also a map we can really walk on, blurring the difference between map and world'.*

Connemara Sculpture (1971), by the British artist Richard Long, was a labyrinth he made with stones in a wild, grassy spot in the west of Ireland. He based it on a pattern he had seen carved into a granite slab in the National Museum in

* In *Wanderlust: A History of Walking*. It is a description that puts me in mind of Borges's story 'On Exactitude in Science', which purports to be a quotation from a seventeenth-century work by one Suárez Miranda, called *Viajes de Varones Prudentes* (*Travels of a Prudent Man*). It tells of an empire in which the art of cartography developed to such an extent that a map of its entire extent was produced at a scale of 1:1. A geographical equivalent, perhaps, of his character in 'Funes, the Memorious', who remembers everything he has ever experienced.

Dublin,* which had perhaps once marked a route for medieval pilgrims. Long's art often involves his walking great distances. En route he might lay down markers: a spiral of seaweed on a beach, a cairn, a depression scratched into desert sand, a line of sticks placed in a field, a cross traced in pebbles on the bed of a stream. These clues may or may not be seen by others; if they are, they may or may not be recognised as 'art'. They are not monumental or permanent; they are the artefact of a passing moment. The walking itself is also the work: the fact that his body has moved through certain places, in a certain pattern.

Maze-maker

When I visited Adrian Fisher in January 2017, he was designing what was going to be the largest maze in the world, in China. The problem was that he'd had a subsequent brief, also for the biggest maze in the world, this time in Indonesia. He was planning to explain to the first client that the important thing was the fact of having held the record at all, rather than the duration of its possession. In his thirty-year career as a maze designer, he had notched up an impressive tally: forty-two hedge mazes and fifty-one mirror mazes. More than a third of the

---

* Long's *Connemara Sculpture* is a work in the Tate consisting of a photograph of the labyrinth, a drawing of the Irish stone, and a short text suggesting that the carving had been made in 2000 BC. Though the stone has often been interpreted as prehistoric, it's in fact more likely to have been made at some point in the medieval period as a marker on the pilgrimage route to the tomb of St Kevin in Glendalough.

world's mirror mazes were designed by him: they use glass set into the walls of tunnels to cast infinite reflections and to bewilder the eye completely. 'They keep coming – good earners,' he said of them. In 1993, he and a collaborator designed the first maize maze, using swift-growing corn to form its walls. Now these summer attractions are a feature of the landscape in parts of the USA and Britain, earning farmers something on the side. The notion of a maze might seem charmingly arcane – a relic, with its cousins the parterre and the knot garden, of the gentlemanly landscapes of a past age. But it seems that plenty of people still want to walk them.

When I arrived at his office – next to his own hedge maze and rambling house on the River Stour in Dorset – he was deep in a Skype conversation with yet another client in China, who wanted a maze as a temporary amusement in a new city square. He had made mazes in castle gardens, in vast air-conditioned shopping malls in the Middle East, and in airports. He had made mazes that let loose spurts of water at the unwary visitor, mazes containing towers and bridges, mazes with complicated storylines worked into them, mazes containing riddles, mazes that floated above water, mazes that snaked through woods.

Fisher also enjoyed talking about navigation, the flow of crowds, puzzles, magic, tessellation, misdirection, spying and ciphers. His conversation was sometimes like his mazes: digressive. He told me about meeting a man who had once worked for the CIA, who had explained to him how you could disguise yourself by putting grains of rice in your shoe to throw off your normal gait. He showed me on a map exactly where he thought the lost turf labyrinth at the nearby village of Pimperne had been laid out (it was a particularly pleasing triangular design, recorded by the nineteenth-century antiquary and maze enthusiast Edward Trollope, but long since gone). He told me about recreational mathematics – a pastime whose enthusiasts gather annually for conferences in Japan, Europe and the US, where a suitable conversational opening might be 'What is interesting about the number 1,729?'* His new joy was his drone – he would have it fly above his mazes so he could film them.

Fisher's mazes occupy an intriguing territory somewhere between puzzle, end-of-the-pier show and landscape art; his own role something between ringmaster, geometrician and impresario. He makes his mazes for families to solve together (in contrast, he explained, to the solitary pleasures of completing a Sudoku or tackling a Rubik's cube). He observes that family members can appreciate each other's skills afresh in a maze – especially if he peppers them with clues to solve or questions to answer as they go. They are compelled to make decisions jointly and agree on a route. 'It is an experience that binds people together. When they come out they've changed – they've had to bury their ego and buckle under.'

He has a little control over how people will behave in his mazes, largely at the beginning and the end of their route, since there are fixed entry and exit points. 'Anything like a rollercoaster

* The interesting thing about the number 1,729 is that it is the smallest number that can be expressed as the sum of cubes in different ways – $1^3 + 12^3 = 9^3 + 10^3$.

The design of the long-lost labyrinth at Pimperne, Dorset.

or a flume ride is like a movie – a linear sequence. As time unfolds you discover them in the order that the designer intends. That's not true in the maze. You might go left and then go right and miss one tower and see the other tower twice. Your twin sister may go another way and see everything I have put in the maze once each. Or I may have designed it so that it's impossible to see everything without going back and seeing some things two or three times.' He can trick visitors with certain moves. For example, imagine a junction that looks like a tuning fork. Were you to approach it from one of the tines of the fork, habit of mind would tell most people to continue broadly in the direction already travelled, joining the handle of the fork rather than branching sharply back onto the other tine; but that counter-intuitive move might in fact be the right path in a maze.

He is good at solving other people's mazes. He told me about visiting the Bridge End Gardens maze in Saffron Walden, designed in 1839 by William Andrews Nesfield.* 'I just went in and felt like doing this and doing that,' said Fisher, 'and then at a certain point it felt right and I went in for the kill.' By which he meant he approached the centre directly, which, true to Mrs Grammatiki's theory of experienced maze-walkers, he knew not to do at once. He had, his surprised companion told him, simply marched to the centre by the most efficient route, as if he knew the design in advance. He didn't, but he had looked at other maze designs by Nesfield, and had simply internalised his likely moves.

There is an adversarial element in a maze: it is as if maker and walker are playing a game together, but with one of the contenders absent. 'It's like chess, only I have to play all my moves in advance,' said Fisher. His aim, though, is not to beat

---

* Nesfield fought at Waterloo and painted landscapes before turning to garden design, planning the great vistas in Kew Gardens. Bridge End Gardens are open, free of charge, to the public every day, meaning that Saffron Walden, taking into account its turf-cut maze on the common, is unusually well off for easily accessible labyrinths.

his adversaries, not to trap or imprison them, nor to confound them too grievously, but to bewilder them just enough to create pleasure. 'I have to entertain you. I have to let you win. And I must let you win just before you've had enough.' One can quite easily have enough: Fisher's wife, Marie, who keeps the business side of the operation in order, stoutly told me that she herself is not a great one for mazes: or rather, she just likes to know she can get out of them.

Fisher has an extremely strong sense of direction. 'Put me down into King's Cross Underground station, and I can tell you I am facing north-east and am roughly so many metres down,' he said. People enjoy solving mazes, he thinks, because they pique our inborn human desire to wander and to explore. 'When you are little you want to know what's behind every corner, every door. That's in us. Doing things we aren't allowed to do.' But there is also the pleasure of the abandonment of control and the joy of being lost (but still held and contained). Being in a maze is like being blindfolded and whirled around for blind man's bluff: so long as you can trust the rules of the game, a little disorientation is thrilling. Fisher is a benign and eccentric wielder of his power, a cunning but kindly Daedalus who makes mazes to confuse – but mostly to entrance.

How to find your way

Mazes are the symbolic link, the halfway house, between human and exploration, between landscape and representation, between earth and map. 'The natural development of the map is the desire which necessity or curiosity imposes on mankind to explore the earth's surface, and to move from one part of that surface to another – working from the known to the unknown – on the path of experience and enquiry,' wrote Herbert George Fordham, the early-twentieth-century authority on cartography.[48] Which also sounds very much like the act of walking a maze.

The question of how we find our way, what is a sense of direction, and how humans understand where we are in the world is one for philosophers, psychologists and neuroscientists as well as poets and painters. Edward Tolman was an American psychologist who taught at Berkeley between 1918 and 1954.* Some of his most important experiments charted how rats navigated their way around mazes of his devising. He contended that the animals were not simply reacting to environmental stimuli that triggered biological responses when they explored a space (as many of his colleagues argued), but rather could learn facts about the world and use them later in a flexible manner. He compared the former view of the brain to a telephone exchange, receiving incoming calls from sense organs, and passing on outgoing messages to muscles. By contrast, he theorised that 'in the course of learning, something like a field

---

* The University of California attempted to dismiss him in the McCarthy era since he refused to swear an oath of loyalty, believing such an oath would impinge on academic freedom. He led resistance, sued the university and won, meaning that other recusants among senior faculty had their dismissals overturned. He now has an important university building named after him.

map of the environment gets established in the rat's brain ... The central office itself is far more like a map control room than it is like an old-fashioned telephone exchange. The stimuli, which are allowed in, are not connected by just simple one-to-one switches to the outgoing responses. Rather, the incoming impulses are usually worked over and elaborated in the central control room into a tentative, cognitive-like map of the environment. And it is this tentative map, indicating routes and paths and environmental relationships, which finally determines what responses, if any, the animal will finally release'.[49]

This theory of a 'cognitive map' held waning interest for psychologists of the next generation, but it was revived in the 1970s by a researcher called John O'Keefe, who is now a professor in cognitive neuroscience at University College London. He studied the hippocampus, the area deep in the brain, curving to a spiral at its tip, that is named for its resemblance to a sea horse. (*Hippos* is Greek for horse, *kampos* for monster). He discovered that when a rat moved around a space, cells in the hippocampus would be activated when it occupied one particular spot – and no other. When it moved to another position, other cells would be activated. These he called 'place cells'. The 'firing' or 'pulsing' of these cells can be translated into a sound in the lab. 'You can imagine that the brain is kind of talking to you or singing to you. One becomes almost addicted to this sound of the cells firing,' he has said.[50] The rat, he argued, would move round a space not just in search of goals (such as food) or in accordance with automatic 'telephone exchange' biological prompts, but out of curiosity, so that the hippocampus could build up a picture of the environment. He published this discovery in 1971, since when he and other researchers have added to and built on his work. It was for the discovery of these 'place cells' that he won a Nobel prize in 2014.

His co-Nobel prizewinners, the Trondheim-based researchers (and married couple) Edvard and May-Britt Moser, worked on a related area of the brain close to the hippocampus, the entorhinal cortex. They discovered 'grid cells' that, when rats move through space, form a kind of coordinate system. Hugo Spiers, a neuroscientist who also works on navigation at UCL, explained to me that these grid cells are like the brain's 'longitude and latitude. They may provide the metric. In a labyrinth they might tell you, for example, how many metres you had walked in'. There are other cells that deal with head direction, telling an animal which way it is facing; others again that seem to signal boundaries and speed. With these elements together signalling place, distance, direction, speed and boundaries, he said, 'You have a map and a compass in your head – and you can use them to imagine where you are going.' He told me of the 'shocking beauty' of the images of the 'grid cells' as they fired, each creating hexagonal patterns of activity across the whole environment. In *The Hippocampus as a Cognitive Map*, the book O'Keefe and his collaborator Lynn Nadel published in 1978, the pair posited that humans had developed Euclidean geometry precisely because the hippocampus itself provided them with 'an a priori Euclidean spatial framework'.[51] The cognitive map, they elaborated, 'is not a picture or image which "looks like" what it represents; rather it is an information structure from which map-like images can be reconstructed and from which behaviour dependent on place information can be generated'.[52]

When O'Keefe began working on the hippocampus, it was well understood that that part of the brain performs an important role in certain kinds of memory. A famous American patient known as HM (Henry Molaison, 1926–2008), who had had much of his hippocampi surgically removed in order to ease his serious epilepsy, afterwards lacked what is known as 'episodic memory', that is, the ability to remember experiences – when, where and with whom a particular event had occurred. Other kinds of memory remained intact: he was able to learn, and retain, new motor skills, for example, without really recalling how he had learned them.

Episodic memory, thinking in the field has it, works in tandem with the 'place cells' to help build up a picture of the world. 'Imagine you are wandering round in a dark cave and have a very unpleasant experience in it,' Spiers said. 'Those place cells were active at the same time as the fear centre in your brain, and if you return to that cave, your map tells you that you don't want to go back into it. The map provides a way of learning about the world and piecing together your construction of it. The view is that this mapping is linked to memory.' So that, on some level, finding our way through life, building up stories about ourselves and making meaningful memories out of our experiences, may be twined together with our ability to navigate. It is something that many people feel instinctively, for to retrieve a memory, it often helps to have that memory positioned within space, within a story. Cicero and other ancient rhetoricians described memory techniques that involved 'placing' facts that one wishes to commit to memory in a certain imagined environment (a town, or a house, for example). The mind can later roam through this space built in the mind, and pluck the memories at will from their positions in the 'memory palace'.

Another team at UCL, led by Eleanor Maguire, has discovered that the hippocampi of London cabbies are larger than those of the regular population. London taxi drivers are required to learn the streets of central London within a six-mile radius of Charing Cross. This is, perhaps, something that will gradually drift out of usage now, in the days of GPS. It takes between two and four years to acquire what is known, with a pleasing aura of mysticism, as the Knowledge. Novices, guided by a document called *The Blue Book*, must ready themselves for an oral examination with elders of the cabbies' tribe, who test their ability to visualise and accurately describe the shortest possible route between any two given points within this radius, also calling to mind landmarks of interest along the way. To aid their memorising of these arcana, they must also learn 320 specific 'runs', one of which is Maze Hill station, SE10, to West Ham Lane, E15, the former perhaps once the site of a turf labyrinth and a reminder, if one were needed, of the involuted nature of the city. Spiers collaborated with Maguire on a control experiment that involved testing the hippocampi of London bus drivers, who have similar exposure to the city's streetscape and its attendant stresses, but no compunction to find their way in it beyond the learning of their set, regular routes. They found that bus drivers had no such enlarged hippocampi.

On the other hand, 'the compass and the map may be the first things to go' in Alzheimer's disease, said Spiers. An early sign is suddenly discovering that one cannot find one's way home – before other dissolutions occur, such as forgetting language, faces, one's family, oneself. He is working on dementia, and has, with collaborators, devised a game* that asks the player to range over an ocean – a kind of maze, according to its designers. Using the data gleaned from the way hundreds of thousands of players navigate the virtual seas, he and his colleagues hope to learn more about how people find their way. O'Keefe too has used virtual environments in order to extend his research beyond the world of rats to that of people. As PET (positron emission tomography) and then fMRI (functional magnetic resonance imaging) technologies emerged, researchers were able to gain a much clearer view of the activity of the human brain: but under a scanner, one cannot physically lose oneself in the streets. In the mid 1990s, however, when virtual-reality computer games became affordable, O'Keefe and his team used a shooter game as a basis for his experiments: it was stripped of its Minotaurish violence, its monsters, its traps and its combatants, and reduced to a harmless 70 x 70 metre streetscape for human subjects to navigate.

I find my way, in so far as I do find my way, by remembering landmarks. I have difficulty visualising my walked routes, and freeze when strangers ask me for directions, always fearing I have set people off on the wrong track even when describing journeys I quite often take. I became disoriented even returning

---

* The game is called 'Sea Hero Quest'. It can be downloaded on any smartphone or tablet, and every minute of play helps Spiers and his team with their work on the brain.

from Hugo Spiers's office to the library where I was working, a distance of about half a mile in a familiar tract of London. The philosopher Walter Benjamin, remembering his childhood adventures in a park in Tiergarten in Berlin, wrote that 'Not to find one's way around a city does not mean much. But to lose one's way in a city, as one loses one's way in a forest, requires some schooling. Street names must speak to the urban wanderer like the snapping of dry twigs, and little streets in the heart of the city must reflect the times of day, for him, as clearly as a mountain valley. This art I acquired rather late in life; it fulfilled a dream, of which the first traces were labyrinths on the blotting papers in my school notebooks'.[53] I share none of this joy of the unknown, this optimistic sense of the pioneer dominating nature. I fear that my hippocampus is, in contrast to those of London cabbies, small and etiolated. I fear that my limited capacities to navigate will be in the process of withering yet more completely as I come to rely on the safe blue thread of my Google Maps directions. The notion that one could disappear under the earth, in King's Cross Underground station, and declare oneself to be facing north-east, I find fantastical.

Follow the Finger That Points

In *The Blue Cross*, G. K. Chesterton's first story about his amateur-detective priest, Father Brown, we encounter the famous French policeman Valentin as he alights from a boat at

Harwich in pursuit of the notorious criminal mastermind Flambeau. On the train up to London he comes across a very short priest with 'a face as round and dull as a Norfolk dumpling' and 'eyes as empty as the North Sea'. The priest is fussing with his brown-paper parcels in the carriage, foolishly telling his fellow passengers that he must take great care, as he is transporting something made of silver with blue stones. Valentin thinks little of it, since he is on the lookout for the criminal: he knows only that Flambeau is six foot four and a master of disguise.

Later, in London, Valentin, having no clues to pursue, follows his own curious method of detection: he strikes at random, going down peculiar cul-de-sacs, knocking on the doors of empty houses, going round every crescent that puts him out of his way: he deliberately, in short, takes long and looping routes in the hope that he will stumble upon something out of the ordinary. At last, having had no breakfast, he stops at a café and orders a coffee, to which he adds sugar. However, it is not sugar that comes out of the basin, but salt.

Valentin demands an explanation. The waiter offers his theory. 'I zink it is those two clergymen,' he says. 'The two clergymen that threw soup at the wall.' Yes, expands the proprietor. There were two clergymen in earlier, quiet and respectable people. One of them hung back as they were leaving – and actually threw half a cup of soup slap at the wall.

This is enough for Valentin. 'In the universal darkness of his mind he could only follow the first finger that pointed.' He sets off in pursuit of the mysterious soup-throwing priests, and pursues a trail that includes oranges mislabelled as brazils in a greengrocer's; an upended box of apples; and a broken window in a restaurant. Valentin, and the London bobbies whom he has enlisted en route, are told by the waiter in this establishment that the clergymen have disappeared up Bullock Street; the journey now 'took them through bare brick ways like tunnels'. Dark is gathering, and even the London policemen are disoriented, until a 'bulging gas-lit window' breaks the blue twilight 'like a bull's-eye lantern'. The light comes from a sweetshop. Valentin gravely buys thirteen chocolate cigars, while the proprietress tells him about a parcel one of the clergymen has left behind, with instructions to post it off to Westminster. The priests have gone on to Hampstead Heath, she says.

Off they dash to the Heath, where the closeness and darkness of the streets opens out into a still-bright sunset over the wide green spaces. There, Valentin finally spots his quarry, sitting on a bench under a spreading tree on the brow of a hill, discussing theology. The taller of the two, gazing out onto the gradually darkening sky, contends that there may be 'wonderful universes above us where reason is utterly unreasonable'.

The shorter priest – whom Valentin recognises from the train that morning – disagrees. 'Reason and justice grip the remotest and the loneliest star,' says Father Brown. 'Look at those stars. Don't they look as if they were single diamonds and sapphires? Well, you can imagine any mad botany or geology you please. Think of forests of adamant with leaves of brilliants. Think the moon is a blue moon, a single elephantine sapphire. But don't fancy that all that frantic astronomy would make the smallest difference to the reason and justice of conduct. On plains of opal, under cliffs cut out of pearl, you would still find a notice-board, "Thou shalt not steal."'

The salt, the thrown soup, the upset apples, the broken window: all of these apparently random and bizarre events have been an Ariadne's trail, a set of clues laid down by Father Brown to draw Valentin towards them. The silver cross with the blue stones – now safely dispatched by post to Westminster, courtesy of the sweetshop proprietor – was bait for Flambeau.

This story was a favourite of Mrs Grammatiki's. She believed in God, and she enjoyed its contention that the world is made up of patterns and shape and reason despite the frequent outward appearance of chaos (metaphorical thrown soup and upset apples being a feature of the world). Reading it, I feel myself wanting to believe, almost ready to believe. But I can't. Mrs Grammatiki could look up into the dark night and see a majestical roof fretted with golden fire; I see a mere congregation of vapours. To me, thrown soup and upset apples are just a consequence of the unreason and erring of the world.

Cretto di Burri

When an earthquake hit the Belice valley in the west of Sicily in 1968, the whole of the village of Gibellina was destroyed. Eventually it was rebuilt some way outside the earthquake zone, with the help of a succession of architects and artists who contributed ideas for the new town at the invitation of the mayor, Ludovico Corrao. When Corrao approached Alberto

Burri, though, the artist refused to contribute an artwork to Gibellina Nuova. Instead, he looked to the shattered and abandoned remains of the old Gibellina.

Burri was an Umbrian born in 1915 who had trained as a doctor and taught himself the rudiments of his art in a POW camp in Texas during the Second World War. Later, he made paintings with jute sacks and with sheets of metal, with plastic blowtorched to open up craters in its surface, and with pigment mixed with resin and kaolin so that the resulting works, when oven-dried, developed a form that resembled the fissured earth of a dried-up riverbed. These last he called *cretti*, or cracks, and these are the works that have the most obvious visual relationship with what he created from the remains of Gibellina.

Visiting the ruins now – known as the Cretto di Burri, the 'Crack of Burri', or the Grande Cretto, the 'Great Crack' – is to enter an impossible world. Above a valley otherwise occupied by olive trees, vines and stubble, was a town that looked as if it had absconded from an Italo Calvino story: a city of silent, doorless walls and empty grey streets. Burri had entombed the ruins of Gibellina's buildings in concrete, leaving its roads and alleyways clear, so that the whole place (which, from afar, resembled a grubby rhomboid handkerchief draped over the hillside) became a maze. A maze not of hedges but of blocks of hard grey matter, uniform in height but irregular in shape.

To step within it was to enter a maze of ghosts, the concrete wedges and slabs mausolea for the detritus of the town. My voice echoed uncannily, at times, against its sharp angles; at one point, I heard the monstrous roar of motorbikes that had come to speed through its enticing empty paths – a sacrilege against the solemnity of the place, which was meant as a memorial to destruction and human pain. When Burri first came to see Gibellina's ruins in the 1970s (the work was partially finished in 1989, and fully completed only in 2015), he also took pains to visit the Greek temple ruins of Segesta and Selinunte, and invested his Cretto with their monumentality and seriousness – and with something else, too, harder to define. I felt my heart thudding as I walked these blank and empty streets, where shadows fell under the white sun with a cruel clarity. There was something deathly about the Cretto di Burri.

I entered at the town's lowest point and the logic of the place drew me up the hill, as if to find the village church or square. But this was a maze without a centre; there was no destination, only a seeming infinity of criss-crossing routes and steep, winding paths that zigzagged between the featureless, expressionless blocks of grey. After the motorbikes disappeared, all was silent, except for the rhythmic thwunk of nearby wind turbines, a sound like a swan's wingbeat. The portion of the work that had been completed in 2015 to mark Burri's centenary was still bone white and pristine. The rest was ageing to grey and succumbing to nature: a swallowtail flitted past my shoulder, alighting on a caper plant; saplings were forcing their way through the concrete, which in places was beginning to crumble away to reveal the metal armature behind it. Left to itself, the Cretto would soon be defeated by nature. Growing things would engulf what had already been engulfed, making a labyrinth of green out of this maze of grey.

The Wilderness of the Streets

Sometimes I offer myself the strange comfort, as I wander the wilderness of the London streets, that it is only a matter of time before these places of human habitation, of human industry and of human vanity will disappear. The parks will go untended. Weeds will grow out of the cracks in the asphalted roads. Tendrils of ivy will finger up the walls of the buildings and snake through the windows, over the dusty, rotting furniture and through all the rooms, pulling them slowly, relentlessly, to the ground. Willowherb and thistles will flower on the rubble. Scrub will invade the houses, the banks, the churches, the flats, the shops, the factories, the mosques, the barracks. Woods will rise, when we are safely gone.

Troy Town, Peckham

Troy: the first labyrinthine city to be described in European literature, a trap of bewildering streets that confounds even Aeneas. All cities are labyrinthine, some more explicitly so than others. Venice is a byword for the disorienting city, Shelley's 'peopled labyrinth of walls'. I have never mastered the simplest routes there despite numerous visits; all my sense of direction, such as it is, departs, leaving me with only the landmarks: turn right at that baker there on the corner, keep that bar there on the left. Like a maze, the city becomes benign and explicable only when seen from above, from the air, when it loses mystery and becomes a mere shape: a fish wearing the idiotic false nose of the projecting cruise terminal.

In a manuscript of a work by the thirteenth-century Arab geographer al-Qazvini, for example, Constantinople is drawn as a labyrinth;[54] in medieval Hebrew bibles the seven-walled city of Jericho is often depicted as one.[55] Roman mosaic labyrinths can sometimes be edged by an image of walls and bastions picked out in tesserae – perhaps to imply the Minotaur's lair, but also suggesting a citadel, a defended place. For Borges, in his story 'The Aleph', London is a 'broken labyrinth'. There is an edition of street plans that can be seen on newsstands or in kiosks in many Italian cities: the cover shows a circular maze, and we quite easily understand that the map book is offering itself as a key to the urban puzzle. The idea that Homer's windy Troy – Troy Town – might be found, symbolically and in miniature, on the side of a B-road in the English countryside, or in the gardens of an Oxfordshire farmhouse, appeals to me.

In Geoffrey of Monmouth's *The History of the Kings of Britain* the story goes that Britain was founded by Brutus, who, like Aeneas, was a refugee from the wreck of Troy. He called his new capital on the Thames Troia Nova, 'New Troy'. Only much later did it become London, writes Geoffrey, when it was renamed after King Lud. But to some of its inhabitants (romantics, fantasists), London is faintly tinged by a shadowy memory of Troy. In Peckham, in the south-east of the city, there is a little street called Troy Town, where once there must have been a turf labyrinth. One cloudless day I went there – an unfamiliar part of the city to me, so I followed the blue thread of my

Google Maps route to get there. The sun was throwing shadows in long black slabs along the pavements. The occasional home-bound worker drifted palely by in shirtsleeves and shades, but the place, nonetheless, had an air of emptiness and ghostliness. People seemed hollowed out by heat.

Troy Town, not even fifty metres long, made a shallow curve. One whole side of it was lined with a bright-purple hoarding that stood about three metres high. It was, it turned out, an enclosure; I followed the garish wall until a gap appeared, and I could see beyond it a patch of waste ground awaiting development, a void in the crowded cityscape. As a boundary, the hoarding had little respect for the street layout: it blocked off an alleyway, Rye Passage, that would normally have acted as a cut-through to the next road, and whose street sign now mockingly indicated nowhere but the solid angle where hoarding met fence. Running along the opposite side of the street were the backs of houses, Virginia creeper and ivy tumbling down them in chaotic profusion, so that gates to hidden yards were half concealed. I lingered for a while. It was a modest and unassuming street. For a moment I imagined it as London's secret omphalos. Troy within Troy.

The arms of Laocoön

Passing *Laocoön* in the octagonal courtyard in the Vatican, visitors pause, or stop to gaze in veneration, or sometimes just give it a glance as they forge a path through the bewildering passageways and corridors of the papal museums. The centre of the court is open to the sky, and the first time I visited the sculpture in my forties, half a lifetime since I had first looked at it, a brief but sharp downpour freshened the air and caused the stones to glisten. I looked at the twisted head and pain-filled face of the priest, the straining shoulders, the helpless boys, the snakes so intricately wrapped around the figures that it was almost impossible to differentiate them. I realised there was something peculiar about Laocoön's right arm: the stone was darker and more weathered than that of the rest of the sculpture, but that was not it: there was something off-key, to me, about the way it bent back behind the priest's head.

Later I understood why. When the sculpture emerged from the soil of the vineyard in 1506, it was in good condition, but nonetheless incomplete: the priest's right shoulder was a stump, as was that of his younger son. The sixteenth-century biographer Giorgio Vasari tells us that after the sculpture entered the papal collection, the architect Donato Bramante held a competition, which Raphael was to judge, to choose the best design for Laocoön's right arm.

That was why I misremembered the sculpture: my most immediate mental image of it derived from copies and reproductions (by, among many others, William Blake) of a previous restoration in which the arm had extended almost straight, forming the highest point of the group, and giving the sculpture quite a different sense of violent upward force. There are hundreds, thousands of these upward-stretching Laocoöns in existence, from the casts in museums such as the V&A in London and the Ashmolean in Oxford, to domestic-scale reproductions in bronze that Grand Tourists bought for their English country houses, and delicate miniature versions made in Meissen porcelain.

Its appearance now is a result of a discovery quite as unlikely as its original emergence from the soil: in 1906, a Prague-born archaeologist called Ludwig Pollak came across a bent-back marble arm in a mason's yard in Rome. Convinced it was Laocöon's lost original appendage, he donated it to the Vatican Museums, but it was only in 1957, after his murder in Auschwitz in 1943, that the group was restored using the limb he had so fortuitously spotted. In fact Laocoön has had, since 1506, several right arms, the result of a series of reconstructions, traceable in Vatican records and through the many drawings of the sculpture made by visiting artists. At one point, Michelangelo is thought to have refused to make a replacement; on another occasion he is believed to have been involved in a mooted restoration that proposed an arm bent back, not unlike the one that Pollak discovered.[56] Looking at image after image of the sculpture copied, reproduced and reimagined, I see now how many Laocoöns there have been, shadowing back into the past in infinite regression, a dance of endless variations.

Eva Hesse's Laocoön

Eva Hesse, the German-born American artist, visited the Vatican Museums eight years after *Laocoön* got his new (or, rather, old) arm. Unlike Pollak, Hesse's immediate family had escaped the camps, fleeing from Hamburg in 1938. A year later, she made a sculpture she called *Laocöon.* It is something over three metres tall, and resembles a ladder, or rather four ladders arranged into a square tower. To construct it, Hesse, who would die six years later from a brain tumour at the age of thirty-four, made an armature of plastic tubing, which she covered in papier-mâché and painted grey. Through and over the 'rungs' she draped coils of cloth-bound, grey-painted wire that she called snakes. It was a condensing of the ancient sculpture into its most essential binary drama: that is, the snakes pull down and the ladders reach up, just as in the board game.

Her fellow artist, Robert Smithson, described it in an article he wrote that year in *Arts* magazine, which he presented in a manner that recalls a labyrinth: four central blocks of text on four pages, each block ringed by footnotes and images. A photograph of Hesse's sculpture was part of this procession of illustrations, a sequence that began with the medieval labyrinth set into the floor of Amiens Cathedral and continued with the anatomical theatre at Padua University; an Egyptian pyramid; a vision of the Tower of Babel; and Kepler's model of the heavenly bodies. In describing what he called her 'vertiginous and wonderfully dismal' work, Smithson wrote: 'In her *Laocöon* ... we discover an absence of "pathos" and a deliberate avoidance of the anthropomorphic. Instead one is aware only of the vestigial and devitalised "snakes" looping through a ladder with cloth-bound joints. Everything "classical" and "romantic" is mitigated and undermined.'

Lucy Lippard, in her 1976 book on Hesse, wrote of how the sculpture developed as she worked on it. In the first version 'there was an element of pathos, that *personnage* aspect of a spindly creature helpless in a tangle of things it could neither control or understand'. But as Hesse moved towards her final version, she stripped the 'snakes' of their animal associations. They become, in her hands, threads. A skein of tangled threads, their involuted pathways trailing, interlacing, trapping.

Spiral Jetty

In 1970, Smithson started work on his own vast coiling monument: a 460-metre-long construction of rock, mud and salt crystals that snails its way through the crimson waters of the Great Salt Lake in Utah. He chose Rozel Point as the site of his great earthwork because in that part of the lake the water is 'the colour of tomato soup', as he wrote in an essay of 1972.[57] (The year after publishing that essay he would die, aged thirty-five, in an aeroplane accident in Texas, while surveying sites for another work of land art.) He quoted G. K. Chesterton: 'Red is the most joyful and dreadful thing in the physical universe; it is the fiercest note, it is the highest light, it is the place where the walls of this world of ours wear the thinnest and something beyond burns through.' At Rozel Point he found a landscape of dilapidated machinery and traces of old oil pumps, a kind of pre-history of lost human remains that 'gave evidence of man-made systems mired in abandoned hopes'. The form of the piece he was to create became quickly obvious as he studied the lake: he submitted himself to the indomitable circularity and swirl of the watery landscape, as if it were a whirlpool sucking him to the centre. He compared the shape of the finished work, his giant red thread in the landscape, to Constantin Brâncuşi's portrait of James Joyce,[58] which consisted simply of three vertical lines and a spiral, which the artist said was suggested by the whorls of Joyce's ear – the creator of teeming universes condensed into these simple, spare gestures.

Brâncuşi's reminds me, too, of the swirls on a snail's shell. I have such a shell that I picked up on Crete: translucent, creamy, faintly ridged like a fingernail, with an ochre marking that threads its way round the delicate structure in eleven loops. The line looks as if it could have been painted by some impossibly deft hand: it is slightly deeper at the outside edge as if a brush had started its stroke densely loaded with colour and paled as it ran its course. In ancient Greek, the word for such a shell is *labyrinthos*. Another is *cochlis*, which gives us the word cochlea, the beautiful spiralling cavern (which really does resemble a shell) within the bony labyrinth of the ear, certain disorders of which, affecting balance and causing nausea, are called labyrinthitis.

The anatomists named the labyrinth of the ear as if it were a palace set in a landscape: within its intricate architecture one finds (thinly veiled in anatomical Latin) chambers and windows, recesses and steps, archways and windows, hallways and tunnels, canals and aqueducts, ridges and pyramids. It even has its own grand instrument, the organ of Corti, which contains the hair cells that translate sound vibrations into nerve impulses. All of which might make one think of something straight-lined, ordered and classical: a Palladian house set about with fountains and elegant geometric gardens. One can forget, simply reading these names, that they are mapping the arcana of the body: things looping and vermicular and pulsating; things red and bloody and impossible.

Ariadne on Naxos

As soon as they arrived at the shore of Naxos the crew set about gathering firewood and collecting fresh water, pitching tents and preparing food. Some of the young survivors mustered themselves to help, as if trying by physical effort to deflect their minds from what had happened on Crete. Even the bright sea light and the fresh salt tang could not banish the memory of the labyrinth's bleakness, its stale and fetid stench, its twining, tangling corridors. From the moment they stepped into it, it had seemed somehow alive, a breathing intelligence, a thing that moved and sighed and changed. Passages seemed to materialise where none had been before. Staircases emerged suddenly from the shadows, leading away to unseen depths or heights. And the scale of it: winding corridors opened out into cavernous hallways, terraces and porticoes. Sometimes they were obliged to crawl on hands and knees through narrow tunnels, edge through tight vestibules and clamber up the narrowest of staircases, as if in a tower; at times the ground fell away from their path into a deep ravine. Sometimes, through the dim light of the place (a ghostly illumination whose source no one could discern), the Athenians stumbled over half-ruined furniture, broken statues, frayed tapestries. On more than one occasion, they saw that the walls were decorated with faded frescoes: in one they saw athletes leaping over the body of a bull; in another, a blue monkey gathering saffron from the blooms of crocuses; in a third, a crowd of beautiful women shown in profile, bracelets pushed up over their arms and hair arranged in elaborate curls.

All this time they knew they were human bait for the monster; that in order for Theseus to battle the beast, they must first allow themselves to be hunted. At last they heard its approaching tread, its snort and bellow and roar as it came into view, emerging from a tunnel into a huge circular chamber like an amphitheatre. Imagine the most tremendous bull you have ever seen. Light dances off its shining coat, its neck is one craggy, knotty mass, its chest a waterfall of muscle. But its horns are what you notice most: they sheer outwards from the creature's head and curve upwards to points, each as sharp as a scimitar. Imagine this bestial strength attached to the body and limbs of a man, a man built on no human scale. Its forearms, feathered in black fur, were thicker than the hero's thighs; its legs were like oaks.

Theseus darted around it, taunting it, teasing it, enraging it. The two creatures, man and monster, seemed to dance with one another. At last it lowered its head and charged, and that was when Theseus moved in, grabbed it by one knifelike horn, plunged the sword into the thick flesh, stabbing and hacking over and over again until the innards gaped open and cataracts of blood flowed. Think of a tower block on the fringe of a great city. It is empty now of hope and inhabitants, but it still soars upwards into misty skies, menacing and solid and vast. Then, at last, explosives are primed and detonated. First its lower parts buckle inwards; then its upper storeys decline with something almost like grace, before they plunge to the ground, engulfed in clouds of rising dust. That's how the creature collapsed to its knees, roaring out its long, shuddering death. Theseus took hold of Ariadne's red thread, and led the others back to the great bronze doors of the labyrinth, the doors that Daedalus had engraved with stories of ancient heroes.

No wonder, then, that the Athenian boys and girls were shaken and silent. Theseus, too. The crew counted themselves glad to be out of there, and without being followed by Cretan ships. The sooner they got everyone back to Athens the better, and it would've been better still if Theseus hadn't insisted on this night ashore. That weird girl from Crete, though: she'd saved them, and you'd got to be grateful, but you'd have to say it was unnatural for her to get her half-brother killed (however much of a monster he was) and to leave her family behind her. You could see that she was obsessed with Theseus, following him around the ship, watching him all the time. But he hardly seemed to notice her, and when he did, you could tell he wasn't that interested. The corridors and passages of the labyrinth seemed to have invaded his mind. He was working everything over in his memory, disappearing into those dark chambers and shaded porticoes, those anterooms and winding staircases.

At length, Theseus seemed to snap out of his reverie. He ordered some of the young Athenians to help him build a little altar, and sent them off in search of something to sacrifice. He would have preferred a bull, but they came back with what they could find, which was a mountain goat. As the sun went down, he slaughtered the animal, then they skewered the fatty bits and flamed them so that the scent of the meat drifted up to the gods. He had brought from Athens a little terracotta statue of Aphrodite, and this he set up and dedicated to the goddess, to be a marker of their safe deliverance. Next he turned to Ariadne – actually addressing her properly for the first time since they'd left Crete – and asked her to teach them the Knossian dance, the one whose weaving steps meant the paths of the labyrinth. It took her a long time to get the Athenians to do it: it was a complicated dance that she and the other young island nobles used to perform for Minos, on the wide terrace outside the palace. But at last, as the moon rose, they were twirling as fast as a potter's wheel spins, then criss-crossing each other in complicated patterns like threads on a loom.

Cleopatra-Ariadne

Laocoön stands on the southern flank of the Belvedere sculpture court. In the north-east corner once stood a classical sculpture of Cleopatra flung backwards over a couch, dying from the bite of the snake that coiled around her arm. Pope Julius II acquired it and placed it there sometime in late 1511 or early 1512. There was symbolism for him in his name (a latter-day Roman hero) when set against hers (the abject, defeated Egyptian queen). An elaborately carved Roman sarcophagus served as a plinth, and the group was made the centre of a fountain installation: Cleopatra lay in a grotto, with water playing around her. She was the dying queen, but also, in her sylvan setting, a sleeping nymph. A curious halfway creature, trembling between identities.

Like Laocoön, Cleopatra has slipped into art history. She sleeps, she dreams, she dies, progenitrix of hundreds, thousands of reclining nudes. She is the sleeping Venus, the one that Giovanni Morelli attributed to Giorgione, that hangs in the Dresden Gemäldegalerie.* She is the sculpted nymph in a woodcut illustration from the beautiful early printed book *Hypnerotomachia Poliphili*:† water runs from her marble nipples, and a priapic satyr stands over her, shading her with a bough of arbutus. I see her lolling, too, in the foreground of Titian's *The Andrians* in the Prado in Madrid; and she is in his *Venus of Urbino* in the Uffizi. I see her transformed even into his Christ, a deathly, limp figure slipped gently into an antique sarcophagus in the Prado *Entombment*. I see her in the same gallery in his *Danaë*, where she is pillowed in ecstasy, Jupiter coming to her in a shower of gold. I see her too in Michelangelo's sculpture, *Night*, on the tomb of Lorenzo de' Medici in Florence; the figure's neck droops heavily like the stem of a poppy. I see her in Bernini's *Blessed Ludovica Albertoni*, in the throes of heaven-sent pleasure or agony in the church of San Francesco a Ripa in Trastevere in Rome. I see her in the nymph in the grotto at Stourhead in Wiltshire, where, in the dark recesses of an artificial cave, water plays over her and she is smudged and

* According to some, it is by Titian; according to others, it is a collaboration by the two artists.

† The text itself is a puzzle, for, though published anonymously in Venice in 1499, it contains an acrostic in the first letters of its chapters that spells out: 'POLIAM FRATER FRANCISCVS COLVMNA PERAMAVIT': 'Brother Francesco Colonna adored Polia'. Colonna is thus assumed to have been its author.

greened with algae. I see her in the Tate in Carl André's sculpture *Equivalent VIII*, reduced and flattened to a rectangular arrangement of bricks.

Cleopatra is no longer Cleopatra. That is, in the eighteenth century it was argued that the sculpture more properly represented Ariadne, sleeping on the shore of Naxos. The more secure identification (though who can be certain?) was made in the early nineteenth century through comparison with similar figures, especially on elaborately carved Roman sarcophagi, where Ariadne is a favourite subject and where there is less room for doubt because of the fuller depiction of her story.

There was another, very similar, antique sculpture of Ariadne that once stood in the gardens of the Villa Medici in Rome, and which is now in the Uffizi. It was painted by Velázquez in its setting in the villa gardens, probably on his trip there in 1629, in a tiny, exquisite work that hangs in the Prado: she lies beneath a triple arch shaded by trees, through which cypresses and hills can be glimpsed; a man near her looks not at her, but out towards the view, while two figures in the foreground seem to be addressing each other. I once bought a postcard of this scene without taking much note of the sculpture lying beneath the arches, and it was only much later that I realised she was one of the Ariadnes of Rome,* as if I had been unconsciously amassing her representations. I have seen

* Velázquez later commissioned a copy of the Vatican *Ariadne* for Philip IV of Spain, and one of *Laocöon*, too – organising casts of the most important antique statues in the Vatican collection was one of the main purposes of a trip he made to Rome in 1648.

another Ariadne, too, in the museum in Antalya, in Lycia on the southern Mediterranean coast of Turkey. Here I overheard a tour guide defending her modesty: she has a bared breast, he said, only because her dress has come undone while she sleeps. We can tell she is truly asleep because, see here: the artist has sculpted a lizard by her foot. It would not have approached so close had she been awake. It was odd to hear such a fervent moral argument on behalf of a lump of marble. There again, these women in stone, who seem to tremble on the edge of life, have been defended, condemned and desired for millennia.

When I visited the Vatican Museums, I could not look at Ariadne. She was in a closed section of the galleries, a long corridor of antique sculpture in the Pio Clementino Museum. She was only just out of sight. I wanted to lift the red-rope barrier and slip to where she lay, on the other side of the hall of the animals (her marble bodyguard of stags, dogs and boars, their ferocity held in stony stillness). I wanted to see her as George Eliot described her: lying 'in the marble voluptuousness of her beauty, the drapery folding around her with a petal-like ease and tenderness'.

De Chirico's Ariadnes

The painter Giorgio de Chirico was born in Volos in Thessaly in 1888, under the shadow of Pelion's peak, mythical site of the building of the *Argo*. His father, who was of Italian ancestry, was an engineer and the family moved often; at one point to Athens, where he attended drawing classes given by Emile

Gilliéron the elder, the artist whom Arthur Evans employed to restore and reconstruct the frescoes and other artefacts of Knossos. 'We copied a lot of prints in his house ... Gilleron [*sic*] was a specialist in drawing the Acropolis, ruins of temples and ancient monuments,' de Chirico recorded in his often splenetic memoirs. He did not put a date to this series of lessons, but it was in the years following the 1896 Athens Olympics – shortly before, or perhaps even during, Evans's Cretan excavations.

Later, after his formal training in Athens and Munich, de Chirico established himself in Paris, where he haunted the salon of the poet Guillaume Apollinaire. At this time, between 1912 and 1913, he made eight paintings that contain Ariadne, all variations on the form of the Vatican *Ariadne*. Here he established his characteristic vocabulary of geometric town squares surrounded by porticoes lit by the still-intense sun of a late afternoon. He had likely never seen the 'original' *Ariadne* in the Vatican, though he must have encountered it through models, casts or illustrations at art school, and there was also a reproduction of the sculpture in the gardens at Versailles. His Ariadnes are enigmatic, sorrowful, caught in stony sleep. An air of enchantment and stillness seems to settle over these mysterious canvases. I used to go to visit one of them – probably the first he made – in a small museum devoted to modern Italian painting, close to where I live. This Ariadne reclined at the centre of a loggia-fringed piazza. *MELANCONIA* was inscribed on her plinth. Shadows fell darkly around her and off her. Behind, the square broadened out into open country. Two small figures seemed to pause, irresolute, in the background.

Later in life, de Chirico and his wife established themselves in Rome, in an apartment high above the Spanish Steps. 'They say that Rome is at the centre of the world and that Piazza di Spagna is in the centre of Rome, therefore, my wife and I would indeed be living in the centre of the centre of the world,' he wrote. Hanging in the apartment is a little copy by him of Velázquez's painting of the gardens of the Villa Medici. He made it in 1944, the year he moved to the city. But Ariadne is not there. He simply removed her from the scene. When I returned to London, I decided to go to see the Ariadne in the museum near my home. It was not on display. When I made enquiries, I was told it had been de-accessioned, the deadly museological word meaning sold. It was now in an American private collection, they didn't know where. It was another Ariadne I could not see, and only an old postcard told me it had ever been there.

ARIADNE ASLEEP

A sleeping sculpted figure is ambiguous: how do we know the figure is not meant to be dead? (Even in the case of church tombs, one prefers to imagine that the figure depicted, perhaps with her feet resting on a stone-carved dog, is meant to be slumbering, rather than a corpse.) It is an old fantasy to imagine life growing from the blank marble, the cold figure waking, Moses pushing himself up from his rocky throne in the gloom of a Roman church. In *Metamorphoses*, Ovid's poem of magical, mythical transformations, Pygmalion is a sculptor who considers real women to be wicked and corrupt, and so lives as a single man. But one day he carves from ivory a figure of a woman so beautiful that he is fired with love for it. He handles it gently, so as not to 'bruise' the delicate white material. He dresses it in lovely clothes, gives it fine jewellery, lavishes it with little gifts as one would a lover. He lays it on a couch of purple silk, supports its head with a soft feather pillow. He then prays to Venus to give it life, and she hears him. When he comes home from the temple, he kisses it and, as it lies there on the bed, its body began to grow warm and soft (like wax mellowed for use with his busy fingers). '*Corpus erat!*' – it is a body; he can feel the thrumming of its pulse. He marries his wax-like, unnamed ivory lady, and we hear no more about her, except that she gives birth to children who are also bound up in metamorphic tales. I wonder what it was like for him once she had taken on her own life and disarranged her limbs from the perfect, frozen pose in which he had sculpted her.

Ariadne in the Vatican sculpture is asleep – perhaps clambering gradually out of sleep. She is vulnerable, undefended. There is an image by the Czech artist Markéta Luskacová of a sleeping figure – a pilgrim in Slovakia – that feels almost transgressive to look at. He is slumbering with his elbow resting in the crook of a tree trunk, leaves carpeting the ground, lost to the wooded world of dreams. I saw the photograph in an exhibition curated by the artist Elizabeth Price in which many figures lay dreaming, sleeping, sickening, dying; there were also images of processions, queues, parades, protests, ice sheets, streamers, and the whirling, floating fabric of an ecstatic dancer's costume. Things, in other words, that naturally ordered themselves into horizontal patterns and planes: such as the layers of earth and sediment that mean, to the informed archaeological eye, not just space but time, the physical remnants of past lives compressed by the weight of soil and centuries into horizontality. Taken to its logical end, its most basic form, a horizontal thing becomes first a stratum, then a line: Ariadne *is* the thread.

For Price, 'the horizontal state ... proposes an interval: a short sleep, a lull, an interruption or respite in labour, gesture, event'. Ariadne will wake.

A Minotaur in Middlemarch

In George Eliot's novel *Middlemarch*, Dorothea Brooke and her new husband, Edward Casaubon, travel to Rome for their honeymoon. Dorothea: the sheltered, idealistic young woman from the Midlands of England whose presence vibrates through the novel, and whom I have always loved since encountering *Middlemarch* for the first time at twenty-one, a rite of passage in itself, since I realised as I did so that I was probably for the first time in my life reading a 'book written for grown-ups', as Virginia Woolf had it. Passionately religious, Dorothea is the sort of person 'who knelt suddenly down on a brick floor by the side of a sick labourer and prayed fervidly as if she thought herself living in the time of the Apostles'. But there is also a pulsing vein of only half-acknowledged physicality in her. Riding, for example, is her great pleasure: 'she felt that she enjoyed it in a pagan sensuous way, and looked forward to renouncing it', Eliot wryly tells us. Casaubon, a man with a smile 'like a pale wintry sunshine', is the emotionally desiccated parson whom she marries in the conviction that she must be his helpmeet, assisting his scholarly work. She is completely out of touch with the emotional and intellectual sustenance she really needs. She has mistaken Casaubon's crabbed pedantry for a thrilling life of the mind.

Dorothea has seen very little, hitherto, in her narrow and provincial life; and what she has seen has been lit in pale, Protestant, English colours. Confronted for the first time with Rome's grandeur, flung down among 'ruins and basilicas, palaces and colossi, set in the midst of a sordid present', she is overwhelmed. The city strikes her as 'an oppressive masquerade of ages'; a funeral procession 'with strange ancestral images and trophies gathered from afar'. Unreal, and deathly, and alien. Unknown worlds heap themselves down upon her with a confounding force. She sees a 'vast wreck of ambitious ideals, sensuous and spiritual, mixed confusedly with the signs of breathing forgetfulness and degradation'. There can, indeed, be something unseemly, something frightening about Rome's ability to flaunt the signs of all its ages so visibly; it is somehow an undecorous place. If many wonders remain hidden beneath the earth, then nonetheless the city has a disconcerting habit of flinging off its layers: a chthonic striptease. Perhaps it is Rome's shameless airing of all its histories, massed together in a state of wreckage and stubborn survival, that can make it a particularly forceful backdrop to the consideration of oneself, one's own history and ruined pasts. So it was for me, at twenty-one and forty-two.

Dorothea had hoped that her husband would prove 'a guide who would take her along the grandest path' and liberate her from her narrow, provincial existence, 'hemmed in by a social life which seemed nothing but a labyrinth of petty courses, a walled-in maze of small paths that led no whither'. But in Rome, space and history radically expand, and her marriage – her ardour for Casaubon founded on bitter misapprehension – is revealed as another dead and crumbled artefact in this parade of decline and loss and grandiose decay, this 'stupendous fragmentariness'.

Eliot has us come upon Dorothea in the Vatican Museums. She is standing next to the sculpture of Ariadne, 'then called the Cleopatra', as the author tells us, scrupulously. A young German painter called Naumann catches sight of her there, watches her, unobserved. She is not looking at Ariadne. 'Her large eyes were fixed dreamily on a streak of sunlight which fell across the floor.' She is beautiful; Naumann is excited. He rushes to fetch his friend to see her, quickly, before she moves, as if she is a rare bird that might take flight. He immediately longs to paint her. Indeed, Eliot often poses Dorothea like an artwork, sometimes as still as a statue, sometimes like a painting of a saint. At this moment, one 'beautiful ungloved hand' pillows her cheek, unconsciously echoing Ariadne. Her reverie is as deep as the sculpture's stony sleep. When Naumann's friend appears, he is disconcerted; for he is Will Ladislaw, Casaubon's cousin, and he has of course met Dorothea before.

Dorothea is not just not looking at Ariadne; she is herself Ariadne. And Will is a curly-haired Bacchus. (I myself see him straight out of a Caravaggio, a 'pretty young sprig' as a gossipy Middlemarcher calls him. When he is first seen in the book, he is mistaken for a gardener – an outdoors spirit, then, like the god.) In time, Dorothea will wake to Will just as Ariadne woke to Bacchus.

For the moment, though, with all her might, she is trying to help her husband, her hapless Theseus, out of the labyrinth in which he has entombed himself. Casaubon's scholarly project, his abiding obsession and quest, is a *Key to All Mythologies*, a work that will show that 'all the mythical systems or erratic mythical fragments in the world were corruptions of a tradition originally revealed'. He does nothing but accumulate countless volumes of notes; it becomes clear that no magnum opus will ever be published. It is the sort of madly encyclopedic, unrealisable project that could exist only as one of Borges's notions of an infinite book – the novel that contains all possible versions of itself, say. Will thinks of Casaubon as 'a dried-up pedant', an 'elaborator of small explanations about as important as the surplus stock of false antiquities kept in a vendor's back chamber'.

Poor Casaubon: his mind is 'lost among small closets and winding stairs', his own confounding maze. Dorothea offers to help her husband in his work; she throws him a thread, but he will not take it. Casaubon is a kind of Theseus. But he is also a sort of Minotaur, threatening to consume her. He is deathly as a catacomb, those mysterious corridors that wind beneath the streets of Rome, lined with now-empty hollows for the bodies of the dead. Later in the novel Dorothea's perspicacious servant Tantripp, who had accompanied her to the city, complains about Casaubon to the butler Pratt, saying: 'I wish every book in that library was built into a caticom for your master.' She sees that his library, his labyrinth, is also his tomb.

In Rome, Dorothea has come to see that the 'large vistas and wide fresh air which she had dreamed of finding in her husband's mind' are absent. She spends lonely days while he pursues his work; he will offer her no emotional bearings, or even any sensible intellectual ones. He suggests that she might like to see the Raphael frescoes of Cupid and Psyche in the Palazzo Farnesina, 'which most persons think it worth while to visit'. Dorothea doesn't really know or mind – she just longs for some kind of heartfelt response from him: 'Do you care about them?' she asks.*

* Why does Casaubon suggest that Dorothea might like to visit the Cupid and Psyche frescoes of Villa Farnesina? His evasive third-person recommendation strongly suggests that he has never, himself, seen them; and Dorothea can't seem to establish whether, if he has, he likes them or not. But if he really means it, it is possible that he is groping towards expressing something vital and physical, trying to clamber out of the dark corridors and gloomy chambers of his mind, though this seems a charitable interpretation. I cannot help wondering what Dorothea would have made of them had she visited. The Villa Farnesina, in the Trastevere district of Rome near the banks of the Tiber, is justly famous for the frescoes commissioned by Alexander Chigi, the Sienese banker, in the early sixteenth century. The visitor now enters via the so-called Loggia of Galatea, painted by Baldassare Peruzzi, Sebastiano del Piombo and Raphael – the last responsible for a famously lovely fresco of the nymph Galatea riding in triumph on a seashell chariot drawn by dolphins, surrounded by exotic and amorous sea creatures and with cupids hovering above. However, it is to the second room, the Loggia

After the encounter in the Vatican, Will calls on the Casaubons, and finds Dorothea alone. He becomes angry as he foresees her future at Lowick (the name is a not-too-subtle hint at the parson's lack of virility). He tells her: 'You have been brought up in some of those horrible notions that choose the sweetest women to devour – like Minotaurs. And now you will go and be shut up in that stone prison at Lowick: you will be buried alive.'

Buried alive

In the catacombs of St Priscilla, thirteen kilometres of passages that snake beneath the streets of Rome near the Via Salaria, I

---

of Cupid and Psyche, that Casaubon was particularly referring. You walk into a room bright with dancing light – the colonnade that forms one of the room's long sides is now glassed in, but would once have given directly onto the garden. And above you and around you is a riot of joyous naked flesh, painted by Raphael and his various collaborators, including Giulio Romano. Its sexy onslaught of bodies seems to be quite the opposite of anything that Casaubon might enjoy. Two enormous scenes decorate the vaults. One is the wedding feast of Cupid and Psyche, and the other is an assembly of the gods, marking the crucial moment in the story when Jupiter gives his consent to the union between the two lovers, one divine, one mortal. The spandrels below are also decorated with episodes from the tale, and among them is a whole menagerie of creatures: tigers, mountain lions, doves, great tits, swallows, woodpeckers, gryphons ... The scenes are divided by luscious swags of foliage, and even they bristle with life and variation: books have been devoted to the marvellous multiplicity of plants and fruits nestling among the leaves: acorns, apples, aubergines, hazelnuts, chestnuts, gourds, melons, pumpkins, squashes and more. These garlands amount to a humanist botanical compendium, delivered in the most charming manner imaginable.

felt disoriented and afraid of the dark, soon sick of the dank and close air, and of the thought of the legions of dead who had once been laid here, before their tombs were robbed and emptied. A guide took us around, leading us down steps that shadowed away beneath a convent, showing us the empty niches, the resting places, he said, of saints. But a catacomb is no place for the living to be. The ceilings are low, the passages confusing. The tunnels are lined and pocked with human-size cavities, stacked two or three high. It is like being in a nightmarish couchette on some sleeper train to the Underworld, or in a giant hive, but there is no dripping golden honey here, no wax, no buzz of living things.

Arthur Conan Doyle wrote a short story called 'The New Catacomb', first published in 1898. Its two principal characters are both young archaeologists and scholars of Rome. One of them is Kennedy: a well-off, complacent, languid young Englishman.* The other is Burger, half German, half Italian: a penniless, clever striver who has struggled to achieve the level of recognition Kennedy's class privilege has allowed him effortlessly to attain. They meet one night in Kennedy's rooms above the Corso, which are richly decorated with his collection of beautiful and ancient things. Burger hints that he has made a stupendous find and Kennedy rightly guesses that he has

* He shares his surname, coincidentally or not, with Victorian classical royalty – Benjamin Hall Kennedy, Cambridge professor of Greek and author of *Kennedy's Shorter Latin Primer*, from which generations of schoolchildren (including me) learned their grammar. The title was commonly mutilated so that it read *The Shortbread Eating Primer.*

discovered a 'new' catacomb that, unlike those one can visit as a tourist to modern Rome, has never been previously discovered and robbed of its treasures. The inscriptions alone, says Burger, could keep a dozen academics going for their entire careers. Kennedy begs his friend to tell him where the catacomb is. You never tell me anything, says Burger. Maybe I'll let you into the secret, but only if you tell me about something in return: your relationship with Miss Mary Saunderson, for example? I suppose you didn't actually love her – or you wouldn't have left her after three weeks.

Kennedy is reluctant to speak at first, but Burger gets up to leave, and he changes his mind. The girl is back in Twickenham with her family, he says. Her father found us in a hotel in London. I was relieved, in a way: I was already pining to be back in Rome at my work. No, it wasn't about love, it was about the adventure. I've chased game in my time, but nothing compares to the excitement of chasing a pretty woman. And she was engaged – I don't know to whom. Which of course made it all the more interesting …

The bargain is made. Since Kennedy has told him about his affair, now it is Burger's turn to show him the catacomb. They meet at midnight, by the start of the old Appian Way. They walk down the ancient road, past the high Roman tombs, and then turn off along a path into the moonlit *campagna*, passing beneath a great aqueduct. At length Burger leads his friend into a tumbledown old barn. They pull away some loose boards from the floor and there it is: a staircase leading down into the inky blackness. Kennedy rushes into the depths, but his friend warns him to be cautious. 'It is a perfect rabbits'-warren below, and if you were once to lose your way the chances would be a hundred to one against your ever coming out again. Wait until I bring the light.'

Off they go, with Burger's lantern to illuminate their path. They walk among the early Christians of old Rome. 'The yellow light flickered over the shrivelled features of the mummies, and gleamed upon rounded skulls and long, white armbones crossed over fleshless chests. And everywhere as he passed Kennedy looked with wistful eyes upon inscriptions, funeral vessels, pictures, vestments, utensils, all lying as pious hands had placed them so many centuries ago.'

At a certain point, Burger fixes a string to a projecting rock in the wall, 'for the passages had become more complex and tortuous than ever'. They arrive at length in a roomy circular hall with an altar in it: an early Christian church, untouched. Kennedy is excited: the bodies of prelates, saints and clergy surround them.

Which is when Burger crosses to the other side of the chamber – and then blows out the lamp. 'It was as if an invisible hand was squeezed tightly over each of Kennedy's eyes. Never had he known what such darkness was. It seemed to press upon him and to smother him. It was a solid obstacle against which the body shrank from advancing. He put his hands out to push it back from him.' Don't you think it's odd, says Burger, the way sound behaves here? You wouldn't know at all where I was standing just from my voice, would you?

I suppose not, answers Kennedy, trying to keep calm. Just stop fooling around, why don't you, and put the light back on. Well, answers Burger, you told me that you love an adventure.

So why don't you treat this as one: why don't you try to get out of here on your own? And while you're at it, why don't you think about Miss Mary Saunderson. There's one part of her story you didn't know, and that's who she was engaged to. I can supply the answer. She was engaged to me.

His voice is already fading. He is disappearing through the tunnels, following his thread. He is leaving Kennedy behind, without a lamp, without matches. He is buried alive. But there is more than one way to be buried alive.

Eliot's web

The great organising metaphor of *Middlemarch* is the idea of the web: the connections that bind people into a community, the subtle threads that trap us. *Middlemarch* is itself a web, and its weaver is Eliot, whose authorial voice at times reminds us of its power and control by breaking through the novel's illusion to address the reader directly. 'I at least have so much to do in unravelling certain human lots, and seeing how they were woven and interwoven, that all the light I can command must be concentrated on this particular web, and not dispersed over that tempting range of relevancies called the universe,' she writes. *Middlemarch* is a microcosm of English life, then. It is a novel of life in the middle, in the Midlands, and in the marches, the edge. An ordinary, peripheral town is made central by her attention and invention.

The web and the labyrinth are first cousins among metaphors. A woven web (whose threads can resemble a labyrinth) is made with the same skill, Minerva's skill, required of the architect of intricate buildings, or poems. Towards the end of *Peliaco quondam*, the Fates appear at the wedding feast of the hero and the sea nymph Peleus and Thetis. They are dressed in white, limbs trembling with age. They spin out human destinies, their left hands holding the distaff, their right drawing down the thread on to the whorl-weighted spindle. They sing: they foretell the future of the Trojan War, the deeds of the son, Achilles, who will be born to the couple. They sing too of his brutal butchering of his enemies, and his own death, his tomb drenched in the blood of human sacrifice. Their art, their stories, become lived lives. Eliot, as the unraveller of human lots in her novel, also takes the role of the Fates: Clotho, spinner; Lachesis, distributor; Atropos, not-to-be-changed. She is the implacable (but wry and knowing) author of destinies; the spider at the centre of the web of *Middlemarch*.

OVID'S SPIDER

Ovid's *Metamorphoses* is a whirling, spinning poem in which bodies transform into animals and waterfalls and trees and rocks. Like the *Arabian Nights*, from which multiple stories sprout as effortlessly as leaves from a seedling, *Metamorphoses* is a profoundly generative poem: stories bloom from stories, the text itself mutating as energetically as the subjects of its tales.

One of the stories concerns the origin of the spider, which came into the world through a young woman's foolish competition with a goddess. It goes like this: Minerva has heard that Arachne, a girl from Lydia whom she had trained in weaving, is failing to acknowledge her as the superior artist. In fact, she is even putting it about that she could beat Minerva in a weaving contest. The goddess decides to pay Arachne a visit. She disguises herself as an old woman, appears at the girl's studio, and advises her – strongly – to stop her boasting. Arachne reacts angrily, and blurts out that Minerva is too cowardly to come and take up her challenge.

At which point, the goddess reveals herself. Arachne is not afraid; she is still proud. But she blushes. The contest begins at once: each of them stations herself at a loom; each chooses her subject; each works with wonderful skill and speed. Minerva's composition is pointed: she depicts the story of how she and Neptune once argued about which of them should be the patron of the young city that would become Athens. Each offered a gift. Neptune struck the rocky Attic ground with his trident and out gushed a spring – but one of briny water, no good for the city. Minerva in turn struck the soil with her spear, and up sprouted an olive tree, productive and sustaining. She was the winner of this face-off: the not-very-encrypted message is that not even gods stand a chance against Minerva. (She is also the goddess of winning, and a temple to Athene Nike – the victor – still stands in Athens.) In each of the corners of the tapestry she weaves scenes that will drive her point home to Arachne, who, of all people, ought not to be dead to the interpretation of art. One shows two mountains, Rhodope and Haemon: once they were mortals, but they dared to name themselves Jupiter and Juno and pretend to be gods. The other corners are also Juno-themed. Two of them show, respectively, a stork and a crane, once women who compared themselves to the goddess. The fourth corner shows a set of temple steps embraced by a king: the steps were once his boastful and arrogant daughters.

Arachne, by contrast, weaves her own meaning-laden scheme: a theologically controversial and pictorially congested design of the sexual crimes of the gods. She begins with Jupiter, disguised as a bull, raping Europa. Then she weaves him perpetrating other assaults – in the form of an eagle, a flame, a swan, a satyr, a shower of gold, a serpent (in this last case, raping his own daughter, Proserpine). She depicts the rapes committed by Neptune, Apollo, Bacchus, Saturn, showing how they disguised themselves – as horse, herdsman, ram; as dolphin, shepherd, hawk. Arachne reveals herself as something of a religious sceptic: her agenda is to show that her talent is not god-given; and that the gods themselves are no more than criminals. When the chattering, clattering looms have finally fallen silent, even Minerva cannot find fault with Arachne's craft or composition. All she can do is rip the tapestry to shreds in a rage, and transform Arachne into a spider.

Ovid's looping story, though, does not end with art being ended. Even in the bewilderment of her transformation, Arachne still makes art, and her daughters make art, for ever and ever. Artist Louise Bourgeois was the daughter of restorers of antique Gobelin tapestries. She made vast bronze spiders, looming, frightening, that referred to the threads so skilfully deployed by her mother. She wrote: 'What is a drawing? It is a secretion, like a thread in a spider's web.'[59] The spider makes a web that is also her dwelling and her art. She sits at the centre, she traps and consumes. She is feared. She is Daedalus, she is the Minotaur.

Spinners

Las Meninas is the acknowledged masterpiece of Diego Velázquez, court painter to Philip IV of Spain. In a way, the work is simple: a portrait of a little princess and her entourage (all of whom can be named, thanks to Velázquez's early biographer Antonio Palomino) in a moment of a domestic intimacy. At the same time it is almost impossibly rich: a deeply self-aware painting that, while never giving up all of its secrets (the paint won't tell!), seems to express so much about making art, about seeing, about the nature of reality and representation: it is a game of elaborate mirrorings and enigmatic encounters. It is probably the greatest painting about painting ever made.

The artist depicts himself in the act of painting, peering out at us as we seem to enter the dark room of the picture, the subject of his work invisible to us since we can see only the back of his canvas. The king and queen are there in the background – or at least their reflections are, spectrally lit in the silvery light of a looking glass that hangs on the back wall, framed as if they were a picture. Also at the back of the painting is a man, a 'real' man, not a mirroring, poised at the entrance of a bright corridor, perhaps encouraging us to walk towards him through this room into which we seem to have intruded. To look at this picture, to lock one's gaze onto Velázquez's, is to allow centuries to crumble and telescope: it is to open a door from our world straight into the Madrid Alcazár in the year 1656, disturbing the painter at his work as his brush hovers between strokes. He has rendered the instrument of this rapturous illusion with the merest flick of pale paint.

Another great painting of his, likewise made not long before he died in 1660, aged sixty-one, is known as *Las Hilanderas*, or *The Spinners*. It hangs, like *Las Meninas*, in the Prado. In the foreground of the painting are three women, perfectly ordinary women of the seventeenth century, working with wool. The figure on the left is at the spinning wheel, its spokes lost in a blur of speed. In her left hand is a spindle from which she draws out the thread, her little finger delicately extended. In the centre, a woman is carding – preparing the fleece for spinning by separating and straightening the fibres. On the right, another is winding the yarn into balls. The group is flanked by two other female figures, aiding the three in their task – one has paused to speak to the spinner; the other brings a fresh basket of, perhaps, fleeces. Energy and concentration, speed and skill: this is what these women radiate. In the centre, among all this industry (it is hot work – there are bare arms and bare legs), lies an indolent tabby-and-white cat, paws tucked beneath itself in perfect stillness and contentment. As I look at Velázquez's *Spinners*, I think of George Eliot, unravelling her human lots. I think of the Fates, allotting the threads of destiny, in *Peliaco quondam*:

Left hand held the distaff, cloaked in soft fleece.
The right, coaxing down the threads,
Shaped them with upturned fingers,
then, twisting with downturned thumb,
twirled the spindle balanced by its polished whorl.

In the background of the picture, another space opens out above and beyond the workshop. It is a grander area, hung with tapestries. In it stands a cluster of women, of whom two, draped in rather classical-looking dresses, stand out. Once these figures were thought to represent a tour party being shown round the royal tapestry factory, their elevated position perhaps alluding to the higher status of the art of tapestry compared with the humble craftwork of the spinning women (and there is surely a tension in the picture between art and craft, between the necessary processes that must occur before the tapestry is made and the making itself). But in the early decades of the twentieth century that interpretation was revised by a succession of scholars. One of these figures in the background, half turned away from us, is wearing a helmet, and pointing fiercely upwards. The other, facing us, is standing right in front of the tapestry, gesturing (defiantly?) towards it with her right hand. They are, in fact, Minerva and Arachne.

I cannot tell you what pleasure it gives me that Velázquez has hidden this magnificent, mythical drama in the background of his painting, and placed the ordinary, sweating, busy Spanish women in the foreground. It is so unlikely, and so beautiful.

Were you to look at the tapestry that Minerva and Arachne are standing before, you would recognise, though it is mostly obscured by the figures, that its subject is the rape of Europa. Look, there is half of the face of a white bull; there is a girl clinging onto its horns as it plunges out to sea; there is her pink shawl wafting up in the breeze behind her; there is a pair of winged cupids bowling through the air overhead. And you might marvel, as I did, how a few translucent brushstrokes can say so clearly 'tapestry', one art form so boldly masquerading as another, textile impossibly woven from paint.

As you stand in front of the painting in the Prado, the moment of gratifying recognition, this 'oh' of comprehension, is easy to come by, because as you look at *The Spinners*, you will also see, hanging on the wall to your right, the selfsame scene of Europa and the bull painted at a grand scale. This *Rape of Europa* is by Velázquez's friend Rubens, and it is itself a loving copy made in the late 1620s of a work by Titian that now hangs in the Isabella Stewart Gardner Museum in Boston. Both paintings, the Titian and the Rubens, were in the royal palace at the time that Velázquez was making *The Spinners*. And so we understand that Velázquez borrowed the form of this great masterpiece – painted almost a century earlier for another Spanish king, later copied by his friend – and transformed it into Arachne's tapestry, a tapestry that outshone the art of a goddess. It is the most joyful, the most knowing homage; an elegant little riddle placed delicately at the centre of this masterpiece.

There's a particular and subtle relationship between *The Spinners* and *Las Meninas*. On the back wall of the room in the latter work hang two paintings, almost lost in the murky browns and dim light out of which the reflected royal faces shine with uncanny brightness. The pictures have been identified. Both were in the Spanish royal collection: copies, by Juan Martínez del Mazo, Velázquez's son-in-law, of oil sketches made by Rubens in the late 1630s of mythological scenes, mostly taken from Ovid. Rubens made a number of such sketches – designs for a series of paintings commissioned to decorate the royal hunting lodge, the Torre de la Parada. The subject of the painting-within-the-painting on the right is the musical competition between Apollo and Pan; that on the left is the contest between Minerva and Arachne. The latter scene shows the moment the goddess dashes the mortal girl to the floor in fury; near her hangs the fateful tapestry depicting the rape of Europa. As the model for this 'tapestry', Rubens slyly used his own *Rape of Europa* from the Torre de la Parada cycle, but in mirror image – perhaps a reference to the weaving process, since a finished textile would normally end up reversing its cartoon.*

What did Velázquez mean by alluding to these contests in the backgrounds of *The Spinners* and *Las Meninas*? Is he telling us that competing with God is a losing game? (In the other canvas, where Pan and the god Apollo are vying together in

* The cartoon would be attached to the loom, against the back of the warp (vertical) threads, and the weavers would work the coloured weft threads from the back of the finished tapestry. Because of this, the final tapestry would show the mirror image of the cartoon. The 'flipping' of the image could be avoided if the cartoon was fixed on the wall behind the weavers, who would then use a mirror set in front of them to copy the design.

a musical contest, King Midas is given a pair of ass's ears for judging the faun a superior performer to the god.) If such a modest avowal is indeed the point, there is a contradiction, since the medium for this message is art. The shadowy canvases on the walls in *Las Meninas* are paintings of paintings of paintings of poems; the 'tapestry' in the background of *The Spinners* is a painting of an imagined textile of a painting that's a copy of another painting that's a poem. To make a poem or a picture about the limitations of human-made art is actually, paradoxically, to proclaim the power of poetry or painting; those dizzying acts of transformation (poem to painting to textile) are surely the work of someone with godlike powers.

One day I looked at my postcard of *The Spinners*, which happened to be sitting on my bookshelf next to another postcard, of Titian's masterpiece *Diana and Actaeon*, a painting that was in the Spanish royal collection until 1704. (It is now owned jointly by the national galleries in London and Edinburgh.) At that moment it seemed to me that they were, to all intents and purposes, the same composition.[60] Titian paints the moment the hunter Actaeon stumbles into a glade where the chaste goddess, naked, is taking a bath: it is yet another scene from Ovid's *Metamorphoses*. Furious, she will, any second now, turn him into a stag to be hunted down and ripped apart by his own dogs. In Velázquez's *The Spinners*, the seated goddess becomes the craftswoman on the right of the picture, winding her thread. An attendant sitting on the edge of the fountain becomes the young girl carding. Actaeon pushing back the curtain becomes the woman who seems to be whispering in the ear of the white-coiffed spinner at her wheel. The hunter's dropped bow becomes the anchor-shaped skein-winder at the spinner's feet. The more I look, the more the correspondences accumulate.

To me, *The Spinners* speaks of the endlessly generative nature of art: it joyfully proclaims that art gives rise to more art and more (endless metamorphoses); that art (even when it is bold and original) is an excavation of the past and a conversation with the dead.

Metamorphoses is about many things, among them art itself. It is about the power of a poet to change people into plants and trees and stags; into rocks and rivers and constellations. It is the artist who is a god; the gods, to an artist, are mere material. Ovid insists on this. It was Arachne, after all, who won the weaving contest. The girl beat the goddess.

In *The Spinners*, Arachne has completed her tapestry. Minerva's hand is raised in anger and – just on the other side of this moment – a spider will be scuttling up the edge of the wondrous fabric that, in human form, she herself has woven. Everything is about to change.

Looking at Ariadne

Finally, I was able to see the sculpture of Ariadne. I had been granted a special permit from the Vatican Museums and went to her one crisp winter morning. I found myself recalling being in Rome that first time, when I had, or so it now seemed, experienced the city with a freshness that was almost acidic in its acuteness. Now, on the other hand, many things felt familiar and there was no possibility of recapturing that earlier excitement. In the Domus Aurea, Nero's stately pleasure dome that covered many acres of the Oppian Hill, with its grand porticoes and courtyards and fountains, my wonderment at the traces of frescoes on the walls had faded. They had lost the power to enthral me, perhaps because I had seen so many better-preserved buildings in Pompeii and Herculaneum in the intervening years and my palate for such things had dulled. Instead, I found myself absorbed by the aesthetics of decay – the rampant, patterning mould on the walls through which the delicate designs could be traced only faintly by the eye.

The symptoms of panic and disorientation experienced by a small number of Japanese tourists visiting the French capital have been called Paris syndrome. Fainting before great masterpieces of the Florentine Renaissance is not unknown, and has been called Stendhal syndrome. My own private Rome syndrome was a feeling of sometimes almost panicky unease at the crowded entrances to famous museums. I became afraid that the fragile memories of my first visit would be crushed and overwhelmed, coarsened by repetition. And yet I wished to return to these places. I had kept for two decades, for example, postcards from the Galleria Borghese. They depicted four of Bernini's seventeenth-century sculptures, their subjects David and Goliath; the rape of Proserpine; Apollo and Daphne; and Aeneas with his father Anchises and son Ascanius. (Creusa, his wife, one assumes, had already been lost to the twining alleyways of Troy.) I had a fixed memory of how Pluto's fingers sank into the cushion of Proserpine's soft thighs as he carried her, a marble tear fixed on her cheek, to the Underworld. I desperately wanted this artwork, and this particular part of this artwork, to revive the same feelings in me at forty-two as it had at twenty-one, but how could it?

In the Vatican Museums that morning, though, I was conducted quickly through the crowds and past the rope barrier into the Hall of Animals. I paused for a moment among its zoological cacophony of hunting dogs, horses, boars, even a lobster; I saw the sculpture of the hunter Meleager past which, in *Middlemarch*, Naumann and Ladislaw pass on their way to gaze at Dorothea. Beyond the Hall of Animals was a long corridor of antique statues, a chilly calvacade of gods, heroes and mortals. Among them stood Paris, prince of Troy, holding out his golden apple, which he was eternally poised to bestow on Venus. Presiding over this stony festival, in a niche at the end of the corridor, was Ariadne, larger than life-size, a giant of generous thighs and fleshy elbows and strong arms. There was the snake-shaped bracelet that had caused her to be thought of as Cleopatra dying from an asp bite rather than the Cretan girl awaking from a sleep. Her bed was a rocky outcrop lightly covered in stony fabric, which itself rested on an antique sarcophagus, doubling as a plinth. Her dress had slipped shy of one breast (there was no lizard, as in the version in Turkey, crouched near her foot to 'prove' that she was asleep). A massive sandalled foot jutted out towards me. There she was, the mother of all those reclining nudes of art from Titian to de Chirico, mental images of which crowded into my mind at that moment.

She was their precursor, but perhaps they were also hers. I saw her in the light of all the other Ariadnes I had ever seen. She was surrounded by the memory of her echoes.

I liked her: she was altogether more massive and robust and less wretched than the abandoned and abject girl my imagination often provided. I thought of this substantial, strong creature brought to life, enacting Catullus's *Peliaco quondam.* In my imagination I lifted the great stony creature off her couch, watched her look about her, heard her call for Theseus, followed her as she hurried to the water's edge and scanned the horizon in disbelief, heard her as she began to shriek and rave at the departing ship. The poem invites us to savour her state of undefended dishevelment, to *picture* her. 'The clothes slide from her body, scattered, / teased at her feet by the salt surf.' And then it tells us that, in her grief and fury at her abandonment, she indeed resembles a sculpture – a sculpture, specifically, of a maenad. The maenads were the ecstatic, maddened worshippers of the god Bacchus, and the comparison provides a hint of what's to come, for real maenads are about to hurtle their way into Ariadne's story. But it's also another imaginative shift. The poem has conjured Ariadne out of text, into textile, and now into marble, as if she's a kind of Proteus of the imagination, a shape-shifter who refuses the stability of one artistic medium.

The poem turns out to be obsessed with the pleasures and the effects of looking. The young Thessalians gathered for Peleus and Thetis's wedding gaze in wonderment at the glorious coverlet on which Ariadne is embroidered, a textile dyed purple with the juice of a million murex shellfish, a coverlet that lies deliciously over a bed 'inlaid with slippery Indian tusk', in the very middle and heart of a house whose rooms, stretching back and back, gleam with gold. The wedding is being celebrated because of the love that flamed between Peleus and Thetis when they first saw each other, he on board the *Argo*, she a sea nymph, her breasts bobbing seductively in the foam. And in turn Ariadne loved Theseus at first sight:

> . . . the second she saw him (desire in her eyes)
> she caught fire, to the core.
> Her body blazed before she'd even dragged
> her flaming stare away.

In a tiny eighteenth-century drawing that I bought many years ago, Ariadne is sitting on an elegant couch improbably erected on Naxos's rocky shore. Its hangings flutter in a faint breeze. She is helpless. Theseus's sail is a fleck of graphite in the distance. Her hand clutches theatrically at her forehead; she is a parody of despair.

A painting of her by the English artist Evelyn de Morgan (1855–1919) is different: here she is looking away from the sea. She bends over herself, her eyes locked in melancholic contemplation of the endless, labyrinthine folds of her own blood-red dress. Looking back on my life, with the steadier gaze of middle age, it sometimes frustrates me that I have, at times, over-identified with Ariadne, thinking myself the abandoned lover waiting for rescue on a rocky shoreline, full of wretched grief and wild fury. Turn your back on the ship and the trackless wastes of the sea, Ariadne, and walk inland. There are farms, and fields, and houses, and people.

Ariadne on Naxos II

At last Theseus seemed satisfied that the sacrifice and the rituals had been carried out properly. Night closed in. The black sea breathed, calm and rhythmic. The full moon gave out her pale light. The Athenians had made up a bed for Theseus and Ariadne on the flat rocks above the shore, some way away from the others. They made love, at last. Afterwards she lay awake for a long time watching the stars, feeling her lover's weight, inhaling his unfamiliar smell as he slept. She thought about how it would be in Athens, how his old father, King Aegeus, would take to her. Perhaps he would give his consent for a marriage. Even if not, what did she care? She'd done the impossible for Theseus. She would carry on doing the impossible. She'd devote herself to him completely. Work for him as a slave if necessary. She'd wash his feet, she'd smooth the coverlet over his body at night, she'd wait for him as long as she had to. Consumed by such thoughts, she finally slept.

She was woken by the sun slanting through trees onto her face. It already seemed deep into morning. She savoured the sensation of the sun on her body, the luxuriousness of it, and lay there half asleep, one arm pillowing her head, listening to the waves and the dipping, mournful cries of the seabirds, and remembering the pleasures of the night. At last she stretched out to feel for Theseus. He wasn't there. She sat up and scanned the beach – no Theseus, no Athenians, no ship to be seen. Just a statue of Aphrodite and a black scar on the ground from the fire where they'd cooked the sacrificial meat.

She quickly pulled on her sandals and dress, and scrambled down the rocks to the shoreline. Out there, on the blue beyond, was Theseus's ship, dark red sails taut with the morning's brisk breeze. It was sailing away. A punch of panic; she felt weightless with dread. Had they forgotten her? Had they left without her deliberately? She waded out, started shrieking, waving her arms. Then she ran along the shoreline, clambered up the rocks at the edge of the cove: if only she could get up to that headland, maybe they'd see her. She managed it with scraped knees and trembling limbs, and stood there high above the water's edge, like a sculpture of a god, like a painting of some nineteenth-century wanderer magnificently posed on a mountaintop. But the wind stole her words and the ship got smaller, smaller. Still she continued to cry out to Theseus. She begged him to hear her, to come back for her. What was she to do, all alone, here on the shore of an island, no one to help, no one to hear, no one to care? It was for this that she'd got her half-brother killed, had left her home, betrayed her father and mother? Even if she could get back to Crete, she would never be able to call it home again. She was going to die here, alone, starve to death, cry herself to death …

Poor girl, she was whirling in a torrent of fear and grief; but then came anger, as cold and bitter as a winter storm. Theseus, she cried, was like a savage mountain lion. He had no heart. He was a monster, one of the yawning, churning, flesh-eating monsters of the deep. He was a sham, a betrayer. He was weak, a coward; he couldn't even look her in the eye and tell her he was leaving her. He was a user and a chancer. No woman should ever believe a man's promises. Once men got what they wanted, that was it: no love, no loyalty, no decency. Their words were as reliable as air was solid. Ariadne's anger strengthened her, it seemed, for at length she stood up straight, switched her gaze from the dwindling rust-red fleck of the sail to the sky and called on Jupiter, called on all the gods of the heavens and the earth and the sea, called on the Furies, the snake-haired, implacable pursuers of murderers and perjurers.

'Make him forgetful,' she cried. 'Make him just as he was when he "forgot" me here on the shore. Make him mindless, make him careless. Let every precept his father taught him, every instruction he was given, drift out of his memory as silently and surely as the clouds that wreathe the mountains waft away in a breeze. When he reaches his home harbour, make him forget to lower those rust-coloured sails, make him forget to hoist the fresh white canvas he's promised to show as a sign he's alive. And when his father sees those bloody sails, let him believe his son destroyed – his darling, treasured son. Let Aegeus's mind dissolve in grief, let him burn with sorrow, let him rave and become wild. Let him in his madness take himself to the topmost tower of Athens and hurl himself to the crags far below. And when Theseus opens the door of his house, let him find inside only grief and confusion – no warm welcome from a father. Then his suffering will be equal to mine. Then he will feel as guilty as me, as lonely as me, and as wretched as me. Jupiter: do this for me!'

As she prayed, the ground beneath her trembled, the deeps writhed and waves slashed the shore. Thunder sounded from a clear sky: irreversible consent from on high. Ariadne sank down, clinging to the juddering rocks until the land and the sea had quietened; then she climbed down from the headland and returned to the beach, exhausted by her anger. She sat down on the sand and she wept: for her monstrous brother, for her parents and sister. For her dead brother Androgeon, killed on Athenian soil. She cried for Daedalus and Icarus and all the people she'd never see again. And when she stopped crying, she stared into herself, gazing at the endless folds and creases of her salt-caked dress.

Which was when she heard sounds coming towards her. First, a strident chorus of wind instruments, a reedy cacophony. Then the clash of hand cymbals, a clattering of metal against metal. Finally she heard the strangest voices: high-pitched, spiralling ululations; yells of elation, of joy, of sheer, unbounded ecstasy. She turned to see.

Tensawalls

It is dead time. Blank eyes are fixed on phone screens. Slowly, footstep by footstep, we wind round this maze, in the basilican loftiness of the arrivals hall. There is nothing devotional about this; it is desultory, it is necessary. We are being controlled, that is all. It is, by the standards of many other queues – for example, those in processing centres, crossing points, refugee camps, food banks – nothing, negligible. We are held in place by Tensawalls, which are stanchions connected by lengths of retractable webbing. Whether you want to manage your queuing space or cordon off access to a restricted area, there will be a Tensawall for your needs. A Tensawall is sold every thirty-four seconds.

There are enough Tensawalls in the world to wind a queue round the moon. They are placed in rows like the furrows of a ploughed field, like ancient Greek text set out *boustrophedon* style, which means ox-turning; that is to say, every other line runs backwards. Tensawalls reduce real and perceived queuing time and manage crowds. They allow you to enhance space, while reducing the risks of costly accidents that could be caused within your business area. Tightly wound, back and forth, we resemble innards, a gut. We are being digested.

Overheard snatches of conversation in French. The French word *queue* means tail. The Italian for queue, for standing in line in single file, is *fila*, from the Latin *filum*, a strand, a yarn, a thread. Italian *filo* means thread. There is also a verb, *filare*. *Il tuo discorso fila* means 'your argument makes sense', for another's thought is a line to be grasped, or a thread to be lost. The English word 'enfilade', meaning rooms threaded together, leading one from another, also comes from the Latin *filum*. And the English word 'file' derives from the thread or wire on which papers were once strung to keep them in order. Ariadne becomes, then, the unlikely patron of digital orderliness, keeping the bestial depths of the internet at bay.

In time, in some time, in nothing time, we reach the head of the queue, the head of the tale; we stand in a row between the gates beneath the illuminated arches. We are at the border. With our right arms outstretched, we place our passports face down, our hands on the books like the row of saints, penitents, prophets or martyrs not many hours earlier seen by me on the glittering mosaicked wall of a Byzantine baptistery, the memory of which, the feeling of which, is now fading, subsumed into the back-and-forth passage of the Tensawall. We are through, or are we? For some the light blinks red.

Ravenna

'*O procul procul este profani*' is written on the lintel of the door to the old monastery next to the church. It is Virgil, it is a warning, it is what the prophetic Sibyl cries out, possessed by the god, standing with Aeneas on the borders of wooded Avernus, about to descend to the Underworld. It means 'Go far, far from here, o uninitiated'. I plunge from spring light into the darkness of the church, the church of San Vitale in Ravenna, just inside which, on the floor, there is one bright square where the sun has penetrated the deep gloom and spotlights a duck, a benign and complacent-looking Roman mallard, depicted in late-antique tesserae.

For a moment, that comical bird is all I can see; then my eyes adjust and take in the golden apse, where a beardless Jesus sits on the blue globe surrounded by angels, solemn senatorial angels dressed in togas, their wings fanning out behind them. And there on the side walls are the Byzantine rulers in all their pomp, here the emperor Justinian and there the empress Theodora, her purple cloak's hem embroidered with images, in gold, of the three Magi. To her right, an attendant pushes back a patterned curtain leading to some dark and secret place, in front of which is a charming, cascading fountain, set on a Corinthian capital. Everything here is green and blue and gold and joyful: no cavalcades of martyrs hacked to death, pocked with arrows, or

The design of the pavement labyrinth in the church of San Vitale, Ravenna.

presenting eyes or breasts on plates. The young church has not yet accrued that kind of gloomy iconography. Instead, dolphins play with tails entwined. In a shady grove, lilies blooming at their feet, two angels sit and eat, served by Abraham in thanks for the gift of a child; his wife Sara stands by, smiling. God's hand emerges from featherlike clouds to stay a death blow, to hand out laws. Peacocks dip their heads to peck in the grass. A sheep nuzzles its soft chin into the palm of Moses.

On the floor, picked out in pale marble and purple porphyry and shards of malachite, is a labyrinth: not ancient, like the glimmering mosaics above, but still venerable, perhaps laid in around 1500. The visitors have kept clear of this circle of stone, as if to tread it carelessly would be wrong; but soon a laughing teenage girl detaches herself from a school party, and, with a mixture of solemnity and good humour, drops to her knees, mock-penitent, and begins to shuffle around it, filmed by her teacher. Later, when the church has emptied, I do the same. I crouch to see the stone up close, the veins in the marble, the striations of the porphyry, the neat triangles that turn out to be made up of tiny glass tesserae, and at the centre, at the very heart, a circle of densely patterned black-and-white marble in which, for a flicker, I can see worlds, the world: a dead shore beached with burnt-out planes, a wood, a willow pattern, a roiling turbulent sea.

Lost in the midst

'Go back,' Mrs Grammatiki told me, more than once. 'If you are disoriented you must return to the place where you lost sight of the signs. If necessary, you must go back to the beginning.' For me, the beginning is, inescapably, also the middle (and maybe the end, of this book at least): the Potteries, in the centre of England, where I grew up.

It is, I think, by filtering my memories of north Staffordshire through the novels of Arnold Bennett that I have made an accommodation with it. Now that I have lived away from the

Potteries for longer than I lived there, Bennett's version of the place has gradually inscribed itself upon me. (Alasdair Gray, the great novelist of Glasgow, once said that a place does not really exist until it is *written* into existence.)

Bennett was born in the Potteries in 1867, and died, one of the most famous men in England, in the grand modern mansion block above Baker Street Underground station in London in 1931. As a young man he left Staffordshire as soon as he could, without a backward glance, to become a lawyer's clerk in London. It was by leaving that he came to see Stoke's potential as material. Distance was necessary. Most of his best novels, such as *Anna of the Five Towns, The Old Wives' Tale* and *The Card*, are set in the region of his birth, of my birth, nicknamed for its one-time position as supplier of ceramics to the entire British Empire. The six towns that form the city of Stoke-on-Trent – Stoke, Hanley, Burslem, Longton, Tunstall and Fenton – become his Five Towns, lightly fictionalised as Knype, Hanbridge, Bursley, Longshaw and Turnhill. Fenton alone he consigned to literary oblivion. The Five Towns lie, he wrote, 'on the face of the county like an insignificant stain, like a dark Pleiades in a green and empty sky. And Hanbridge has the shape of a horse and its rider, Bursley of half a donkey, Knype of a pair of trousers, Longshaw of an octopus, and little Turnhill of a beetle.' The Potteries were made poetic by his pen, almost heroic. Like Joyce's Dublin (written into being from Paris), his Stoke-on-Trent was a loving and careful re-construction from afar.

I resisted reading Bennett (whom I dismissively regarded as a mere 'local author') until after I had left Staffordshire. It was then, as a young woman living in London, that I saw my error and fell in love with his books – not just the fiction, but his brisk and spirited self-help volumes such as *Journalism for Women* and *How to Live on 24 Hours a Day*, which brim with the energy of a man who has 'got out' and is forcefully making his way in the world. His drive was remarkable, his output vast. His journals are the record of a world that presented itself rivetingly to his greedily observant eyes; they are also logbooks of prodigious daily word counts, with episodes of extreme productivity followed by predictable attacks of ill health. He was a man who had made good by the power of his pen, and wrote as furiously as if he were constantly staving off the danger of slipping back to a life of lawyer's clerking in Burslem.

Of course Bennett's Five Towns – a nightmarish region of black-smoked horizons, mountains made of pottery sherds, and red-flamed nightscapes – had transformed by the time I was born, forty-one years after his death. The skies were no longer filled with the stench and fug of a thousand coal-fired pottery kilns, the pavements no longer filmed with mud. The snow fell to earth white, not black. But there were still a lot of jobs in the pottery industry. My parents' friends and neighbours among the Potteries bourgeoisie were people whose names you could see on the front of factories or the back of plates. The fathers of my two closest school friends made bricks and kilns. Mrs Thomas, who lived in our street in Newcastle-under-Lyme (a town that, according to the fine lacings of snobberies and inverted snobberies of the area, is very definitely not Stoke, though contiguous with it on the map), had once been told she had 'the best white body in the Midlands'. Her family firm manufactured the mixture of clay and bone and minerals that is used to make pottery: my best white bone-china cups are, as it were, made with her body. When such families got together for a meal, it was polite to turn over your plate to inspect the backstamp, a habit I can't (and don't wish to) shake.

Stoke-on-Trent was ugly. It was ugly in Bennett's day, black and ugly. It was ugly when I was growing up, the era of decline. It is ugly now that so many of the potteries have closed, and the coal and steel have gone. Now that pound shops and betting shops and empty shops cluster together on sorrowful high streets while the grand old potbanks elide into ruin, or have been pulled down, leaving wilderness behind them. Staffordshire was, somehow unsurprisingly, the very last volume of his canonical county-by-county guide to the architecture of England to which Nikolaus Pevsner turned. He undertook the research for the book in 1971, the year before I was born. 'Stoke,' he wrote bluntly, 'is an urban tragedy. Here is the national seat of an industry, here is the fourteenth-largest city in England and what is it? Five towns – or, to be correct, six – and on the whole mean towns hopelessly interconnected now by factories, by streets of slummy cottages, by better suburban areas. There is no centre to the whole, not even an attempt at one, and there are not even in all six towns real local centres.'

On the opening page of his masterpiece *The Old Wives' Tale*, Bennett offers this description of Staffordshire, skewering, with gentle irony, the curious combination of pride and immoderate modesty shown by its inhabitants: 'In the county excess is deprecated. The county is happy in not exciting remark. It is content that Shropshire should possess that swollen bump, the

Wrekin, and the exaggerated wildness of the Peak should lie over its border. It does not desire to be a pancake like Cheshire. It has everything that England has, including thirty miles of Watling Street; and England can show nothing more beautiful and nothing uglier than the works of nature and the works of man to be seen within the limits of the county. It is England in little, lost in the midst of England.'

Can it be that Staffordshire contains something of everything of England? Can it be that Staffordshire is England in miniature? That is how George Eliot makes us feel about Middlemarch: all life is here. (Eliot's own home town was Nuneaton, over Staffordshire's southern border in Warwickshire, her 'Loamshire'.) What is true is that Stoke is a place in the middle of England that lacks a middle. It is a geographically central place that is anything but central, a place whose force is centrifugal and that seems to consist entirely of peripheries and edges. A place that, at times, does not know whether it is really in the middle at all, for it lurches in its geographical allegiances, sometimes abjuring its connection to the Midlands and claiming kinship with the north of England. (As in Arnold Bennett's first published novel, *A Man from the North*, though any 'proper' northerner finds this laughable, if not vaguely insulting; on the other hand, north Staffordshire bridles at being confused with the Black Country and Birmingham to its south, the 'real' Midlands.) When John Wain, later Oxford professor of poetry, set his 1958 novel *The Contenders* between his native Potteries and London, between the provinces and the centre, his narrator called Stoke 'the town I mustn't name'. It was 'that place you stop at on the way to Manchester – the one where you look out of the train window when it's slowing down, and think, "Well, at least I don't live here."' When Gustave Flaubert mentioned Stoke in a diary entry, making notes on Minton tiles he saw in the South Kensington Museum (now the V&A), he couldn't even spell it. 'Stroke-upon-Trend' is what he wrote.[61]

As for me, I went to university, my parents moved away and for many years the ties were completely severed. In this departure I claim allegiance to Bennett, and to 'local' poet Charles Tomlinson, who made a habit of naming his poems after the definitely-not-Potteries locales he haunted: 'On Eleventh Street'; 'The Oaxaca Bus'; 'Ode to San Francisco'; 'Macao'. All the same, Tomlinson made his return to and his peace with a place that he had once thought 'Too desolate, diminished and too tame / To be the foundation for anything'.[62] Perhaps, in fact, Stoke's 'sedimented air'[63] ran through all his poetry, whether written in Basford (where he was born in 1927) or Brooklyn. Perhaps it is important for me, too, to concede that the Potteries are my middle. They formed me, they modelled me, they fired me. And (conversely) as a child I grubbed about in their soil, which was a soft red clay that I can still feel between my fingers, and that hardened into the shapes I gave it.

Borges in Stoke

Jorge Luis Borges was the great Argentinian writer of philosophically dense, laconically expressed short stories, full of the sly leafing-together of real and invented material (po-faced footnotes making punctilious references to non-existent books; structures borrowed from detective fiction; stories falsely claiming to be faithful records of actual events). Like James Joyce, he wrote from what was then the periphery and changed the map of literary history, the forerunner of a great generation of Latin American novelists. He once wrote of an 'aleph' in a basement of a suburban Buenos Aires house into which you could look and see every single thing on earth, including the aleph, and the aleph in the aleph: he made this unpromising place his centre, as surely as the maker of the *mappa mundi* placed Jerusalem in the middle of his vision of the world. He wrote about a land called Uqbar, which he said had been described in a certain single copy of a standard encyclopedia. The only other evidence the narrator, a version of Borges himself, can find to support its existence is a bookseller's catalogue listing of a work called *History of the Land Called Uqbar* by one Silas Haslam – who was also the author, according to a footnote, of *A General History of Labyrinths.* (The author and his works are invented; Haslam was the name of Borges's paternal grandmother.) The labyrinth is a recurrent image in Borges's literature: it is, for him, something endlessly circular, endlessly self-reflective, like the aleph in which you can see all the world, including the aleph. Or it is like two mirrors placed opposite each other ('all you need to make a labyrinth', he once said). Or it is like *A Thousand and One Nights*, in which tales are stacked and nested inside each other, and (in one version of which) a character begins to narrate the story of *A Thousand and One*

Nights so that the book becomes infinitely regressive, a loop without an end.

Borges was a lover and a connoisseur of English literature, in large part owing to the influence of that paternal grandmother. She was the redoubtable Frances Haslam, who was born on Christmas Eve 1842 in Hanley, Stoke-on-Trent, the daughter of a schoolmaster, and died in 1935. She emigrated to Argentina as a young woman with her father to join her elder sister, Caroline, whose husband was an engineer with various business concerns in the country; she married a dashing colonel who was posted on the frontier of Buenos Aires province, but who died after three years of marriage, leaving her a widow with two small sons. Haslam took lodgers to help her scrape by, and raised her boys in what was, according to Borges's biographer Edwin Williamson, 'to all intents and purposes an English household'. Borges's father, Jorge Guillermo, was, in turn, bookish and intellectual, the owner of a large collection of volumes in English. 'If I were asked to name the chief event in my life, I should say my father's library. In fact, sometimes I think I have never strayed outside that library,' wrote Borges. In the summer of 1923, when he was about to turn twenty-four, he joined his family on a trip to Europe that included a visit to Stoke; it was Haslam's first return home for half a century. That was the year that Arnold Bennett published *Riceyman Steps*, one of my favourites among his novels. Haslam was, Borges remembered in his autobiographical sketch,[64] 'a great reader. When she was over eighty, people used to say, in order to be nice to her, that nowadays there were no writers who could vie with Dickens and Thackeray. My grandmother would answer, "On the whole, I rather prefer Arnold Bennett, Galsworthy and Wells."'*

Not long before his death in 1986, Borges was asked by an Argentinian publisher to select a 'personal library' of books that he loved, to each of which he would offer a brief introduction. Among his choices were *A Thousand and One Nights*, Robert Graves's *Greek Myths*, Virgil's *Aeneid*, Henry James's *The Figure in the Carpet*, and G. K. Chesterton's *The Blue Cross*. Also among them was a work by Arnold Bennett – or Enoch A. Bennett, as Hyspamérica Ediciones has it, using his first name. The Bennett story Borges chose was not *The Old Wives' Tale*, or *Clayhanger*, or *Riceyman Steps*, but a less well-known short comic novel called *Buried Alive* (in the Spanish translation, *Enterrado en vida*). 'The whole story,' wrote Borges in his introduction, 'with all its light and shade, arises from one single act of shyness,' and so it does. The hero, Priam Farll, is a reclusive, diffident, incredibly famous painter who returns incognito to London after living abroad for many years. The only person in the city who knows who he really is is his valet, Henry Leek,† who promptly falls ill of pneumonia. Farll summons a doctor, but when he opens the door, he is mistaken for the valet, and the ailing Leek is assumed to be the master.

* Coincidentally or not, these are, however, authors deprecated by Virginia Woolf in her famous 1923 essay 'Mr Bennett and Mrs Brown', which asserted the claims of the modernist 'Georgian' writers of her own generation over the old-fashioned 'Edwardians'.

† The surname Leek is taken from the name of a town in the Staffordshire moorlands, on the edge of the Peak District.

Farll finds himself too abashed to correct the error (and at the same time, of course, too rash – it is a moment of both great timidity and great boldness). After Leek dies, the painter lets the error persist, and so he has the interesting experience of reading his own obituaries, attending his own funeral at Westminster Abbey and sloughing off his old identity. He starts again, takes a different path and slips into a new existence. His art, though, will find him out in the end.

Forking paths

One of Borges's most celebrated stories is 'The Garden of Forking Paths', first published in 1941. The story begins with an allusion to an unimportant episode in the 1914–18 war, supposedly noted by the historian B. H. Liddell Hart, when an Allied offensive was delayed by three days because of bad weather. The narrator promises to shed light on this event by presenting a fragment of a document purporting to be the transcribed confession of a Chinese professor of English, Dr Yu Tsun, who had been employed as a spy for the German government.

Yu's document – the first two pages of which are said to be missing – is now laid forth. We join his narrative just as his cover has been blown. He is alone, in Staffordshire. He has an important secret in his possession and must devise a way of communicating it to his masters before his (surely imminent) arrest. Thinking fast, he leafs through the telephone book. He finds where he must go: to a suburb of Fenton called Ashgrove. I remember vividly, the first time I read this story, my astonishment at the fact that the great blind storyteller of Buenos Aires should have set a narrative not only in Staffordshire, but in the astoundingly modest town of Fenton; and not even in Fenton itself, but in the absolutely impossible location of a suburb of Fenton, the very notion suggestive of a grandeur that Fenton is very far from possessing.* Later, when I learned of Borges's admiration for Arnold Bennett, and of his Potteries grandmother, it occurred to me how pointed the choice of Fenton was: it was Bennett's non-town, the one he expelled from his fiction when he chose to write about five rather than six Potteries towns. A suburb of Fenton, then, is a nowhere of a nowhere. Ashgrove does not exist on the real map of north Staffordshire. In his story 'Tlön, Uqbar, Orbis Tertius' Borges has a character called Herbert Ashe, an Englishman, supposedly an intimate of his father's, who 'suffered from unreality'.

Yu takes the train. As it pulls away, he catches sight of a British officer, his pursuer, stranded on the platform, thriller-style. In his compartment he sees a young boy reading Tacitus's *Annals*. He gets off the train and asks directions to the house of Dr Stephen Albert. The instructions ('turn left at every crossing') remind him of a method of solving certain types of maze. He is put in mind of his great-grandfather, Ts'ui Pen, a governor of Yunan province, who renounced temporal

* The only mention of Stoke I had hitherto come across in a novel, outside Bennett, was in Evelyn Waugh's *Decline and Fall*, in which the rascally schoolmaster Grimes is said to have lost his leg in a tram accident in Stoke-on-Trent. Such an incident in such a location is understood to represent the very pinnacle of comic ingloriousness. He allows his pupils to imagine it a war wound.

power in order to construct a novel and a labyrinth. For thirteen years Ts'ui Pen laboured away, until he was murdered by a foreigner, but afterwards the novel made no sense and no one could ever find the labyrinth. Yu speculates about this lost maze. 'I pictured it perfect and inviolate on the secret summit of a mountain; I pictured its outlines blurred by rice paddies, or underwater; I pictured it as infinite – a labyrinth not of octagonal pavilions and paths that turn back upon themselves, but of rivers and provinces and kingdoms . . . I imagined a labyrinth of labyrinths, a maze of mazes, a twisting, turning, ever-widening labyrinth that contained both past and future and somehow contained the stars.' Yu's imaginary labyrinth is nothing other than the universe.

When he arrives at his destination, he is met at the gate by Albert, who conducts him along meandering garden paths to the house. Albert reveals himself to be, by marvellous coincidence, a sinologist, and an expert on the very Ts'ui Pen who was Yu's ancestor. As they talk, he reveals that he has solved the mystery of the labyrinth and the novel. His clue was the discovery of a fragment of a letter from Ts'ui Pen himself that read, 'I leave to several futures (not to all) my garden of forking paths.' This hint has caused Albert to conclude that the novel *was* the labyrinth. Its apparent meaninglessness – its internal inconsistencies, its dead hero in chapter three who is suddenly alive again in chapter four – arose from the fact that, though incomplete, it attempted to contain all the available outcomes of its story. (Imagine, for example, Arnold Bennett's *Buried Alive* if it contained every version of itself – a version in which Priam Farll corrects the doctor when he mistakes him for his valet

Henry Leek, a version in which Leek survives his bout of pneumonia, a version in which Priam's true identity is perceived at his funeral ... It would be an infinite book, for every possible branch of the story would sprout its own possibilities.) Albert explains: 'Unlike Newton and Schopenhauer, your ancestor did not believe in a uniform and absolute time; he believed in an infinite series of times, a growing, dizzying web of divergent, convergent and parallel time.' Borges also lays down delicate clues about the contingency of this Chestertonian detective story he is telling, with its hints that under other circumstances, in other versions of the tale, Albert and Yu would be friends ...

Yu shoots Albert dead, thereby drawing his masters' attention, via newspaper reports, to his secret: the location of the Allied artillery park, in the French town of Albert.

UNDERGROUND

The artist Mark Wallinger was commissioned to make a permanent artwork for the London Underground, to celebrate the 150th anniversary of its opening in 1863. His first idea was to position a pair of round mirrors opposite each other at certain points in each of the 270 stations.[65] Had he installed these panels of infinite reflection, he would have interposed his own bewildering superstructure onto the already complex map of the Underground, creating illusory tunnels leading nowhere. The idea was abandoned – not least, Wallinger told me, because it was 'viewed as impractical and somewhat dangerous'. The presence of the mirrors and the phantom passages would, it was felt, cause passengers to become disoriented and bewildered in their navigation of the subterranean galleries and chambers.

Instead, Wallinger decided to express the infinite entanglement and complexity of a traveller's path through the city by installing, at every station, a plaque depicting a labyrinth, each subtly different from the last. The plaques are simply present, without explanation, in ticket halls or on platforms or in subterranean corridors, the circular form of the labyrinths echoing the familiar shape of a London Underground roundel. They have an official look about them – they are manufactured by the same firm that produces the Tube's standard signage – but their obscure significance, at least to the uninitiated, lends them

Mark Wallinger's labyrinth at Highbury & Islington Underground station, London.

a vaguely esoteric air. Every time I sight one of them, in my peregrinations about the city, I feel a tug of familiarity and relief. The one I see most often – affixed to a tiled wall near the top of the escalator at Highbury & Islington – is like a banner that welcomes me as I emerge from the deeps.

And yet part of me mourns that his original idea was never (and indeed could never have been) realised. After all, mirrors have particular and uncanny qualities. As a child I was gripped, at night, by the fear that I would look into the bathroom mirror and see unfamiliar, frightening faces looming out of the reflection next to mine. 'The Fauna of Mirrors' is a story from Borges's *Book of Imaginary Beings.* In it, he recounts a supposed Chinese myth. Once upon a time, the world of humans and the world of mirrors were not separate – the two zones, specular and secular, could be freely entered by all. But one day the mirror people invaded the human world. At the end of a period of bloody war, the Yellow Emperor succeeded, through his magic arts, in trapping the mirror people inside their own world, and forcing them slavishly to imitate the actions of the world of people. Nonetheless, a day will come when the mirror people will break the spell. They will force their way out from the mirrors, and the clatter of their weapons will presage their emergence.

In Flann O'Brien's novel *The Third Policeman*, de Selby, the savant to whose learnings the narrator of the story devotes so many footnotes, is said to have formulated the notion that it would be possible, if one were possessed of sufficiently keen eyesight, to perceive our younger selves – as children, or babies even – when staring at our own reflections in parallel mirrors, since light takes a certain time to travel between the reflective surface and the eye. He claimed, for example, to have seen himself as a child of twelve, thanks to the use of a powerful telescope: his own past, trapped in the centre of the labyrinth of mirrors.

Arnold Bennett in the Underworld

The Underground, to the native Londoner, feels like a haven, a hive, a home. Wallinger was brought up at the eastern extreme of the red Central line, on the section known as the Hainault Loop, between Grange Hill and Chigwell. He considers himself 'a child of the Tube': its reassuring rattle was the first thing he heard in the morning and the last thing at night. For me, a provincial from the centre of England, the Tube was a new language that had to be acquired when I moved to London. It took months, if not years, to get it by heart, to understand the quirks of the Northern line's branches, to match actual geography with the diagrammatic representation of Harry Beck's map (to learn, for example, that some stations are 'close together', like Leicester Square and Covent Garden, and that others, such as those on the Victoria line, are 'far apart'). Wallinger has talked of the trust with which he sees Londoners using the Underground – they fall asleep in it, they dream in it, they seem not to mind that they are observed. There is an odd play between intimacy and distance in the way travellers ride the Tube. We very often face each other, but we hardly ever acknowledge that we are not alone, and stare through our fellow passengers as if they were ghosts circling Hades.

I still (after twenty-one years) feel a faint unease when travelling on the Underground. I bought my copy of Arnold Bennett's novel *Riceyman Steps* in 1993, two years before I moved to the capital. It is set in Islington, King's Cross and Clerkenwell – the neighbourhoods in which I would end up living and working. The book contains an account of the calamity that occurred during the building of the Metropolitan Railway – the first section of the London Underground – in 1862. One night that spring, the ground was seen to be subsiding near Clerkenwell Green. Cellars filled with foul water. Pavements sank. The earth buckled. And then came a great collapse of the subterranean works. Scaffolding and beams 'were flung like firewood into the air and fell with awful crashes'. After that, 'a dark and fetid liquid appeared, oozing, rolling, surging, smashing everything in its resistless track, and rushed into the mouth of the new tunnel'. The Underground may feel tame to its native users, but there is still part of me that believes that its terrifying chthonic force could somehow be unleashed. The shadow world that exists underneath London – with all its passages, tunnels, pipelines and secret dead worlds – could erupt and engulf us, like Borges's mirror people, freed at last.

Loop Line

Arnold Bennett's stories run on the railways. An exceptionally brash or wealthy character might occasionally pull up in a motor car, but for the most part it is trains that rattle his creations around the Five Towns. They sweep characters off for a summer by the sea in Llandudno, and they convey them north to Manchester, south to Birmingham and to London. More enterprising persons might even get as far as the Continent. For the inhabitants of the Five Towns, the most significant, the most emotionally laden railway line is the Loop Line. In Bennett's fiction, and in real life, it was a curlicued, rococo flounce of a railway that wound its way through all the towns of the Potteries, joining up with the main line at Stoke (Bennett's Knype). The Loop Line, with its creaking, circuitous passage through the unlovely industrial landscape, is practically a character for Bennett: parochial, somewhat eccentric, faintly unreliable, sometimes thrillingly ready to carry its passengers on to the world beyond north Staffordshire; sometimes stubbornly causing them to 'miss the connection'. Bennett loves scenes in which the anxiety and high emotion of an extraordinary journey – a young man's leaving home for the first time; a groom on the way to his bride – is set against the daily passage of the ordinary Loop Line users, who are only going on to Turnhill or Longshaw and not towards a higher destiny. 'Catching the Train' is a glorious short story of his that conveys, like nothing else I have read, how time stretches and contracts when one is travelling by train – the heart-pumping madness of running for a train, the light-headed panic when one realises one is on the wrong train, the stomach-gnawing feeling of impotence when one is on a late train, the becalmed blankness of waiting on a platform to change trains.

In *The Old Wives' Tale*, the two sisters at the centre of the book, Constance and Sophia, are reunited as old women. Sophia has lived in France for decades (her 'Odyssey', as Bennett called her wanderings in his journal). Constance has remained in the same square in Bursley all her days. Their reunion takes place at Knype station, where the sight of Sophia's absurdly coiffed poodle, bedecked with a pink bow, administers something of a shock to Constance's more sober sensibilities. The sisters' first, halting attempts at conversation take place in a second-class Loop Line compartment, whose door Sophia has slammed shut with continental assurance. 'Same smoke!' she says, complacently. 'I must have forgotten how dirty it was!' She is astonished, though, to see through the carriage window two camels and an elephant 'amid manufactories and warehouses and advertisements of soap'. A new depot, explains Constance, for Barnum's circus. She proudly points out that it is there because the Potteries are the centre of England – and there can be only one centre, after all. Privately, Constance thinks that the terrible clipped French poodle ought to be left there with the camels. The Loop Line is the third party in this reunion, in this dance of familiarity and estrangement that the two redoubtable women perform in the middle of England.

By contrast, in Bennett's story 'The Death of Simon Fuge', it is a complete stranger – a Devon-born, Cambridge-educated Londoner – who takes the Loop Line, giving Bennett the opportunity to describe the scene before the narrator, as he travels from Knype to Bursley, with a wonderment proper to the occasion. It was a 'singular scenery of coal dust, potsherds, flame and steam, through which the train wound its way. It was squalid ugliness, but it was squalid ugliness on a scale so vast and overpowering that it became sublime. Great furnaces gleamed red in the twilight, and their fires were reflected in horrible black canals; processions of heavy vapour drifted in all directions over the sky, over what acres of mean and miserable brown architecture! The air was alive with the most extraordinary, weird, gigantic sounds. I do not think the Five Towns will ever be described: Dante lived too soon.'

The Potteries Loop Line closed in the 1960s, before I was born. The coal and steel industries it served as a carrier of freight were declining, and the potbanks themselves were on the wane; ordinary passengers were increasingly in a position to drive, or take buses, rather than wind their way slowly by train.* One former passenger and historian of the line[66] describes a route of steep climbs and reverse curves as it rambled along its seven-mile length – a distance that, with six stops along the way, took half an hour to cover. After Stoke, the train's first calling point was Etruria, a steep valley cut through by railway lines and the Trent and Mersey Canal and, most obviously, by the great hulk of Shelton Bar – a steelworks and several coal mines. Even when I was growing up, the scale of the industrial assemblage was impressive; when rounding the hilltop from the suburb of Basford, one could suddenly see it laid out, glorious and terrifying: the blast furnaces, the vast grey sheds, the depots, the coal conveyors, the slag heaps, a landscape pitted and bleak.

* The local bus company when I was growing up was called Potteries Motor Traction, meaning the letters PMT were emblazoned on the sides of all its vehicles, to the amusement of visitors.

The valley had got its name from Josiah Wedgwood's first great factory, which opened in 1769, and which he christened in honour of the region of central Italy where so many beautiful ancient pots had been discovered. On the factory's first day, Wedgwood threw six pots himself. They were then decorated with elegant classical figures in red, copied from the catalogue of antiquities compiled by the collector and diplomat William Hamilton. Beneath the figures ran the words '*Artes Etruriae renascuntur*', 'The arts of Etruria are reborn'. Some of the pots I like the best from the early years of Wedgwood are in this style – black-basalt and *rosso antico* copies of red- and black-figure Greek vases. It was only, I think, when I first visited Tuscany when I was twenty or so that it seemed comical or incongruous that the sylvan, cypress-studded home of the ancestors of Maecenas, the elegant cradle of Rome, should have lent its name to this unlovely valley in Stoke-on-Trent; and that Stoke-on-Trent might be so bold as to claim to be its artistic successor. But then we had a Dresden, too. We specialised in acts of geographical dislocation.

THINKBELT

There is a little town called Stone just south of the city of Stoke-on-Trent, not far from the hamlet, Beech, to which my family moved when I was eight years old. In 1934, Cedric Price was born there, potters' blood flowing in his veins. Stone has its curious name because, it is said, a Saxon queen of Mercia raised a church and a tomb there to her Christian sons, who had been murdered by their pagan father. Appropriately, given

Velázquez's *View of the Gardens at the Villa Medici*, c. 1630.

Ariadne has become Melancholia, or melancholy, in de Chirico's painting of 1912, which once hung in the Estorick Collection, London.

Markéta Luskǎcová's *Sleeping Pilgrim, Levoca, Slovakia* (from the series *Pilgrims*), 1968.

Velázquez's *Las Meninas*, 1656

The Spinners, 1655–60

Titian's *The Rape of Europa*, 1560–62.

Rubens's *Minerva and Arachne*, 1636–67.

(*above*) Titian's *Diana and Actaeon*, 1556–59.

(*left*) Rubens's *Daedalus and the Minotaur*, 1636–37.

Paolo Uccello's *The Hunt in the Forest*, c. 1465–70.

Picasso's *Le Minotaure une coupe à la main*, May 17, 1933.

Titian's *Pardo Venus*, c. 1524–27

Manet's *Le Déjeuner sur l'herbe*, 1862–63.

(*above*) One of Picasso's Minotauromachie etchings, 1935.

(*left*) Picasso wearing a bull's head designed for a bullfighting training, La Californie, Cannes, 1959.

(*below*) An Attic black-figure amphora, c. 550 BC.

Titian's *Bacchus and Ariadne*, 1522–23.

this story, Price grew up to be an architect; and, in fact, his father had been an architect too, part of the design team that built Odeon cinemas in the 1930s, including the one in Hanley I went to as a teenager and student.

Price died in 2003 and I wish I had met him. Photographs show a big, splendid man, cigar trembling on his lip, always turned out smartly in an Eton collar and knitted tie. He was puckish, full of stories and jokes; a bon viveur who might take more than a nip of brandy at breakfast. The room into which he departed to think or talk at his office was called East Grinstead, a long-standing joke. ('No, I'm afraid Cedric is not available. He's in East Grinstead.') His life partner was the actor Eleanor Bron. 'We had very little in common,' she has written, 'apart from ... the fact that we were both freelance and knew the meaning of the word "vicissitude".'[67] He was, it was said, light on his feet, and once asked Cyd Charisse to dance, a story that reminds me of Arnold Bennett's novel *The Card*, in which the irrepressible hero Denry, the son of a washerwoman, asks the Countess of Chell to dance, thus earning himself a reputation of almost unspeakable boldness and dash.*

---

* Price had good tales about Staffordshire, too. One anecdote he told about Stone was that it was the first place in which Georgy Malenkov, who was briefly Stalin's successor, spent the night outside the Soviet Union: after his demotion to minister for power stations in 1956, he visited the English Electric Works in Stafford, and was afterwards hosted at the Crown in Stone. (This may have seemed luxurious in retrospect, since he ended his career running a hydroelectric power station in Kazakhstan.) This is noted in Patrick Keiller's account of a road trip with Price, chauffeured by Nick Barley. The essay appears in Price and Obrist's *Re: CP*.

It is hard to think of a more influential architect who built less than Price. His best-known work is the angular aviary at London Zoo, visible from the towpath of the Regent's Canal, which he built with Lord Snowdon and structural engineer Frank Newby. There was also an arts centre called InterAction in Kentish Town, London, which was pulled down in 2003. Price believed in getting rid of things when their useful life was over, and hated the thought of his few works being listed. Why shouldn't York Minster be demolished, or the stones of Stonehenge recycled? These were typical provocations. He believed that architects should free themselves from the egotistical notion that buildings should be monuments – erected to serve the designer's vanity and desire for immortality. He also held that just because you approach an architect, the answer to your problem may not necessarily be a building. The client might be better off leaving their marriage, for example; building can be a displacement activity. Instead, he believed in thinking. He was an idealist. His projects, according to Bron, 'represented . . . a way of being in society – his pressing sense that architects ought to be useful . . . Sometimes, when things were hard, someone would make him an offer he couldn't refuse. Yet at the same time he would refuse. I admired the cut of his jib'.

In the early 1960s, Price and the theatre impresario Joan Littlewood worked together on her idea for a 'Fun Palace'. It was to be a completely new kind of arts centre, rejecting top-down notions of culture. They described it thus: 'Arrive and leave by train, bus, mono-rail, hovercraft, tube, car or on foot at any time you want to – or just have a look at it as you pass. The information screens will show you what's happening. No need to look for an entrance – just walk in anywhere. No doors, foyers, queues or commissionaires. Look around, take a lift, a ramp, an escalator … if it's too wet, the roof will stop the rain but not the light … We are building a short-term plaything in which all of us can realise the possibilities and delights that the twentieth-century environment owes us. It must last no longer than we need it.'

It could have been built, and should have been built, but wrangles over possible sites in London meant it never was. Instead, it had a powerful influence on Richard Rogers and Renzo Piano's Pompidou Centre. Price was, too, the first to think of building a big wheel on the South Bank in London – he put the idea into the unrealised master plan he was commissioned to draw up in 1983 by the Greater London Council, and it eventually inspired the London Eye, which opened seventeen years later. He was full of odd prophecies. There is a 1968 magazine cover designed by him showing a wrist wearing something uncannily like the Apple Watch, which is meant to be showing a TV broadcast. Of all the qualities of architecture, perhaps delight (Vitruvius's '*venustas*') was the one most dear to him. Asked by the Earl of St Germans to think about ways the family estate in Cornwall could be revivified, he suggested making 'the whole of Port Eliot, whether estate, park, garden or house [into] one giant life-toy'. He proposed building a maze, the one element of his ideas that was realised. An annotated sketch anticipates the reactions of children as they find their way through it: 'Saved and home at last. What relief! – what excitement!'

To the issue of *New Society* magazine dated 2 June 1966, Price contributed a long article titled 'Potteries Thinkbelt'. It was a bold proposal for the future of higher education: a university (though he rejected the term) on rails. It would establish itself on the curvaceous, sinuous route of the Potteries Loop Line, which was still running but had been marked down for closure by the chairman of British Railways, Dr Beeching. Instead of carrying coal and steel and a decreasing number of passengers, the Loop Line would carry mobile lecture theatres and teaching rooms, academics, researchers and students; it would carry facilities and equipment that could be built and used for as long as they were needed, and dismantled when they were not. It was precisely those aspects of the Loop Line that rendered it uneconomic as a passenger service, he noted – numerous stations at extremely short intervals – that made it 'well suited to Thinkbelt working'. The Thinkbelt would have no 'landmark' new buildings. It would have no discernible inside or outside – it would welcome twenty thousand students, and it would house its students, too, along with local people, whose 'slummy cottages', as Pevsner would call them, were so unsatisfactory. ('As regards buildings', wrote Price, the Potteries was 'a disaster area'.) The Thinkbelt would connect to other forms of transportation including, at its southernmost point, an airport (an old wartime airstrip that was in use until the early 1970s).

The Thinkbelt was Price's radical answer to the new universities, so often placed in what he called 'gentlemanly seclusion' outside urban areas, with their architect-y buildings by Basil Spence and Denys Lasdun that distantly echoed the grandeur of Oxford and Cambridge. (In particular, it was a rebuke to north Staffordshire's Keele University, just outside Stoke, which he envisaged would be rendered obsolete by the Thinkbelt.) His Thinkbelt would reach out into the community; in fact, it would be entirely of the community. 'The Thinkbelt's information and learning facilities are for general use,' he wrote. 'The system by which "the public" is self-consciously invited to take part, on sufferance, in certain activities in present-day universities will not obtain.' The Thinkbelt was another Pricean act of prophecy, for he foresaw in this project what British higher education has indeed become – a post-industrial industry in itself, though I am not sure he would have liked the neo-liberal turn it has taken. In the *New Society* article, he wrote that as Stoke's economic base of pottery, steel, coal and rubber further contracted, 'the Thinkbelt will add a major industry providing a wide range of employment for the present and future population of the Potteries ... The Thinkbelt will encourage a desperately needed tuning up of the amenities.' He anticipated, too, the importance of digital technology and online learning. The Thinkbelt 'makes full use of technological resources (like computers) now reserved largely for activities outside the universities', he wrote. 'Electronic, non-physical links will be constructed between student and information store ... this lets students develop their own pattern of study.'

The Thinkbelt was, indeed, a thoroughgoing examination of what education was for. It was more than just a thought experiment, too: Price undertook his research rigorously, meeting rail executives repeatedly, for example, to discuss the weight and size of the potential mobile teaching units, and seeking data on subsidence from the Coal Board. Stephen Mullin, who worked with Price in the 1960s, and who ended his career many years later in Whitehall, spoke about the project at an event held soon after Price's death.[68] He recalled visits to the Potteries with Price, where they witnessed 'a terrible, terrible lack of decent housing. This was compounded by the fact that the gouging and the mining into the landscape had been done underground as well as overground'. What stood out above all, said Mullin, 'was [Price's] desire to return something to the area where he had been brought up. There was an emotional attachment to the Potteries, which went far beyond any sort of clinical or forensic analysis of the site, and which came out very strongly indeed'. Mullin remembered a 'rail network still ... functioning with steam trains. They rattled round very tight curves. This web of rail network, which served the original industry of Britain, overlaid the canal network, overlaid the road network ... It was a most extraordinary landscape, utterly gutted, mined, gouged for clay – for the potteries, for steam, iron, coal, everything'.

A photograph taken by Price to illustrate the *New Society* article shows a landscape pitted and bare and laid waste, hollowed out and despoiled. Sink holes used to open up in Stoke. Buildings could lapse gradually into the earth. In his poem 'Gladstone Street', Charles Tomlinson wrote, as if the inhabitants of Hades were at hand:

> People were sure the street was going downhill.
> It literally was: cracks in our hall

> Opened as the house started to subside
> Towards the mines beneath. Miners were everywhere
> Under that cancerous hill. My mother swore
> That you could hear them tapping away below
> Of a quiet night ...

There is a famous Stoke story about how one day, in December 1903, a man called Thomas Holland was walking to work along St John Street in Hanley, singing a hymn. All of a sudden the road simply gave way beneath him. He disappeared, plummeting into what turned out to be a disused mineshaft. It is assumed that Holland met his death buried beneath tons of earth; the shaft, judged to be 121 feet deep, was anyway filled with poisonous gases, so no one could attempt to search for him. A burial service was held for him later, on the spot. There were sometimes small earthquakes, too, caused by the subterranean traumas of mining.* Tomlinson wrote of 'a landscape of disembowellings, underworlds / Unearthed among the clay'.[69] It was truly an infernal ground, one whose surface seemed at any moment to be threatened with inundation by the world beneath, a ground so ruined that it was almost magnificent. Dante did indeed live too soon.

---

* Several when I was growing up. QUAKE ROCKS STOKE ran the headline in the local paper on one occasion. Beneath the banner, in smaller letters, 'My parrot fell off its perch'. My father won £5 from *Private Eye* when he sent in the cutting.

Dante's Minotaur

In Dante's *Inferno*, the Minotaur is half man and half bull, but his head is a man's and his body the animal's, so that in illustrations of the text he often has a look of a centaur about him. Dante calls him the '*infamia di Creti . . . che fu concetta nella falsa vacca*' – 'the infamy of Crete, who was conceived in the pretended cow'. The Minotaur inhabits the steep side of a boulder-covered ravine and is a creature made of fury, '*ira bestial*'. He gnaws at his own limbs in his rage; he bucks and plunges about like a bull that has received a mortal blow.

Rubens's Minotaur

For one of his designs for works to hang in the Torre de la Parada, Rubens sketched the Minotaur. Like Dante's Minotaur, he has the body of a bull and the head of a human. Daedalus, his sleeves rolled up, a set square and compasses tucked into his belt, lays a protective hand on the creature's flank. With the other hand he gestures in front of him, towards a lightly described network of interlaced walls – the labyrinth. This Minotaur, whose face we can see in half-profile, has nothing of fury or anger about him. He looks noble and melancholy, as if accepting the inevitable. Daedalus might be protecting him – or tricking him.

THE WAND'RING WOOD

The *Inferno* begins, famously, like this:

> *Nel mezzo del cammin di nostra vita*
> *mi ritrovai per una selva oscura*
> *ché la diritta via era smarrita.*

> At one point midway on our path in life,
> I came around and found myself now searching
> through a dark wood, the right way blurred and lost.

The narrator is wandering, disoriented in a 'wilderness, savage, brute, harsh and wild'.[70] He has, somehow, sleepwalked his way to this pass – '*tant' era pien di sonno*', 'I was so full of sleep'. It is not only a literal wood but an allegory: a state of confusion and sin. He sees, far off, a beautiful mountaintop and attempts to make his way to it, but his path is barred by first a leopard, then a lion and a wolf. He is despairing: but then he catches sight of a figure, a man who says he was once a poet – '*poeta fu*'. It is Virgil, who will be Dante's guide on the first stage of the journey towards that far-distant hilltop, the earthly paradise. Not by the direct route, for that is impassable. Virgil will first lead the Florentine on a tortuous, difficult path that brings him through the depths of the earth past all the inhabitants of Hell, lower and lower into its vast, spiralling, funnel-shaped abyss, through its 'appalling and ruinous' topography, as Borges described it, with its 'crypts, pits, precipices, swamps and dunes'.*

Dante probably began to write the *Inferno* at the age of forty-two. He set it, precisely, at the Easter of 1300, when he was thirty-five. Some thirty years after his death, Boccaccio recorded an anecdote about the poet. One day in Verona he was said to have overheard some ladies saying to each other: 'Isn't that the man who goes down to Hell, and comes back when it pleases him, and brings back news of them below?' Reading the poem, with all its precision and biographical detail about him and those he knew, it feels as if Dante really does want us to believe he went there – on some level.

The wood and the Underworld: these are both kinds of labyrinth, especially in Virgil's *Aeneid.* You need a tour guide, someone to conduct you safely through, to explain the weird geography, the nightmarish monsters, the stories and lessons of the journey. These places engulf you, disorient you. Gaston Bachelard, in his *Poetics of Space,* wrote about the peculiar experience of being in a forest: 'We do not have to be long in the woods to experience the always rather anxious impression of "going deeper and deeper" into a limitless world.'[71] Once

---

* In an essay about Dante, collected in *The Total Library,* Borges suggested that in order to contemplate the poet, we should think of a panel painted many years ago: perhaps we might think of its illustrating all the stories of the *Arabian Nights,* or as a Chinese novel containing hundreds of thousands of characters. All of human history is contained here and 'awaits us somewhere in this serene labyrinth', he wrote. He continued: 'I have fantasised a magical work, a panel that is also a microcosm: Dante's poem is that panel whose edges enclose the universe.'

inside the woods, it is quickly impossible to discern the edge. They bewilder us.

Borges thought that labyrinths, literature and woods shared an edgeless, borderless, knotted quality. 'I think of the world's literature as a kind of forest, I mean it's tangled and it entangles us but it's growing . . . it's a living labyrinth, no? A living maze.'[72] A hedge maze, on the other hand, is a rationalised forest, tamed and trimmed and grown for domestic use, but still exuding the scent of wild leaves and damp earth, and still capable of trapping the unwary.

Virgil's *Aeneid* is a poem full of dark woods, forerunners of Dante's *selva oscura*. They confound and baffle those who wander in them. They are places of deep shadows, confusing paths and erring footsteps.[73] In Book 9 of the poem, a pair of Trojan warriors, the young lovers Nisus and Euryalus, attempt a night-time sortie. The refugees have reached Italy by now, but their forces are under siege by the Rutulians, led by the hero Turnus. The lovers, fuzz barely growing on their cheeks and hot for war, want to prove their prowess by getting a message through to Aeneas, who has lately been absent from the main force, surveying the future site of Rome with his new ally, Evander. But after an initial success – the pair slaughter a number of sleeping Rutulians – things go terribly awry. A troop of enemy forces, three hundred strong, comes riding by. They catch sight of Euryalus's helmet (looted from a dead Rutulian) glinting in the moonlight. Nisus and Euryalus rush into the woods and 'trust to night':

The dense woods
spread far, the thickets and black ilex bristle,

> briars crowd the entire place, with a rare track
> showing a faint trace through the thick blind glades.
> The dark branches, the heft of the plunder, all weigh down
> Euryalus – fear leads him astray in the tangled paths.[74]

The pair are separated, and when Nisus finally looks back, Euryalus is gone. Despairingly, Nisus gropes his way back through the '*fallacis silvae*', the 'deceptive wood', retracing his steps. But Euryalus is found by the Rutulians and killed, and when Nisus attempts to avenge his lover, he is killed too: so the wood has been nothing but a place of error and deception, futility and death. Amid the complicated structure of the *Aeneid*, with its multiple mirrorings, echoes and internal resonances, this passage evokes that earlier climactic scene of loss and being lost when Aeneas heedlessly leaves his wife Creusa behind among the complex paths of the city of Troy. Like Nisus, he only belatedly realises his beloved is gone; and then he fruitlessly searches for her as he attempts to retrace his steps.

The most significant and most deeply described wood of the *Aeneid*, though, is the forest that girdles the Underworld – which Aeneas will visit in Book 6 of the poem, soon after he has made landfall in Italy. When he lands at Cumae, he meets the Sibyl – the prophetic priestess of Apollo who will be his guide to the Underworld, just as, in the *Divine Comedy*, Virgil becomes, in turn, Dante's guide. 'The entire heartland here is thick with woods,' she tells Aeneas, and the ghastly River Cocytus glides around it, holding the kingdom of the dead in its coils as if it were a black snake. Just as in Dante, the woods must be navigated before the deeper labyrinthine mysteries of the world of the dead can be tackled. She continues:

> man of Troy, the descent to the Underworld is easy.
> Night and day the gates of shadowy Death stand open wide,
> but to retrace your steps, to climb back to the upper air –
> there the struggle, there the labour lies.[75]

The labour: '*hic labor est*'. In the Middle Ages, writers would make much of a speculative etymology for the Latin for labyrinth, '*laborintus*', connecting it to the phrase '*labor intus*', which means 'labour inside'.[76] The labyrinth became a proxy for the labour of life; the work of knowing the self; and the struggle to tread the labyrinth of the world.

Before Aeneas can descend to the Underworld, he has a task to perform, instructed by the Sibyl: he must pluck the mysterious Golden Bough, which itself grows at the heart of a 'deep-shaded tree' obscured by a grove, folded over and closed in by dusky valleys. Dusky: '*umbra*', or shadow, is one of Virgil's most beloved words, the very last word, indeed, of the *Aeneid.* Sometimes I feel that the whole poem takes place in the dusk, an epically unending gloaming that darkens a work that operates, too, in shades of ethical grey: a twilight of doubt and regret and moral uncertainty.

Once Aeneas has seized the Golden Bough, and made appropriate sacrifices, the Sibyl shrieks out her warning – '*Procul, o procul este profani*' – 'Away, away, unhallowed ones!' – and leads the hero into a 'vast cave deep in the gaping, jagged rock, /

shielded well by a dusky lake and shadowed grove'. It is the tree-encircled entrance to the Underworld:

> On they went, those dim travellers under the lonely night,
> through gloom and the empty halls of Death's ghostly realm,
>
> like those who walk through woods by a grudging moon's
> deceptive light when Jove has plunged the sky in dark
> and the black night drains all colour from the world.[77]

It might be a description of the territory in Tarkovsky's 1979 film *Stalker* – in which three men enter a deserted landscape called the Zone in search of a mysterious enclave known only as the Room, in which one's innermost wishes are said to come true. The Zone is an infernal, deserted place, full of swamps and industrial wreckage and poisoned-looking rivers, in which the Stalker of the film's title takes the role of a capricious guide, leading the Writer and the Professor through tunnels and ruins and overgrown meadows. Their destination is close at hand, the Stalker tells the two travellers, but 'to go straight ahead is fatal'. They must 'go around'; 'there is no going straight here'. The Zone, like Dante's *Inferno*, lets pass only those who have abandoned hope. And like the epic wanderings of the *Aeneid*, the journey of the men is involuted, confusing, often apparently pointless, and shrouded in a fog of doubt.

Aeneas follows the Sibyl into the ghastly night of the Underworld, encountering Death and Disease and raging Strife; passing harpies, scyllas, centaurs; sighting the crowds of the dead who flock at the shore of Acheron's river, desperate to cross, as numerous as the falling leaves in autumn forests, or flocks of migrating birds. He meets the ghosts of the dead, including the lover he left, Dido. After he sailed away from her without explanation, leaving her, as Theseus did Ariadne, heedless in the dead of night, she clambered onto a funeral pyre and stabbed herself to death with the sword he had given her. She now wanders among endless woods, '*errabat silva in magna*'. The trackless forest is her eternal territory of non-being. She will not speak to Aeneas when he tries to address her. At least for him there is a route out: Dido must stay in the wood, condemned to an abandoned lover's fruitless meanderings, but he will meet the shade of his father, Anchises, who will both prophesy a proudly linear future for Aeneas's descendants, and conduct his son swiftly out of the realm of the dead, albeit via the disconcerting route of the ivory gate of false dreams. Anchises will predict Rome's destiny as an '*imperium sine fine*', an 'empire without end'. But the empire would always have edges, and sometimes those edges would be marked by walls and ditches (as well as by time and history), however vast and unknowable it might have seemed from the inside, from the notional centre of Rome.

Woods, caves, dreams: these are places between the worlds, between the surface and the interior. Caves lead inwards, towards the earth's belly; they are vestibules between the known, familiar surface and the mysterious, uncontrollable regions that lie within. The woods and forests of folklore and fairy tale are a territory of refuge or enchantment or threat or confusion, zones that operate under their own tangled magical logic. In the *Aeneid*, Dido and Aeneas fatefully make love in a cave, where they have sheltered from a storm – an act with baleful consequences. In the fifteenth-century Italian romance *Hypnerotomachia Poliphili*, the narrator, Poliphilio, falls into a deep sleep and dreams that he is in a forest. 'Scarcely had I entered than I realised that I had carelessly lost my way,' he recounts.[78] He had discovered the forest's immediate, complete immensity. 'I realised that no track or side-path was to be seen in this thorny wood – nothing but dense thickets, sharp brambles, the wild ash that vipers shun, rough elms that suit the fruitful vines, thick-barked cork-oaks apt for woman's adornment, hard Turkey-oaks, strong roburs, acorn-bearing oaks and ilexes with their abundant branches. They did not allow the sun's welcome rays to reach the damp soil, but covered it like a vaulted roof with dense leaves that the nurturing light could not penetrate.' The wood, with its enveloping canopy of branches, becomes something like a bewildering building, even a prison. In this opaque and oppressive zone Poliphilio fears for his life and, recognising the 'rough and pathless wood' as a maze from which escape is impossible without help, prays 'to the blessed Ariadne of Crete, who had given the ingenious thread to deceiving Theseus, so that he could kill her monstrous brother and come from the tangled Labyrinth, that she might likewise deliver me from this dark forest'.[79]

At the beginning of Edmund Spenser's *The Faerie Queene*, the English, Elizabethan successor of Italian epic romances by Tasso and Ariosto, the Redcross Knight and his steadfast and pure companion Una also find themselves in a 'shadie groue'. They have taken refuge here in a storm, just as Aeneas and Dido sought refuge in a cave from a tempest. Spenser's forest, like that of the *Hypnerotomachia Poliphili*, is at least initially an Ovidian rather than a Virgilian wood:[80] the arboreal catalogues of both texts have a common ancestor in the description of the trees that gather around Orpheus to listen to his wonderful music in the *Metamorphoses*. Here are (among other trees)

> The Birch for shaftes, the Sallow for the mill,
> The Mirrhe sweete bleeding in the bitter wound,
> The warlike Beech, the Ash for nothing ill . . .[81]

But it quickly shades into a Virgilian wood, confusing and frightening: 'They cannot finde that path, which first was showne, / But wander too and fro in wayes vnknowne.' At length Una explains: 'This is the wandring wood, this Errours den.' Errour is a monster: a Virgilian creature, at least by way of her naming and her slinking, deceptive form, with her long tail 'in knots and many boughtes vpwound'.

Some poets find that even Ovid's woods – transformative places, but lacking the melancholic atmosphere of Virgil's – can contain hints of the Dante-esque when read in a later age. In his *Tales from Ovid*, loose translations from the *Metamorphoses*, Ted Hughes begins his story of Actaeon, the hunter who is ripped apart by his own dogs after he accidentally spies Diana at her bath, by recording that 'It is no crime / To lose your way in a dark wood.' This 'dark wood' is not really Ovid's; it is Dante's *selva oscura*. Ovid, by contrast, places us firmly on a mountainside in these opening lines of the episode, before we stumble, with Actaeon, into the goddess's secluded grove. But one can see why Hughes can't resist glancing at Dante in his version. It is tempting to remark, as Borges once did when writing about the art of coaxing text from one language to another, from one era to another, that the original is unfaithful to the translation. In some poems, as in labyrinths and woods, time may loop and spiral, and abjure the kind of straight linearity promised, though not necessarily delivered, by heroic epic.

Mazed world

Those who have read certain stories instinctively understand a forest's magical properties and its ability to transport one into another world, for good or ill. Think of the thickets of the Grimms' fairy tales: they are both havens of magical creatures and witches, and impenetrable, unnavigable. You might try to leave a trail of stones or crumbs to get back to your house if you were an intelligent child being led by your father and stepmother deep into the woods to starve. In Shakespeare's *A Midsummer Night's Dream*, the metaphorical labyrinth of the story is the 'wood outside Athens', whose king, Theseus, is about to celebrate his marriage to the Amazon Hippolita. (In Shakespeare's wonderfully free and careless use of mythology, Theseus has, as it were, transported the labyrinth, or a dim memory of it, with him from Crete.) The story opens, as G. K. Chesterton put it in his essay on the play, 'in the sane and common world'. But night falls, and as the four young lovers advance 'into the tangled wood of young troubles and stolen happiness, a change and bewilderment begins to fall on them'. In this 'mazed world' (as Titania calls it), they wander, they sleep, they dream, they are enchanted. 'They lose their way and their wits for they are in the heart of fairyland. Their words, their hungers, their very figures grow more and more dim and fantastic, like dreams within dreams, in the supernatural mist of Puck.' For Chesterton, to read Shakespeare was as if to wander a Dickensian city. He 'lets us come upon his splendours by accident, as we come upon an old City church in the twist of a city street', he wrote.

In C. S. Lewis's *The Lion, the Witch and the Wardrobe*, the children find themselves in a thick forest, pines bowed down by snow, when they step through the rustling fur coats of the wardrobe into Narnia. In *The Magician's Nephew*, Digory encounters Polly – a girl who seems half awake, half dreaming – in an endless wood in which pools serve as portals. If you leap into one of these pools wearing a magic ring, you can travel to a different universe. I remember the first time I saw Paolo Uccello's fifteenth-century painting *The Hunt in the Forest* in the Ashmolean Museum in Oxford. I was about seventeen. Immediately and secretly (I was too old to think this officially) I imagined it as the wood between the worlds, and on some level I still cannot believe that C. S. Lewis, Oxford professor, did not think so too. A few years later, as a student journalist, it was the first picture I dared to try to write about. It depicts a malachite-coloured wood in which scarlet-clad huntsmen, some on horseback and some on foot, chase deer with dogs. The trees are tall, elegant and arranged on the panel with the kind of evenness and regularity that one would normally associate with architecture rather than nature. The figures and trees recede with perspectival precision, and indeed technical analysis has revealed Uccello's under-drawing, which used a gridded layout heading towards a single vanishing point on the horizon: the picture is deeply concerned with the illusion of depth and distance.

The trees are like pillars in an endless cathedral. They remind me of the many columns in the forest of Córdoba Cathedral in southern Spain, once a mosque: 856 of them, in granite, jasper, onyx and marble. But there is no telling how many columnar trees there might be in Uccello's forest. There is no glimmer of relief, no 'something else' to be seen beyond the canopy that stretches away into the dark. There is no 'edge' in the world of the painting, though the picture itself is safely contained and bounded by the edges of its rectangular panel. As the scene stretches away, smaller and smaller are the horses with their crimson bridles and reins, smaller and smaller are the leaping deer and their snapping, supple pursuers. All this under a night sky: a pale, thin new moon throws a flicker of golden light onto the leaves of innumerable trees.

C. S. Lewis once contrasted the way that we in the modern world look at the night sky compared with our medieval forebears. For us, with our post-Romantic, post-Enlightenment worldview, staring at the stars gives us a sense of the awe-inspiring immeasurability of the universe. The experience is, he wrote, 'like looking out over a sea that fades away into mist, or looking about one in a trackless forest – trees forever and no horizon'. On the other hand, for the medieval watcher of the skies, there was a sense that the heavenly bodies were affixed into a kind of ceiling, albeit one a great distance away. 'To look up at the towering medieval universe is much more like looking at a great building,' he wrote.[82] He added that Dante, on his journey through the cosmos, was 'like a man being conducted through an immense cathedral, not like one lost in a shoreless sea'. I wonder what it must have been like, to feel so contained in the universe, so held in pattern and structure, in *texta.*

In the Woods

The lane wound down from our house towards the farm, passing only one cottage on the left, where old Miss Holmes lived with a rough-haired collie, an outside bathroom and an ancient iron range. She had visits, sometimes, from a man she called her nephew, really her son. In her front yard double opium poppies flowered in profusion. My mother sowed their descendants – frilly, pink, dissolute – in all her gardens, drying the heads each autumn and shaking out the tiny black seeds as if from old-fashioned pepperpots. Three decades on, still the poppies grew, while Miss Holmes lay in her grave in the Catholic churchyard. On the other side of the lane, hidden by an overgrown hawthorn hedge, was a field of daffodils. Miss Gosling, the farmer, had once tried growing them for profit, but florists, she said, preferred early blooms. If you knew where the gap in the hedge was, she let you squeeze through and take as many as you wanted, under the eye of an indignant saffron-beaked blackbird. I'd go there each morning for a fortnight and fill my arms with yolky blooms, and for those two weeks of the year they glowed in all the rooms of the house.

Miss Gosling kept a flock of sheep, two ponies and two horses, a herd of goats, two dogs, several cats, some chickens and some pigs. The horses were called Carly One and Carly Two; I cannot recall the names of the ponies, the dogs, or the cats. Miss Gosling wore a brown cotton coat tied with string, brown corduroy trousers, a headscarf and a pair of wellington boots. For rainy weather, she had a voluminous and battered waxed coat. Her face was deeply lined but fine-boned, and when she smiled (which was often, since she was kind), you noticed how few teeth she had. As a girl, I collected warm eggs from among her hay bales. She let me feed the orphaned lambs. I can still feel now the needy tug of their jaws on the nipple of the bottle, the soft insides of their sucking mouths, and the downy, curled fleece on their blunt foreheads. She taught me how to milk the goats, firmly but carefully squeezing the teat, using the pressure of my little finger to bring the milk into the bucket in a thin, hard stream.

Sometimes we would go into the farmhouse: there was a back kitchen, with dark green shelves against the walls lined with yellowing strips of newspaper cut into a zigzag frill. The front kitchen had a table where cats slept on piles of old copies of *Farmers Weekly*. One day I came into the front kitchen and a man was sitting there, engulfed by a winged armchair. It was a shock, but on the other hand I'd heard noises from upstairs before, and even thought I'd seen a face looking out from an upper window. He was dressed in a brown three-piece suit with a collar too big for his neck, and a watch chain round his chest. He had the pallor of someone who never went outdoors. It was Joseph, Mary Gosling's brother, kept away from the world. I still have no idea what word one would correctly use for his condition. As I recall, he did not form much in the way of words, but he was friendly. His concealed existence seems much odder to me now than it did then. Secret relatives were not uncommon in books; I had probably not yet read *Jane Eyre*, but I had read *The Secret Garden*.

One afternoon I came to the bit of yard outside the back kitchen – there was a ledge there where I'd often sit with the quieter of the two dogs. I saw a man who used to come each year to help with the sheep shearing: each ewe would be turned on her back and cradled like an enormous baby while she was shaved in muscular strokes, until, finally, the whole fleece came away in a shaggy heap and the animal struggled away, suddenly ridiculously small and cleanly white. Today he was here because of the pig. Lately it had been snuffling and honking in one of the ramshackle stables at the back of the yard, as big as a man. It had been the runt of a farrow I'd watched the morning after they were born, wriggling at their mother's udders in the straw. I remember Miss Gosling telling me how the sow could accidentally crush a piglet to death when she rolled. Newborn piglets have an immensely particular smell: warm, babyish, musky. Today the pig was dangling head down, trussed by its hind feet, as blood dripped from its throat. Its body was steaming – it had just been scalded to remove its bristles – and bloodstained water was running in rivulets down the yard. Where it gathered in puddles, the cats scooped up the red liquid with busy tongues, their bony shoulders skywards.

There had been more land, Miss Gosling once said, in her father's day. She used to ride one of the forefathers of Carly One and Carly Two to dances, and then return asleep, or half asleep, trusting to the horse. The Miss Gosling of the parties must have been, I thought, very different from the one I knew. I imagined her, beautiful, in some wide-skirted dress that she had made herself, drifting home at dawn across the valley. By the time I was young, that valley was torn through by the motorway, whose hum I cannot remember having heard, much; but when I went back there, at forty-two, it seemed to me a bestial and threatening roar. Beside Miss Gosling's farm were woods that stretched down towards the great road. They cannot have been very big woods but they felt so to me as a child. Each May they were thick with bluebells, their faint green scent hanging in the air. I loved those woods, but they frightened me. Whenever I went into them I could feel them closing in. The freedom of the fields and the low, rolling hills would be lost. The sky would disappear.

OUT OF THE WOODS

Epic poems are like woods, like the Underworld. Easy to enter, hard to escape. Their edges cannot be perceived when one is lost within. The classicist Don Fowler wrote: 'The middle of a work, especially of a large work like an epic, is labyrinthine in its complexity, with many false trails and dead ends. We enter at the beginning and hope eventually to find a way out, but the essential experience of the work is the experience of the middle, before anything becomes clear.'[83] In such a way epic poems are also like life. We cannot remember our beginnings, nor, generally, do we have a feeling for how things are going to end. We experience life as the middle.

Epics often have problems with endings. The end of the *Aeneid* certainly feels like the end in one sense, for its final line is a death – that of Aeneas's enemy, the Rutulian leader Turnus. On the other hand, it has been claimed since antiquity that Virgil left the poem unfinished; in any case, those last lines are an abrupt and unsettling conclusion. Turnus, having been defeated by Aeneas in hand-to-hand combat, pleads for mercy. Since the ghost of his father had, during their encounter in the Underworld, instructed Aeneas to spare the defeated, one might have expected him to give Turnus his life. But no: the fired-up, furious Aeneas stabs him through, and 'His life breath fled with a groan of outrage / down to the shades below.' No funeral rites as for Hector in the *Iliad.* No wedding between Aeneas and his Italian wife-to-be, Lavinia. No calming endgame. Just the wielding of a brute and violent power – followed by the literary equivalent of an abrupt theatrical blackout.

The *Odyssey* has a notoriously peculiar finish. Its conclusion seems ludicrously protracted. After Odysseus and Telemachus have slaughtered Penelope's suitors, after Odysseus and Penelope have been reunited, it turns out there is still quite a lot of poem to go: Odysseus reveals himself to his father; the suitors' allies plot insurrection against their newly returned king; we even follow the dead suitors on their one-way journey to the Underworld. There are several endings, in fact, yet the poem always feels to me to lack that sense of utter completion that Charles Dickens delivers in *Oliver Twist*, any of whose concluding few chapters might serve as a fitting finale, and which almost obsessively doles out to each character their deserts (just or not), up to and including Bill Sikes's suicidal hound.

In the *Odyssey*, even when the goddess Athena has separated the warring factions and the poem grinds to a halt, we have the sense that the story will continue beyond the borders of its lines, since Odysseus has been instructed by the prophet Tiresias that he must, after his twenty years of wars and wandering, now set out on another journey, this time carrying an oar from his ship, venturing so far inland that the inhabitants cannot identify his burden and mistake it for a winnowing fan. As the anthropologist Mary Douglas wrote in *Thinking in Circles*, her book on ring composition, 'There is nothing final about homecoming. Any recognised kind of ending is loaded with intimations of other endings. After a rest, the home-comer will set out again, and return again. Nonetheless, with the sight of the place and the familiar smells and sounds, everything announces "home". No matter how many more expeditions there will be, each successive return to the start is an ending.'[84] The stem is ready to grow new stories.

The end of *Peliaco quondam* is bewildering, its tone hard to read. First (as it were, at the beginning of the end) comes the wedding song that the Fates perform at Peleus and Thetis's marriage feast, which combines joyful praise of the couple's mutual love with a disturbing prophecy about the violent life and death of their future son, Achilles. Then comes an abrupt (wistful? knowing? deeply felt? devastating?) envoi: since mortals have now become so utterly corrupt, turning away from piety and all that is good, the gods now refuse to frequent their gatherings. The last two lines are evanescent, hard to fathom, probably impossible to translate:

Quare nec talis dignantur visere coetus
nec se contingi patiuntur lumine claro.

And so the gods no longer deign to come among us,
nor let themselves be touched
by our clear light,
our eyes.

Lumen carries the meaning of both eye and light. Humans are wicked and corrupt, but there's something so beautiful about that phrase, '*lumine claro*' – and it belongs to us, to our human realm.

As for the *Iliad*: I love its end, which takes the form of a series of dirges over the corpse of Hector, Helen of Troy's the last. The final line, 'And so the Trojans buried Hector, breaker of horses', has always seemed to me to contain a plangent beauty: no more swift horses for the hero who lies dead and stilled on his pyre. But in some versions of the manuscript there follows an extra pair of lines – 'And there came an Amazon, the daughter of great-hearted Ares'[85] – which suggests a continuation, the start of another epic story in the endless cycle of epic stories. Hector's death does not signal the end. There is always another beginning, someone else's beginning.

THE DOORS OF DAEDALUS

The Trojans' arrival in Italy, halfway through the *Aeneid*, marks a homecoming and a fresh beginning. The first thing that Aeneas sees at this climactic moment, after five books of fruitless meanderings over the Mediterranean, is an image of a labyrinth. This is what happens. He moors his fleet at Cumae. His men go off in search of timber. The hero, alone, seeks out the temple of Apollo. It was here, we are told, that Daedalus, once upon a time, alighted after fleeing the kingdom of Minos on wings of his own making. His son Icarus had died on the journey: despite his father's warnings, he flew too close to the sun, so that the wings' wax fixings melted in the heat and he fell to his death. Daedalus himself built the temple, dedicating his wings there to Apollo in thanks for his safe deliverance. And on the doors he carved stories: he carved the death of Androgeon, prince of Crete. He carved the people of Athens, obliged to send young men, chosen by lot, as sacrifice to the Minotaur. And he carved the urn, standing ready to receive its lots. On the facing door he carved the land of Crete rising from the sea. He carved Pasiphaë coupling with the bull – becoming a kind of double traitor, for she tricked both the animal and her husband. He carved the Minotaur, a living memorial to the monstrosity of the queen's passion. He carved the labyrinth: the house of labour, the endless blinding maze. He carved himself, taking pity on the princess's love, untangling the bewildering labyrinth's forking paths, guiding the hero's blind footsteps with thread. And he might have carved you,

Icarus, too, falling from the sky, had not his hands dropped to his sides, useless ... Twice he tried to depict you in gold, and twice he failed.

It is a deeply strange scene. Though we see the artwork through Aeneas's eyes, we seem to be very close to the narrator's voice, which twice breaks through the poem to be heard directly – once addressing the god Apollo, once addressing Icarus. We're alerted to the fact that a poet writing about an artist might be telling us something about the nature and purpose of art, right here in the middle of his greatest creation. The effect seems especially pointed since Daedalus has carved events from his own life; his own autobiography, if you like. On one side of the doors he depicts something of a backstory: events not controlled by him. On the other side he has carved representations of objects he himself made. First the fake cow that enabled Pasiphaë to couple with the bull. Then the labyrinth, the building he designed to keep the consequence of their mating hidden. Neither Theseus nor Ariadne is named, and Ariadne's role in saving Theseus is suppressed: this is a different story from the one we know (and Virgil knew) from *Peliaco quondam.* Here it is Daedalus who is the protagonist, unravelling the secret of his own labyrinth out of pity for Ariadne's love. Then there is the death of Icarus: a scene he cannot bear to finish. We are looking at an incomplete artwork. I imagine the carved reliefs just petering out. (If that is precisely what they are – Virgil is vague, except for telling us that Daedalus tried to depict Icarus in gold.) The highly worked surface simply smooths away into nothingness at its edge.

Why are these the very first things that Aeneas sees when he arrives in his longed-for Italy? What is he expected to understand by studying them? As it turns out, it is difficult to tell what Aeneas might or might not absorb from his solitary contemplation of the works. He is abruptly dragged away when some of his men arrive with the Sibyl. Now is no time for gazing at the sights, she tells him. Better to sacrifice to the gods. He has heroic and epic concerns to attend to and cannot dawdle like a *flâneur* or a tourist. Perhaps the Sibyl regards these scenes as somewhat unedifying and unheroic, apt to set a bad moral example. It is perhaps significant that later in this book of the poem, when the ghost of Aeneas's father Anchises is prophesying the destiny of the empire, we are told that the arts of Rome will be government and empire and war. It will be for others to 'forge the bronze to breathe with suppler lines, / draw from the block of marble features quick with life'.

We, the readers, nevertheless may pause to admire these miraculous doors. We may ponder why Virgil (via Daedalus) is showing us, in the centre of his labyrinthine poem, an image of a labyrinth. On one level, it is a preview of Aeneas's trip to the Underworld: both are places of traps and difficulties, of confrontation with monsters, or ghosts, or one's past, or one's future. On another level, the labyrinth is also a fabrication, and we might reflect on how, like Daedalus's other creations – the fake cow, the sham wings – it brought great harm and grief. His contrivances, taken together, are terribly bound up in destructive desires: harmful sexual passion in the case of Pasiphaë, disastrous overconfidence and recklessness in the case of Icarus. Above all, Daedalus's capacity for artistic expression simply peters out when faced with the truly unspeakable reality of the loss of a son. We are being told a story of art's failure and art's deceitfulness.

And yet: it turns out that the only way to express this destructive pointlessness, this incapacity, is through making art. The void on the surface of the sculpted doors is, paradoxically, the perfect artistic expression of art's inadequacy. Unfinished, the work makes precisely the point it needs to make. It is a confession that, even in the face of his work's aesthetic, practical and ethical shortcomings, in the face of its complete impotence and even its destructiveness, it is the only thing Daedalus can do. He is an artist, and art is his life. At the same time, that incomplete, perfectly inadequate artwork is only part of another artwork – a poem that is itself simultaneously incomplete, and perfect, and a labyrinth, and deceitful, and true.

Picasso's Minotaurs

1. A Minotaur lies on a couch, holding a wine glass aloft. Beside him is a naked woman. His weird little tail spreads behind him.
2. A Minotaur grips a naked girl. One hand prods at a nipple. Here are the girl's breasts, buttocks and vulva. She has no face. A flautist plays.
3. A Minotaur makes a toast, his glass held high. Beneath him is a tangle of limbs, a girl's lolling head. Next to her is a man (hairy, legs splayed, almost a satyr) clawing at a woman's breasts.

4. There is the gauze of a wind-teased curtain. A Minotaur sleeps. A girl, her face registering what might be pity, keeps watch.
5. A Minotaur topples a woman, and gores her arms, her breasts. She is dead, or as good as.
6. A Minotaur, on all fours, tail to sky, claws at the ground. He is close to death, watched by three pairs of eyes.
7. A young man plunges a knife into a Minotaur. The monster's body is balled up and his hands hang limp and useless. An audience is seated above, as if watching a bull-fight.
8. A dying Minotaur has plunged to his knees, his head angled towards the sky. Beside him is a knife. A girl reaches out from the audience to touch his back, perhaps tenderly.
9. A curtain wafts in the breeze. A Minotaur lies among cushions, with a girl in his lap. They seem pensive, or afraid.
10. A Minotaur, a man and two women lie together, their naked limbs entwined. The face of the Minotaur is aglow with lust. The women seem bored.
11. A Minotaur, vast-headed, looms over a sleeping girl. It is hard to know whether he is about to kill her, or burst into tears.
12. A blind Minotaur carries a staff. A little girl, her arms full of flowers, leads him. The monster raises his face to the sky and bellows.
13. A streaming-haired girl cradles a dove. She guides the blind Minotaur. Ferrymen stare from a boat. A boy observes. The monster raises his face to the sky and bellows.

14. A streaming-haired girl cradles a dove. She guides the blind Minotaur. Ferrymen stare from a boat. A boy observes. The monster raises his face to the sky and bellows.
15. Night: a star-filled sky. A streaming-haired girl cradles a dove. She guides the blind Minotaur. Ferrymen stare from a boat. A boy observes. The monster raises his face to the sky and bellows.

PASTORAL INTERLUDE

One of the scenes that Arachne, in Ovid's *Metamorphoses*, stitches into her tapestry is the rape of the mortal woman Antiope by the god Jupiter, disguised as a satyr. This is – possibly – the subject of a somewhat enigmatic painting by Titian that hangs at right angles to the *Mona Lisa* in the Louvre; the work, when it is not known as *Jupiter and Antiope*, is referred to as the *Pardo Venus*, after the Spanish palace where it was once hung. (It was the first canvas that Titian produced for Philip II. He himself, in a letter to the king's secretary, simply referred to it as 'the naked woman with the landscape and satyr'.) If you want to spend time looking at the painting now, the experience is somewhat like standing in a fast-running river – you are constantly buffeted by the flow of people behind and in front of you, some of whom pause to join you in contemplation of the work, some of whom may wonder why your back is so resolutely turned to *La Joconde*.

In the right-hand half of the picture, a woman lies asleep, her arm folded back over her head. Whether she depicts Venus, or Antiope, or just a 'naked woman', she is one of the many artistic offspring of the Vatican Ariadne. At her side are grapes, pomegranates, an empty wine jug. A satyr is crouched beside her. He has lifted the diaphanous white material covering her limbs and is gazing greedily at her body. He wears some kind of skin jerkin over his shoulders, and his legs are the wild hairy limbs of a goat. Cupid is on the wing above, shooting an arrow at this lascivious creature. Facing away from this scene, on the left of the painting, a fully clothed young woman and another satyr sit together on the grass. She has flowers in her lap; his head is wreathed with leaves. Among all this is a hunting scene – dogs on leashes and men who gesture towards the woods and the river and the far-off mountains. There are more huntsmen, further back in the picture; their dogs are setting about a stag, about to rip it apart. The whole thing is a strange combination of rural pleasures and rural violence: a picnic and wine, and, in the offing, rape and blood.

The picture reminds me of *Déjeuner sur l'herbe*:* the works have the same bosky atmosphere, the same picnic strewn carelessly on the grass, the same play of nudity and clothed-ness, though Manet has undressed both of his women and allowed his men the bourgeois black suits of the 1860s. And at the same time, I think of one of the works from Picasso's *Vollard Suite*, a series of etchings made by the artist in the 1930s, some of which depict the Minotaur in various invented settings and

* Although the major sources for the painting are generally agreed to be Titian's *Concert Champêtre*, also in the Louvre, and Marcantonio Raimondi's engraving after Raphael's *Judgement of Paris*.

poses. The image I am thinking of has the Minotaur and a girl reclining together on cushions. The beast, in half-profile, holds aloft a glass of wine. His animal tail is what I think of; it curls out and rests on the cushions in just the same way as one of the satyr's in the Titian. Because of these echoes, Manet's men in *Déjeuner sur l'herbe*, notwithstanding their sober suits, seem to me lascivious, priapic satyrs, just like the priapic satyr that looms over the sculpture of the sleeping nymph in the *Hypnerotomachia Poliphili.*[86] Or like Minotaurs, violent and bestial.

Françoise Gilot, one of Picasso's lovers, wrote in her memoir about her first visit to the artist, in Paris in 1944. She was a young painter – in fact she'd studied at Cambridge and the Sorbonne, but she was determined to pursue art. He'd spotted her in a restaurant, and now he had invited her over to see his etchings – the *Vollard Suite*. According to Gilot, he talked as he leafed through them, eventually arriving at the sequence depicting the Minotaur. She recalled that he told the story of these images through a highly charged personal mythology. The setting for the etchings was an island like Crete, he told her. The Minotaurs (not one, but many) were the rich seigneurs of the island, who lived all along the coast. 'They know they're monsters and they live, like dandies and dilettantes everywhere, the kind of existence that reeks of decadence in houses filled with works of art by the most fashionable painters and sculptors,' he told her. 'They love being surrounded by pretty women ... They get the local fishermen to go out and round up girls from the neighbouring islands. After the heat of the day has passed, they bring in the sculptors and their models for parties, with music and dancing, and everybody gorges himself on mussels and champagne until melancholy fades away and euphoria takes over. From there on it's an orgy.'

One of the works of the *Vollard Suite* depicted a Minotaur watching a woman as she slept. The creature was, Picasso told Gilot, trying to decide whether the girl loved him *because* he was a monster. She remembered him saying, 'Women are odd enough for that, you know ... It's hard to say whether he wants to wake her or kill her.' After their conversation, he took Gilot to a bedroom and asked her to strip naked.

MINOTAUROMACHY

There is a photograph of Picasso dating from 1959, in which he wears one of the enormous woven bull's heads used by bullfighters in training. The head has basketry horns and silly tufty ears and blank circular eyes. The artist's shirt is off and his hairy chest and thickened stomach are exposed; in his left hand a cigarette burns down. He looks monstrous. He has become a Minotaur.

Picasso drew bulls throughout his life, from his twenties to his eighties. But in the 1930s – when he was enduring an especially turbulent period of his life, leaving his wife, the dancer Olga Khokhlova, for his mistress, Marie-Thérèse Walter – he drew Minotaurs over and over again. It is hard to avoid the thought that sometimes these Minotaurs are him – in all his sexual voraciousness, in all his abjectness. He once said, 'If all the ways I have been along were marked on a map and joined up with a line, it might represent a Minotaur.'[87] Sometimes his Minotaurs are blind, which seems the cruellest fear for an artist. Sometimes they are pathetic, sometimes bestial. They are hairy, squat, big-balled. Their faces often look stupid, or uncomprehending. They never seem to be enacting the myth of the Cretan Minotaur exactly, though sometimes they are seen being killed in an arena, or there's a hint of a shoreline that might be Crete. In 1933, Picasso designed the cover for the first issue of the surrealist journal *Minotaure*, the title of which was chosen for the monster's association with the free, unbridled unconscious. In 1937, he drew a Minotaur running: looking at this work, you can see the shine of the graphite, feel the pressure of the pencil where he scribbled shadow under the arm and between the buttocks, sense his thumb blotting the page to shade the elbows and thighs, the muscular back.

In 1935, as Spain slid towards civil war, he started to work on several versions of an etching called *Minotauromachie* – an invented word adapted from the Greek *gigantomachia*, meaning the mythical battle between gods and giants, so that *minotaur-omachie* means the battle with the Minotaur. At the left, a bearded man climbs a ladder. Beside him, a little girl holds a candle radiating a web of light, and a bunch of flowers. Towards her careens a horse, with a dead or wounded *matadora* splayed over its back. At the right is the Minotaur, one monstrously vast arm spread out in front of him, his head a swollen mass of curled fur surmounted by tusk-like horns. From a window above, two women gaze down serenely upon this scene of combat and death – the Minotaur's untriumphant triumph. A pair of doves stand on the windowsill before them. In the background, the sail of a boat hovers on the horizon.

It is as if Picasso borrowed shards and fragments of myth and transformed them into his own dense narrative, far removed from the original stimulus. But what is the nature of this narrative? It is a scene that has seemed to many viewers to be a riddle, one that could be solved, if, for example, its characters could be identified. The little girl, it has been suggested,* could be his sister Conchita, who died when he was a child. The bearded man might be his father, the *matadora* Marie-Thérèse, the horse Olga . . . maybe. When I look at the *Minotauromachie* etchings I myself see echoes of *The Spinners*: the ladder at the left-hand side resembling the ladder in Vélazquez's painting; the upper window recalling the background space occupied by the goddess and her entourage; the Minotaur's arm reaching out like the wool-winder's; the creature's grotesque horned woolly head like the clump of wool attached to the spinners' wall (and in turn like the stag's skull in the grotto in Titian's *Diana and Actaeon*). But if Picasso had a metamorphosis in mind in his *Minotauromachie*, it is opaque: it happens beyond the confines of the picture.

---

* By Picasso's biographer John Richardson in his essay in the exhibition catalogue for *Picasso: Minotaurs and Matadors*, held at Gagosian, London, in 2017, for which Richardson unforgettably brought together Picasso's images of bulls, bullfighters and Minotaurs.

Minotaur

One night I dreamed I was trapped in a dark place. It was a cave, perhaps, but I could not make out its edges. I felt that people were nearby in the close gloom, since I had the sense of vague shapes moving somewhere on the periphery, but my face felt peculiar, muffled and constricted, and my vision blurred.

Someone showed me some golden tablets – sheets of metal that shone bright in the darkness. They were inscribed with swirls and shapes. I had the feeling that they contained important information – rules, laws. But I could not decipher them. I could not make sense of anything.

After a while someone forced me to look into a mirror. There was a feeling of something alien, something terribly wrong. I saw my reflection: I was the Minotaur. I felt terror, terror, terror.

Seven ways to kill the Minotaur

1. You straddle the Minotaur, you grab his neck, you twist the horned head. Scattered on the ground are human skulls and bones.
2. You straddle the Minotaur. Scattered on the ground are human skulls and bones. Nearby, two young women embrace; one wears a yellow robe behind which a child shelters, sneaking a glance at the fight. You twist the horned head.

3. Your hand takes the Minotaur's wrist. Others, if they saw this detail, noticed nothing else, might think the gesture almost delicate. You poise your sword to sink into his flesh. Winged Victory holds up her skirts, as if dancing.
4. The Minotaur, thrown to the ground, resists, thrusts up towards your chest. Too late: your swordpoint plunges in, blood cascades. Ariadne's red thread is wound round your chest. The Minotaur's face is almost placid: it is a farmyard creature.
5. You have the Minotaur's neck by your right hand. He stumbles to his knees as you plunge in your sword. A bird (unless it's some god in disguise) darts past.
6. You cup the Minotaur's muzzle. The monster pushes back at the sword blade, kicks at your knee. But he is already dying: blood drips from his bovine neck. Ariadne smiles and holds a sprig of leaves to her nose. You wear her red thread.
7. The Minotaur grabs a boulder, prepares to throw. Your sword is already at his flank. Minos raises a hand. Ariadne holds high the red thread.

Theseus the Hero

Pittheus of Troezen tricked Aegeus, king of Athens, into having sex with his daughter Aethra. Aegeus told the girl, 'I will hide my sandals, and my sword, under this stone. If you have a boy, bring him here when he's grown and ask him to move this rock, which no one but a son of mine could do. Then let him come to Athens bringing me the sword and the sandals as signs.' Aethra indeed had a baby, whom she called Theseus. When he grew up, she showed him the great rock, which no one else had been able to shift. But he bowled it away as if it had been a child's ball. Then he snatched up the sword and put on the sandals, and set off for Athens. On the road he was stopped by Periphetes, a thug wielding an iron club. Theseus killed him, and took the club for himself. Then he encountered Sinis, a man who murdered people in a cruel and unusual way: he'd challenge them to bend pine trees, saying he'd help them do it. But he'd let go of the tree just as it was arched to the ground, and it would catapult the unfortunate traveller to their death. Theseus tricked him in turn, so that he died by means of his own bad joke, flying into the air and falling from a great height. Then he chased the man's daughter, Perigune. She was young and afraid. She hid by a stream, among the wild asparagus and the reeds, whispering to the very plants to help her. He raped her there.

Next he encountered Sciron, who used to sit on the rocks by the sea, and compel passers-by to wash his feet; after they'd done it, he'd kick them into the water. But Theseus took Sciron by his feet and flung him into the waves, where he drowned. After this he met Cercyon, who forced travellers to wrestle with him. Theseus took him on, and killed him. Finally he came across Procrustes, a man who lived near the road and would invite people into his house to rest for the night. Procrustes had two beds, one small, one big. When tall guests came he put them on the small bed and sawed off their legs at the shin to fit the bed. When small guests came he hammered and struck them until they stretched to fit the big bed. Theseus killed him. And then the hero came to Athens.

The queen in those days was Medea. She was a princess of Colchis who had helped Jason to steal the Golden Fleece. She had sailed back on the *Argo* with Jason and lived with him in Corinth, bearing him two children. But Jason had tired of her and wanted to marry Glauce, the king's daughter. In her fury, Medea had killed Glauce with a poisoned crown, then stabbed her own children to death in order to punish Jason. She had then fled to Athens in the chariot of Helios, the Sun. Here she married Aegeus, with whom she had a baby, Medus. Thanks to her magical powers, she foresaw the arrival of Theseus, whom, as the elder son of the king, she didn't want around. She convinced Aegeus that the young man meant to plot against them, and so he sent Theseus off to tackle the seemingly impossible challenge of killing the Marathonian boar. When he succeeded, survived and returned, she gave him a cup of poisoned wine, but just as he was raising it to his lips, Aegeus noticed Theseus's sword and his sandals – tokens of his true identity – and dashed the cup out of his hands. Medea's plotting was discovered, and she was expelled from Athens along with her son.

Theseus volunteered to go to Crete as part of the tribute of seven girls and seven boys demanded as fodder for the Minotaur. Ariadne fell in love with him and decided to help him by giving him a sword and a length of red thread.

On their journey back to Athens, they put in on Naxos. But Theseus departed in secret during the night, leaving Ariadne asleep on the shore. Whether he did so because he was already tired of her, or because he was afraid of Minos's pursuit, or because some other god had shadowed his mind in forgetfulness, no one can tell for sure. But Ariadne cursed him, so that when he sailed near to Athens, he forgot to raise the white sails that would signal to his father that he was safe. So Aegeus, seeing only rust-red sails, despaired and flung himself from the citadel.

Daedalus, meanwhile, who had built the labyrinth, was punished by King Minos by being shut into it with his son, Icarus. But the craftsman devised an escape by means of wings he had designed, made from feathers and wax. He warned his son: don't fly too near to the sea, or the waves will wet the feathers and they won't carry you any more. And don't fly too near to the sun, or the heat will melt the wax and you will drown. But Icarus, overjoyed at the freedom of flying like a bird, soared higher and higher until the sun melted the wax. He plunged into the deathly deeps and drowned near the island of Naxos, where, wheeling around the seaways in his grief, Daedalus saw Ariadne, abandoned by Theseus, alone on the shore. But Daedalus flew west to Italy, where he built a temple to Apollo and dedicated his wings. On its doors he made carvings of the story of Pasiphaë's cow and the labyrinth, his destructive and terrible inventions. But in his despair he could not finish his carvings of Icarus.

Theseus joined the expedition that Hercules was mounting against the Amazons, the tribe of one-breasted female warriors. There, he abducted and raped Melanippe. The Amazons laid siege to Athens to try to recover her, but he defeated them. Melanippe bore him a son, Hippolytus, and they lived together for a time. But later, Theseus entered into an alliance with the new king of Crete, Deucalion, and agreed to marry his sister, Phaedra, who was also the sister of Ariadne and the half-sister of the dead Minotaur. At the wedding, Melanippe and the other Amazons appeared, armed and ready to fight. But Theseus and his men killed them. The boy Hippolytus was sent to Troezen. When he grew up and returned to Athens, Phaedra became obsessed by him, although he was not only her stepson, but an abstainer from sexual relations, being a follower of Artemis. One day she tried to entice him to her bed, but, horrified, he refused her. Phaedra tore her clothes and dishevelled her hair and accused him of trying to rape her; she then hanged herself. Hippolytus, denounced by his father, took his chariot and hurried back to Troezen, but a monstrous bull emerged from the sea and frightened his team, so that his chariot was overturned and he perished, trampled to death by his own terrified horses.

Theseus now made a pact with his friend Pirithous that they would both marry daughters of Zeus. Theseus went to Sparta, from where he abducted Helen – a daughter of Zeus, and a child of twelve. Her brothers, Castor and Pollux, waged war on Athens and recovered her. Later she married Menelaus, but was abducted by Paris, on account of which the Greeks besieged Troy for ten years. Many fighters, including Hector, prince of Troy, and Achilles, son of Peleus and Thetis, died; and at the end of the war, the surviving Trojan women were raped and enslaved, and their babies flung from the towers of the city.

Pirithous, Theseus's friend, decided to try to abduct Persephone, who was also a daughter of Zeus. She was living in the Underworld as its queen, since, long before, Hades had raped her and taken her to his grim realm. Hades greeted them cordially and asked them to sit – tricking them, for this was the Seat of Forgetfulness. As they rested there, snakes coiled over them and trapped them. Hercules heard of the plight of his friend and freed Theseus, though he left Pirithous there for all eternity. When Theseus returned to Athens, he found it convulsed by violence and split into factions. So he went to Scyros, where he had lands, and where the people were friendly to him. Its king, Lycomedes, led him high up a steep crag, saying that from there they would be able to see the extent of his territory. Whether because he was afraid of Theseus, or whether for another reason, he pushed him from the crag. And so Theseus died.

Pictures at an Exhibition, Rome, 1 March 2017

Theseus abandoned Ariadne. And Apollo flayed Marsyas. And Medea killed her children. And Hades raped Persephone. And Tarquin raped Lucretia. And Bireno abandoned Olympia. And Tancredi sent Ghismonda the bloody heart of her lover. And Judith decapitated Holofernes. And Salome demanded John the Baptist's head on a platter. And David killed Goliath. And the old men spied on Susanna at her bath. And Cleopatra committed suicide. And Potiphar's wife falsely accused Joseph of rape. And Jael crushed Sisera's head with a hammer.

AN EDGE

Borges once said, of Henry James and Kafka, 'I think that they both thought of the world as being at the same time complex and meaningless.' For them, no pattern. The story will not tell. How different from Chesterton, with his many jewelled worlds, each of them bounded by the rules of reason, each of them proclaiming with iron certainty that 'Thou shalt not steal'.

You are, on the whole, with James and Kafka. But still, is it not possible to live in the complex and meaningless world? The labyrinth is something that you cannot help entering. Once inside it, you have no idea where you are, you feel lost, you are robbed of a sense of direction, but perhaps that does not matter. You will never see the whole design, but you can live with that. There are terrors within the labyrinth but there is also love. The centre may not be where you think it is or where you want it to be. But humans are creatures who desire pattern and shape and design. They spin thread, they tell stories, they build structures (and ships with which to explore the unknown wilderness of the seas). There is meaning to be made, meaning to be excavated.

In her last email to me, Mrs Grammatiki wrote this: 'I sometimes imagine that Daedalus, when he designed his labyrinth, must have re-created the ridges and convoluted folds of his own brain in the form of a building, as if it were a self-portrait. Do you not find that an image of the human brain resembles a labyrinth? And If Daedalus's labyrinth is a diagram of the brain, it is therefore also a symbol of the imagination.

It represents the manner in which humans make associations, one thought following another in a long procession, from the edge to the centre to the end. Stories have this comfort to them: they have a beginning and an end. They find a way out of the labyrinth.'*

Bacchus and Ariadne

The first thing is blue. Blue sky, lightly cloud-scudded; morning-blue mountains; blue sea rushing Theseus's ship towards the edge of the frame and out of the picture, its twin sails umbrella'd in the stiff breeze. Blue is Ariadne's robe, which has slipped down, its red sash dragging in the sand. Blue are the maenads' loose gowns. Delicate blue iris, elegant blue columbine push up through the grass at the front of the painting. These flowers would have grown wild in the hills above Venice, Titian's home ground.

The second thing is a leap: Bacchus's leap from his chariot, his pink cloak parachuting up above him, his stare locked on

* The reader may have suspected a little slippage between truth and invention, between excavation and creation, in this book. The sibylline Sophia Grammatiki (her name means 'wisdom of a teacher') is, as hinted, more or less a figment of my imagination – like the elderly Italian whom 'Ivan Lermolieff' met in the Pitti Palace in Florence. Nonetheless, there really was a guide who gave me three postcards, many years ago, in the museum at Heraklion, and to whom I remain profoundly grateful for sparking my imagination. The impetus for this book came, in fact, from a dream.

to Ariadne. She's just been looking out to sea, that ship as it gusts away from Naxos without her. Now she's spinning round, clutching at her drooping garments, interrupting the right-to-left momentum of the picture that (without that sudden turn of hers) might make you think of a Roman relief, a frieze. Full in the face she stares back at him, this god with forehead wreathed in ivy, this girlish god with golden hair, this dangerous god, this nearly naked god, this sexy god who has arrived in a chariot drawn, extraordinarily, by cheetahs. The leap is oddly still and arrested: his front foot is concreted down on thin air.

Behind the god comes clamour: a frenzy of cymbals (frenzy of symbols!) and tambourines. There's a whole rowdy crowd of the god's followers: a pair of maenads, a dark-skinned, bearded wild man with snakes twining round his naked body; a faun leaping and stamping and yelling and waving the butchered leg of a deer, which he has no doubt torn apart in ecstatic, god-inspired, drunken madness. A little dog (charming, collared, perhaps a real dog belonging to Alfonso d'Este, who commissioned this picture) yaps at a child faun, scented jasmine crowning his hair, who is dragging behind him on a string, as if a toy, a calf's trunkless head, a head that any minute now is going to crush and stain with gore the long white stamens and stigma of the pinkish-white caper flower that's growing at his feet. Silenus the satyr trundles along in the distance on a donkey, his enormous belly drifting; he's slumped across the man who is trying to steady him. And amid the raucous, drunken, chaotic crowd, the god and the girl are magnetised together, compelled to the centre by all the logic and illogic of the world. Behind, the pale sun illuminates tranquil hills, farms, a man out hunting with his dog. Above, stars cluster in the dawn sky, a celestial crown for Ariadne. Below, a golden cup lies thrown to the ground, engraved with the word TICIANUS.

Ariadne

As for Ariadne, there are different accounts. Some say that in her despair, abandoned on the island of Naxos, she took the red thread, twisted it around her neck and hanged herself from a pine tree. Some say that Bacchus, love-struck, deliberately clouded Theseus's memory, so that he could marry her himself. Some say that after the god found her, he flung her into the heavens, transforming her into a constellation. Some say that Ariadne merely watched him and his rowdy followers passing by, but did not go with them. And that later she stopped crying, stood up, and walked inland from the beach, where there were farms, and fields, and houses, and people.

CODA: *PELIACO QUONDAM*

Once upon a time,
pines rooted on the peak of Pelion
they say,
swam through Neptune's waves
to currents of Phasis, borders of Aeetes,

when hand-picked youths, Argive oak-strength,
lusting to steal the golden fleece from Colchis
dared to run their swift hulls through the salt surf,
sweeping the turquoise straits with pinewood hands.

Minerva (who keeps high citadels safe)
herself made a vehicle fit to fly on the light breeze,
Lashing woven pine to a curvaceous keel.
That prow inured shy Amphitrite to voyages.

As soon as it slashed the sea with its beak
and, with twisted oars, turned the waves foam-hoary,
fierce faces emerged from the shimmering deeps:
Sea-nereids, amazed at the freak of nature.

Then, only then, under that day's sun,
did mortals glimpse the ocean nymphs,
their bare breasts seen in the spumy waves.

Then, at that moment,
they say,
Peleus raged with love for Thetis,
Thetis stooped to a human marriage,
father Jupiter himself saw
they should be twined together.

O heroes, born in a time I pine for much too much,
I salute you!
Offspring of gods, sons of great mothers,
I salute you once more!
I shall call on you often in my song,
and on you above all, Peleus, pillar of Thessaly,
made greater yet by a lucky marriage.
You, to whom the father of the gods
gave his cherished daughter.
Didn't Thetis, loveliest sea nymph,
fall into your arms?
Didn't Tethys and Ocean
(who belts all Earth with his waters)
let you marry their granddaughter?

As soon as the longed-for day arrives, the appointed time,
all Thessaly – a joyful crowd – fills the house,
gifts proffered, faces wreathed in smiles.

Cieros is deserted. From Phthoptican Tempe,
from Crannon's houses, from Larisa's battlements,
they pour and converge on Pharsalus,
throng in the halls of Pharsalus.

(The soil's untilled, the bull-necks soft,
no vine is tamed with the rake's curved claws,
no ox tears the clod with a down-faced plough,
no blade thins the shade of the fronded trees,
abandoned ploughs grow filthy with rust.)

The palace, though: as far as the royal rooms stretch in
splendid enfilade
they glimmer with lustrous gold and silver.
Ivory shines on thrones, goblets shimmer on tables.
The house exults in the royal treasure's dazzle.

And truly, there,
at the heart of it all,
stands the goddess's own bridal bed,
inlaid with slippery Indian tusk,
spread with a textile dipped in rosy murex, Tyrian purple.

This cover, stitched with figures from long ago,
picks out with wondrous skill brave deeds of heroes.

Look, there,
gazing over the wave-sounding shore of Naxos:
Ariadne. Raging fury roils in her heart,

as she sights Theseus in his swift ship, vanishing,
and she can't believe her eyes
when, just then, as she wakes from deceitful sleep
she finds she's alone, left behind, on an empty beach.
But the heedless boy thrashes the waves with his oars,
flinging false oaths to the storm-winds.
And the Minoan girl far away on the sand
like a stone sculpture of a raving maenad
watches,
watches,
and storms break in her heart ...

Her light cap falls from her golden locks,
her filmy dress slips ...
Full breasts are bared of their twisted band.
Clothes slide from her body, scattered,
teased at her feet by the salt surf.
She ignores her cap and floating frock –
but thinks only of you, Theseus,
hangs on to you with her heart and soul,
her tormented mind.

Poor girl!
Venus of Eryx shook your mind with sorrow,
sowing thorns in your heart
right from the moment when fierce Theseus
cast off from the curved harbour of Piraeus
and anchored at Gortyn's temples, home of
unjust Minos.

For, they say,
once upon a time,
forced by plague to pay for Androgeon's murder,
Athens sent hand-picked youths, glory of girls,
as a feast for the Minotaur.

But when this dreadful price
brought anguish to her slender walls,
Theseus preferred to die for his darling Athens
than the dead/not dead be shipped to Crete.
And so, borne on the gentle breeze in a light ship,
he came to the lofty palace of great-souled Minos.

Ariadne was still held in the fond embrace of a virgin bed,
sweet-perfumed, like the myrtle that Eurotas's stream
    coaxes forth,
like spring air, teasing multicoloured buds to bloom –
But the second she saw him (desire in her eyes)
she caught fire, to the core.
Her body blazed before she'd even dragged
her flaming stare away.

God-child! Yes you, cruel Cupid,
who stirs frenzy with your savage heart,
who adds pain to pleasure,
and Venus, queen of Golgi and bosky Idalium –
they were rough waves on which you tossed
that girl with the smouldering mind
when she sighed over the blond stranger.

What terrors she bore in her failing heart!
How often she paled more than gold's gleam
when Theseus, lusting to battle the savage beast,
sought death or the prize of glory.
She promised little offerings to the gods,
she kindled her prayers on silent lips –
and it worked.

Think of an oak, or pine with resinous bark,
shaking its branches on Taurus's peak.
A fierce gale twists its doughty trunk,
topples it. It lies prone, uprooted,
ripped out, everything under it
smashed. Theseus downed
the beast like that, felling
its devastated body.
It waved its horns
pointlessly
in thin
air.

Theseus the famous, the invulnerable,
swerved round, guiding his steps
(which would otherwise stray) with thread,
so the inscrutable trap of the building
should not bewilder him
as he escaped the tendrilling labyrinth.

But why am I taking this turning?
Why should I tell how she left her father's care,

her sister's embrace, abandoned her mother's love
(who desperately wept for her daughter)?
How she put her desire for Theseus first?
How, on his ship, she came to Dia's foam-strewn beach?
How that husband of heedless heart
left her behind when sleep had her trapped?

Over and over again
they say,
heart flaming, furious, she poured out sobs,
and in her frenzy climbed steep crags,
scanned the horizon, the boiling ocean,
ran to the shivering brine, braved the waves,
hitched her light clothes over her bare thighs.
And the grief-struck girl, face damp,
choked cold tears, and spoke:

'Is this how you drag me from my home, monster,
leaving me here, on this deserted beach?
Is this how you vanish, indifferent to me,
to the gods? All you're shipping home is lies.
Could anything have changed your cruel mind?
Is there no kindness inside?
No way your unsweet heart could have pitied me?
This wasn't what you promised me.
You flattered me, told me to expect a wedding day,
happy marriage, not this misery.
The winds have scythed your words to the skies.
No woman should ever trust man, any more,

or imagine his word is his bond.
When he's thirsty for sex he'll swear anything,
But when he slakes his lust, he'll forget
    his vows,
and never think twice about lies.

'When death's vortex had you spinning,
I plucked you out. I preferred to let
slip a brother than let you down
when you were on the edge, liar.

'And for all that, I'm to be thrown away,
picked over by carrion,
no one to throw dust on my bones.
What lion birthed you under a desolate crag?
What sea conceived you, spat you out?
Spew of Syrtis, Scylla, Charybdis –
is this what I get for saving your precious life?

'If you didn't want marriage, flinched
from your father's old-fashioned precepts,
you still could have brought me home.
I would gladly have been your slave,
washed your feet in spring water,
smoothed your bed with a purple cover …

'Oh, why am I flinging my words into thin air?
Dumb wind doesn't hear, doesn't speak.
He's way out there on the seaways
and no one's here on the weed-clogged shore.
Fate denies me even a listening ear.

'All-powerful Jupiter! If only that Cecropian
prow had never grazed our Knossian shore,
Bearing its tribute for the indomitable bull!
If only that faithless mariner had never lashed
his line on Crete, never slept as a guest in our house –
Theseus, his bitter heart hidden in a lovely husk.

'Where should I go? Is there no hope for me?
Should I make for Ida's mountains?
The savage sea-deeps lie in my way.
What if my father sends help? I left him
behind for a boy drenched in brother-blood.
Can a husband's care bring me comfort?
He's sailing away, waves buckling his oars.

'The island's deserted, no exit from the sea-maze.
No help, no hope, all's dumb, all's bare, all's death.

'But my eyes will not fade in death,
feeling will not slip from my worn-out limbs
before I have called down justice from the gods
and prayed Heaven it may come to pass . . .

'Furies!
The snakes that crown your foreheads
only hint at the seething anger within.
You bring dire punishment for men's deeds.
Come now, come, hear my grievances!
I've dragged them from my deepest entrails,
birthed them in my bones.

Do not allow my agony to go for nothing!

'(For I'm miserable, I'm helpless,
I'm blind, out of my mind with anger.)

'Heedless, he abandoned me.
Heedless, may he destroy himself, his family.'

As she poured out those words from her sorrowful heart,
in distress praying justice for merciless deeds,
the heavenly lord gave a nod in consent. Irreversible.
The earth and the bristling deeps writhed and shook,
The firmament shivered the stars in the sky ...

But Theseus, mind jungled with blinding dark,
let flutter from his forgetful heart
all the commands he'd held firm.
As his home harbour hove to sight,
he failed to hoist the lovely sails
that signalled safety to his fretful father.

For, they say,
once upon a time,
when Aegeus entrusted his son to the gales
as he set forth from Minerva's city,
the old king held the boy in his arms,
and gave him these commands:

'My only son, dearer to me than life,
son whom I must send on a doubtful mission,
son only just returned to me, at the edge of my span –

my ill-luck and your ardour rip you from me, unbearably.
My failing eyes are not yet sated with the sight
of your dear face. I shall send you, not glad,
not with flags and banners, but with my grief.
I shall soil my white hair with earth and dust.
To show the anguish that flames in my mind
I shall hoist sails from that roving mast
that are dirtied and stained with Spanish ochre.
But if Minerva – she who lives in sacred Itonus,
protects our people and Erechtheus's city –
lets you souse your hands in bull's blood,
then keep these orders fresh and safe in your mind,
unblotted by time, so that the moment you glimpse
our hills, you lower the deathly sheets,
and hoist from every twisted rope a white and shining sail.
Do this that I may lift my heart, rejoice to see you safe,
when a glad hour brings you home to me.'

Theseus had kept these words close to his heart.
But now they drifted, just as a veil of clouds
on a mountain's snow-capped summit
is wafted away by the faintest breeze.

His father, eyes devoured by endless tears,
scanned the seas from Athens' topmost tower.
And when he saw that swollen sail,
thinking Theseus lost to an unsweet fate
he hurled himself from the steepest crag,
headlong.

So it was that savage Theseus,
as he walked through his father's door,
found a house struck down by death.
The precise weight of pain his heedless mind
had brought to Ariadne, he endured.

And she gazed out at the dwindling ship,
spinning in her wounded heart unspeakable griefs.

But on another part of the textile,
ivy-wreathed Bacchus was leaping –
on the hunt for you, Ariadne,
flaming with love for you.

All around him gangs of satyrs,
Indian silenes, ecstatic thyads,
out of their heads, tossing their heads,
singing the god song.

Some brandished thyrsus, tendrilled with vine-leaves,
some chucked the limbs of a dismembered deer,
some circled themselves with a writhing of serpents,
some worshipped the secrets held safely in caskets,
secrets that ordinary men may not hear.
Some banged at tambours with fingers extruded,
some clattered clamour from smooth-polished cymbals,
some raucously blew up a racket of piping,
barbarous flutes shrieked a horrible song.

The textile was stitched with figures like this,
spread over the couch, embracing it close.

When the young Thessalians had looked their fill,
they began to disperse, and immortals appeared.

When Dawn treads the threshold of vagabond sun,
the gentlest of zephyrs will pucker quiet waters.
Slowly at first, the waves swell and ruffle.
Gusts lightly ripple them. Sound as of laughter.
The wind gets stronger. Waves breed, grow bigger,
glinting with faint purple light as they glide.
That's how it was when the guests took their leave,
billowing out from the halls of the palace,
scattering back to their own humble homes.

Then the first to come from Pelion's peak
was Chiron, the centaur, with gifts from the forest:
all that Thessaly bears in her meadows,
flowers she grows on her grandiose mountainsides,
blooms the warm breezes unfurl by her riverbanks:
he brought them himself, woven and plaited in untidy crowns.
The house itself, caressed by the perfume, laughed in delight.

Peneus comes next, from viridian Tempe,
Tempe, encircled by overgrown woodland,
where Haemonian dryads are dancing their rituals.

He's not empty-handed:
brings an uprooted beech tree;

a slender-stemmed laurel;
a wind-fretted cypress;
a poplar, sister of flame-engulfed Phaethon;
a shivering plane.
He arranges them all in the palace's forecourt,
a green-stippled light and a soft-verdant bower.

Behind comes crafty Prometheus,
still showing scars from his age-old penance,
paid off with his stone-chained limbs
dangling from a sheer cliff.

Then the father of gods and his holy wife Juno
arrive from Heaven, with all their children.
Except for you, Phoebus, and Diana your twin
(the goddess who dwells on the Idrian peak).
For you and your sister alike despise Peleus,
refuse to honour the nuptials of Thetis.

The gods reclined on the snow-white couches,
tables heaped lavishly, dish after dish.

Meantime,
age-old, tremble-limbed Fates
began to sing their truthful song.
Robes of white, purple-hemmed, ankle-length,
clung to their quivering bodies,
rose-red chaplets adorned their snowy hair.
Their hands performed the everlasting task:

left held the distaff, cloaked in soft fleece.
The right, coaxing down the threads,
shaped them with upturned fingers,
then, twisting with downturned thumb,
twirled the spindle balanced by its polished whorl.
All the while they bit the thread to smooth it out,
as tufts of wool snagged on their dry old lips.
White fleeces stood in baskets at their feet,
and as they plucked the fleeces, so they sang –
clear, prophetic, true, words no age will disprove.

'You who heap valour on virtue,
guardian of Emathia, darling of Ops,
hear on this bright day what the sisters
unwind for you, a truthful oracle.
But you, whose paths men's destinies tread,
spindles – run, run, drawing out the thread.

'The longed-for evening star will shortly rise.
And with him will come your wife,
to dissolve you in desire, to love you,
to share your languorous dreams,
cushioning your strong neck in her slim arms.
Run spindles, run, drawing out the thread.

'No house has ever wreathed around such love,
No love has ever bound itself so strong
as the love that now entwines the two of you.
Run spindles, run, drawing out the thread.

'There will be born to you a fearless child,
Achilles. Enemies will know his face, not his back.
He'll run faster, faster than a fiery-footed hind.
Run spindles, run, drawing out the thread.

'No hero will be his equal in war
when Phrygian fields are clotted in Teucrian blood.
After a long-drawn-out siege, the third heir
of perjuring Pelops shall shatter the Trojan walls.
Run spindles, run, drawing out the thread.

'Mothers will sing of his egregious
virtues and famous deeds, when they undo
their greying hair and bruise their breasts
with feeble fists, mourning their dear sons' deaths.
Run spindles, run, drawing out the thread.

'For as a reaper clips the close-packed corn-ears,
gathering a golden harvest, under a burning sky,
Achilles will crop Trojan corpses with his fatal blade.
Run spindles, run, drawing out the thread.

'Witness to his virtues: Scamander's waters,
which flood into the swift Dardenelles.
He'll choke its course with slaughtered flesh,
warm its deeps with crimson currents.
Run spindles, run, drawing out the thread.

'The last witness to his prowess will be a prize

won after his death: on his high-built grave
will be heaped the pale, butchered limbs of a girl.
Run spindles, run, drawing out the thread.

'For when luck shows the shattered Greeks
a way to loose the chains of Neptune's Troy,
his tomb will be drenched in Polyxena's blood.
She will plunge to her knees like a butchered beast,
    decapitated.
Run spindles, run, drawing out the thread.

'Come now! Loose your limbs in love.
The mortal takes the willing goddess,
the bride is given to the lustful groom.
Run spindles, run, drawing out the thread.

'When nurse comes at dawn she'll try, and fail,
to tie a ribbon round the young bride's neck:
a sign! No fractious daughter sleeping alone,
no need for a mother to fret and doubt –
she can hope for darling grandchildren.
Run spindles, run, drawing out the thread.'

It was long ago
that the Fates sang their inspired song,
foretelling joy for Peleus.
For they used to visit the chaste homes
of heroes, show their faces at mortal nuptials,
before men scorned to think of the gods.

Jupiter, seated in his gleaming temple
on his feast days, would often watch
a hundred oxen toppled in his honour.
Dionysus would lead his wild-haired,
shrieking gang from Parnassus' summit,
and Delphians, all of them, would rush from the city,
happily receiving the god, altars smoking.
Often Mars, or Minerva, or Diana
would appear in death-bringing battle,
urging on battalions of men.

But then,
Earth was soaked in evil and crime,
people chased justice from their greedy minds.
Brothers drenched their hands in their brothers' gore;
children, when their parents died, forgot to mourn.
Fathers prayed that sons in their prime might die,
so they could take their own sons' brides as wives.
Mothers indulged their incestuous desires,
daring to desecrate the household shrines.
Right and wrong tumbled in grotesque disarray,
and the angry gods turned their faces away.

And so the gods no longer deign to come among us,
nor let themselves be touched
by our clear light,
our eyes.

ENDNOTES

1 See Burgin, p.86.
2 My thanks to Lucy Worsley, chief curator of the Historic Royal Palaces, for allowing me to read her unpublished paper on the maze.
3 Defoe, Vol. 1, p.255.
4 *Iliad* 18 599–604 (Robert Fagles' translation for Penguin Classics, 18 700–5).
5 Tom Holland's translation for Penguin Classics, 2, 148ff.
6 Flinders Petrie, p.91.
7 *Natural History* 36 13 19 84 (D. E. Eichholz's translation).
8 For example, Mario Tomelli in Shapiro et al., p.89; ibid., Lezzi-Hafter, p.6 of plates section.
9 Translation: Stanley Lombardo.
10 Myles, p.151.
11 A point made to me by Tim Whitmarsh.
12 Robert Fowler alerted me both to Acusilaus/Akousilaos, and to the truth claims in *Gilgamesh*. See his *Early Greek Mythography*, Vol. 2, p.623.
13 *Odyssey* 13 296–9 (Robert Fagles' translation for Penguin Classics, 13 335–9).
14 Macaulay, p.112.
15 Pashley, p.209.
16 Evans, *The Palace of Minos*, Vol. 1 (1921), p.24.
17 See MacGillivray, p.180.
18 Evans, *Time and Chance*, p.350.
19 Evans, *The Palace of Minos*, Vol. 3, p.145ff. See also Evans, 'The Ring of Nestor'. Gere subjects Evans's interpretation of the ring to a detailed analysis, p.133ff.

20 Gere, p.130.
21 An intriguing possibility floated by Mary Beard in her 2009 review, in the *New York Review of Books*, of Gere's *Knossos and the Prophets of Modernism.*
22 Evans, *The Palace of Minos*, Vol. 3, p.440.
23 Gere, p.129.
24 See Sherratt.
25 Lapatin, *Mysteries of the Snake Goddess*, p.136.
26 In his travel book, *Labels.*
27 Evans, *The Palace of Minos*, Vol. 3, p.49.
28 Ibid., Vol. 4.2, p.385.
29 Quoted in Momigliano, p.37.
30 Evans, *The Palace of Minos*, Vol. 3, p.61.
31 Momigliano, p.39.
32 Macaulay, p.111.
33 Ibid.
34 Quoted in Hood.
35 Viereck, p.36. George Viereck was a German-American, an enthusiastic supporter of Adolf Hitler.
36 In Bourgeois.
37 Translation: David McLintock.
38 Freud, *Civilisation and its Discontents*, pp.7–9.
39 Translation: Alice Sedgwick Wohl.
40 Doob, pp.123–4.
41 *Room 237* (2012), directed by Rodney Ascher.
42 In his *Paris Review* interview: The Art of Fiction no. 39, the *Paris Review* issue 40, winter–spring 1967.
43 A point made by Barkan, p.19.
44 *Aeneid* 5 588–93 (Robert Fagles' translation 5 647–50).
45 As Schief and Svenbro point out in *The Craft of Zeus*, p.45.
46 See Kern, p.141.
47 In Solnit.
48 *Maps: Their History, Characteristics and Uses* (1921).
49 Tolman.
50 *The Life Scientific*, BBC Radio 4, 10 March 2015.
51 O'Keefe and Nadel, p.6.
52 Ibid., p.78.

53 Benjamin, p.352.
54 Kern, p.119.
55 Kern has various examples, p.130 ff.
56 Tracked by Barkan, p.10 ff.
57 Smithson, p.143.
58 Published in 1929 as a frontispiece to *Tales Told of Shem and Shaun*, a volume of work-in-progress for *Finnegans Wake.*
59 Quoted in Bourgeois, p.50.
60 However, in *The Vexations of Art*, Svetlana Alpers has written rather about *The Spinners'* relationship with another masterpiece, Titian's *Diana and Callisto.*
61 This crushing detail is noted by Julian Barnes in *Flaubert's Parrot*, p.188.
62 'At Stoke', Tomlinson, p.243.
63 'The Marl Pits': ibid., p.248.
64 'An Autobiographical Essay', in Borges, *The Aleph and Other Stories.*
65 Wallinger, p.20.
66 Allan C. Baker, in his book *The Potteries Loop Line.*
67 In her prologue to Hardingham's *Cedric Price Works 1952–2003.*
68 Hardingham and Rattenbury's *Supercrit #1* contains Mullin's memories and many other reactions and responses to the project.
69 'At Stoke', Tomlinson, p.243.
70 Translation: Robert Kirkpatrick.
71 Bachelard, p.203.
72 Burgin, p.16.
73 See Philip Hardie's commentary on *Aeneid* 9, and Don Fowler's essay 'Epic in the Middle of the Wood', in Sharrock and Morales. They both have much to say about woods, shadows and labyrinthine moves in Virgil. Doob importantly reads the *Aeneid* as a labyrinthine text.
74 *Aeneid* 9 381–5 (Robert Fagles' translation 9 441–6)
75 *Aeneid* 6 126–9 (Robert Fagles' translation 6 149–52)
76 Doob, pp.97–100.
77 *Aeneid* 6 268–72 (Robert Fagles' translation 6 307–11).
78 Colonna, p.13.
79 Ibid., p.15.

80 See P. Hardie, 'Spenser's Vergil: the Faerie Queene and the Aeneid', in Farrell and Putnam.
81 *The Faerie Queene*, Book 1, Canto 1, ix.
82 Lewis, p.99.
83 D. Fowler, 'Epic in the Middle of the Wood', in Sharrock and Morales.
84 Douglas, pp.134–5.
85 See P. Hardie, 'Closure in Latin Epic', in Roberts, Dunn and Fowler.
86 Colonna, p.73.
87 Quoted in Dor de la Souchère, p.54.

Bibliography

Alpers, S., *The Vexations of Art: Velázquez and Others*, New Haven and London, 2005

Armstrong, R. H., *A Compulsion for Antiquity: Freud and the Ancient World*, Ithaca, 2005

Bachelard, G., *The Poetics of Space,* trans. M. Jolas, Boston, 1994

Baker, A. C., *The Potteries Loop Line*, Burton-upon-Trent, 1986

Barkan, L., *Unearthing the Past: Archaeology and Aesthetics in the Making of Renaissance Culture*, Yale, 1999

Barnes, J., *Flaubert's Parrot*, London, 2009

Bartsch, S., '*Ars* and the Man: The Politics of Man in Virgil's *Aeneid*', *Classical Philology*, Vol. 93, no. 4 (Oct. 1998)

Beaton, R., 'Minoans in Modern Greek Literature', in Y. Hamilakis and N. Momigliano (eds), *Archaeology and European Modernity: Producing and Consuming the Minoans*, *Creta Antica*, Vol. 7 (2006)

Benjamin, W., *Selected Writings*, Vol. 3, 1935–1938, Cambridge and London, 2002

Bergstein, M., 'Moses of Michelangelo: Vasari, Photography and Art Historical Practice', *The Art Bulletin*, Vol. 88, no. 1 (2006), pp.158–76

Borges, J. L., *Labyrinths*, Harmondsworth, 1970

Borges, J. L., *The Aleph and Other Stories 1933–1969*, 2nd edn, Harmondsworth, 1973

Borges, J. L., *Collected Fictions*, Harmondsworth, 1998

Borges, J. L., *Selected Poems*, Harmondsworth, 2000

Borges, J. L., *The Total Library. Non-Fiction 1922–1986*, London, 2001

Bourgeois, L., *Louise Bourgeois*, London, 2000

Brown, A. (ed.), with K. Bennett, *Arthur Evans's Travels in Crete 1894–99*, Oxford, 2001

Brown, J., *Collected Writings on Velázquez*, Madrid, 2008

Burgin, R. (ed.), *Jorge Luis Borges: Conversations*, Jackson, 1998

Carr, D. W., with X. Bray, J. H. Elliott, L. Keith and J. Portús, *Velázquez*, London, 2006

Catterson, L., 'Michelangelo's Laocoön?', *Artibus et Historiae*, 52 (2005)

de Chirico, G., *The Memoirs of Giorgio de Chirico*, trans. M. Crosland, New York, 1994

Colonna, F., *Hypnerotomachia Poliphili: The Strife of Love in a Dream*, ed. and trans. J. Godwin, London, 1999

Defoe, D., *A Tour Thro' the Whole Island of Great Britain*, 6th edn, 1762

Doob, P. R., *The Idea of the Labyrinth: from Classical Antiquity Through the Middle Ages*, Ithaca, 1990

Dor de la Souchère, R., *Picasso in Antibes*, London, 1960

Douglas, M., *Thinking in Circles*, Yale, 2007

Evans, A. J., *The Palace of Minos: A Comparative Account of the Successive State of Cretan Civilization as Illustrated by the Discoveries at Knossos*, 4 vols, London, 1921–36, with an index by J. Evans

Evans, A. J., 'The Ring of Nestor: A Glimpse into the Minoan After-World and a Sepulchral Treasure of Gold Signet-Rings and Bead-Seals from Thisbê, Boeotia', *Journal of Hellenic Studies*, Vol. 45, part 1 (1925)

Evans, J., *Time and Chance: the Story of Arthur Evans and His Forebears*, London, 1943

Farrell, J., and M. C. J. Putnam (eds), *A Companion to Vergil's Aeneid and its Tradition*, Oxford, 2010

Felman, S., 'Turning the Screw of Interpretation', *Yale French Studies*, no. 55/56 (1977), *Literature and Psychoanalysis. The Question of Reading: Otherwise*

Flinders Petrie, W. M., *Ten Years' Digging in Egypt, 1881–1891*, London, 1892

Flinders Petrie, W. M., G. A. Wainright and E. Mackay, *The Labyrinth, Gerzeh and Mazguneh*, London, 1912

Fordham, H. G., *Maps: Their History, Characteristics and Uses*, Cambridge, 1921

Fowler, R., *Early Greek Mythography*, 2 vols, Oxford, 2001-13

Freud, S., 'Moses of Michelangelo', in J. Strachey (ed. and trans.) with A. Freud, A. Strachey and A. Tyson, *The Standard Edition of the Complete Psychological Works of Sigmund Freud*, Vol. 13 (1913–14), *Totem and Taboo and Other Works*, London, 1955

Freud, S., *Civilisation and its Discontents*, trans. D. McLintock, London, 2002

Gamerro, C., 'The Aleph and the Labyrinth', *Brazilian Journal of Irish Studies*, no. 11 (2009)

Georgievska Shine, A., and L. Silver, *Rubens, Velázquez and the King of Spain*, Farnham, 2014

Gere, C., *Knossos and the Prophets of Modernism*, Chicago, 2009

Ginzburg, C., 'Morelli, Freud, and Sherlock Holmes: Clues and Scientific Method', in U. Eco and T. Sebeok (eds), *The Sign of Three*, Bloomington, 1983

Griffin, N. E., 'The Greek Dictys', *The American Journal of Philology*, Vol. 29, no. 3 (1908)

Hadis, M., *Literatos y excéntricos: los ancestros ingleses de Jorge Luis Borges*, Buenos Aires, 2006

Hamilakos, Y., 'The Colonial, the National and the Local: Legacies of the "Minoan" Past', in Y. Hamilakis and N. Momigliano (eds), *Archaeology and European Modernity: Producing and Consuming the Minoans*, *Creta Antica*, Vol. 7 (2006)

Hardingham, S., *Cedric Price: Opera*, Chichester, 2003

Hardingham, S., and K. Rattenbury (eds), *Supercrit #1: Cedric Price: POTTERIES THINKBELT*, Abingdon, 2007

Hardingham, S. (ed.), *Cedric Price Works 1952–2003: A Forward-minded Retrospective*, London, 2017

H. D., *Tribute to Freud*, New York, 1956

Hood, S., 'Collingwood on the Minoan Civilisation of Crete', in D. Boucher and B. Haddock (eds), *Collingwood Studies*, Vol. 2, *Perspectives*, Swansea, 1995

Jaffé, D. (ed.), *Titian*, London, 2003

Kallendorf, C., *In Praise of Aeneas: Virgil and Epideictic Rhetoric in the Early Italian Renaissance*, Hanover, 1989

Kern, H., *Labirinti. Forme e interpretazioni, 5000 anni di presenza di un archetipo. Manuale e filo conduttore*, Milan, 1981

Lapatin, K., *Mysteries of the Snake Goddess: Art, Desire and the Forging of History*, Boston, 2002

Lapatin, K., 'Forging the Minoan Past', in Y. Hamilakis and N. Momigliano (eds), *Archaeology and European Modernity: Producing and Consuming the Minoans, Creta Antica*, Vol. 7 (2006)

Lessing, G. E., *An Essay on the Limits of Painting and Poetry*, trans. E. A. McCormick, Baltimore, 1984

Lewis, C. S., *The Discarded Image*, Cambridge, 1971

Litinas, N., 'Looking for the Labyrinthos: Exploring the Maze of Evidence', in M. Andreadaki-Vlazaki and E. Papadopoulou (eds), Proceedings of the 10th International Cretological Congress (Chania, October 1–8, 2006)

Lombardo, S., and D. Raynor (trans.), *Callimachus: Hymns, Epigrams, Select Fragments*, Baltimore, 1988

Lyons, M. C. (trans.), *The Arabian Nights: Tales of 1001 Nights*, Vol. 1, 2nd edn, London, 2010

Macaulay, Rose, *Pleasure of Ruins*, London, 1953

MacGillivray, J. A., *Minotaur: Sir Arthur Evans and the Archaeology of the Minoan Myth*, London, 2000

Mathews, S., *From Agit-Prop to Free Space: the Architecture of Cedric Price*, London, 2007

Matthews, W. H., *Mazes and Labyrinths: Their History and Development*, London, 1922

Momigliano, N., 'Modern dance and the seduction of Minoan Crete', in S. Knippschild and M. G. Morcillo, *Seduction & Power: Antiquity in the Visual and Performing Arts*, London, 2013

Morelli, G. (I. Lermolieff), *Italian Painters: Critical Studies of their Works. The Borghese and Doria Pamfili Galleries in Rome*, trans. C. J. Ffoulkes, London, 1892

Myles, E., 'Long and Social', in M. Burger, R. Glück, C. Roy and G. Scott (eds), *Biting the Error: Writers Explore Narrative*, Toronto, 2000

O'Keefe, J., and L. Nadel, *The Hippocampus as a Cognitive Map*, Oxford, 1978

Orvieto, P., *Labirinti Castelli Giardini: Luoghi Letterarari di Orrore e Smarrimento*, Rome, 2004

Padel, R., 'Labyrinth of Desire: Cretan Myth in Us', in *Arion: A Journal of Humanities and the Classics*, 3rd series, Vol. 4, no. 2 (1996)

Palomino, A., *Lives of the Eminent Spanish Painters and Sculptors*, trans. N. A. Mallory, Cambridge, 1987

Pashley, R., *Travels in Crete*, Vol. 1, Cambridge, 1837

Phillips, A., *Houdini's Box*, London, 2001

Portús Pérez, J., 'Las Hilanderas como fábula artística', *Boletín del Museo del Prado*, Vol. 23 (2005)

Powell, D., *The Villa Ariadne*, London, 1973

Price, C., *Works II* (Architectural Association), London, 1984

Price, C., and H. U. Obrist (ed.), with contributions by A. Isozaki et al., *Re: CP*, Basel, 2003

Roberts, D. H., F. M. Dunn and D. Fowler (eds), *Classical Closure, Reading the End in Greek and Latin Literature*, Princeton, 1997

Roessel, D., 'Happy Little Extroverts and Bloodthirsty Tyrants: Minoans and Myceneans in Y. Hamilakis and N. Momigliano (eds), *Archaeology and European Modernity: Producing and Consuming the Minoans, Creta Antica*, Vol. 7 (2006)

Sarlo, B., *Jorge Luis Borges: A Writer on the Edge*, 2nd edn, London, 2006

Schief, J., and J. Svenbro, *The Craft of Zeus*

Settis, S., *Laocoonte, Fama e Stile*, Rome, 1999

Shapiro, H. A., Mario Iozzo and Adrienne Lezzi-Hafter, *The François Vase: New Perspectives*, Kilchberg, 2013

Sharrock, A., and H. Morales (eds), *Intratextuality: Greek and Roman Textual Relations*, Oxford, 2000

Shaw, C., *Julius II: The Warrior Pope*, Oxford, 1993

Sherratt, S., *Arthur Evans, Knossos and the Priest-King*, Oxford, 2000

Smithson, R., *Collected Writings*, New York, 1979

Solnit, R., *The Faraway Nearby*, London, 2013

Taylor, M. R., *Giorgio de Chirico and the Myth of Ariadne*, London, 2002

Tolman, E. C., 'Cognitive Maps in Rats and Men', *Psychological Review*, Vol. 55.4, 1948

Tomei, M. A., 'Nota sui Giardini Antichi del Palatino', *MEFRA*, Vol. 104.2 (1992)

Tomlinson, C., *New Collected Poems*, Manchester, 2009

Vasari, G., *The Lives of the Painters, Sculptors and Architects*, trans. A. B. Hinds, Vol. 4, London, 1966

Viereck, G. S., *Glimpses of the Great*, London, 1930

Villedieu, F., *Il Giardino dei Cesari*, Rome, 2001

Wallinger, M., *Labyrinth: A Journey Through London's Underground*, London, 2014

Webster, T. B. L., 'The Myth of Ariadne from Homer to Catullus', *Greece and Rome* 13, 1966

Ziolkowski, T., *Minos and the Moderns: Cretan Myth in Twentieth-century Literature and Art*, Oxford, 2008

Illustrations

Plate section I: Three postcards from Greece (© Sophie Hay); Cup-bearer Fresco (© Ashmolean Museum, University of Oxford); The Ring of Nestor (© Ashmolean Museum University of Oxford / Bridgeman Images) • Snake goddess (Heraklion Archaeological Museum / Tarker / Bridgeman Images); Our Lady of the Sports (with permission of the Royal Ontario Museum © ROM); Moses, Michelangelo (Granger / Bridgeman Images) • Chartres Labyrinth (Sonia Halliday Photographs / Bridgeman Images) • *Laocoön* (Musei e Gallerie Pontificie, Musei Vaticani, Vatican City / Bridgeman Images); *Mappa mundi* (detail), (The Dean and Chapter of Hereford Cathedral and the Hereford Mappa Mundi Trust) • *The Dying Slave*, Michelangelo (Jörg Bittner Unna); *The Rebellious Slave*, Michelangelo (Louvre, Paris, France / Mondadori Portfolio/Electa/Sergio Anelli / Bridgeman Images); *Bacchus and Ariadne* (detail), Titian (National Gallery, London, UK / Bridgeman Images) • Cretto di Burri, Alberto Burri (Gabriel Valentini); *Laocoön* (Musei e Gallerie Pontificie, Musei Vaticani, Vatican City / Alinari / Bridgeman Images) • *Spiral Jetty*, Robert Smithson (© George Steinmetz); *Portrait of James Joyce*, Constantin Brâncuşi (Christie's Images / Bridgeman Images © Succession Brâncuşi. All rights reserved. ADAGP, Paris and DACS, London 2017); The anatomy of the inner ear (Wellcome Collection) • Ariadne (Musei e Gallerie Pontificie, Musei Vaticani, Vatican City / © Sophie Hay); *Sleeping Venus*, Giorgione/Titian (© Staatliche Kunstsammlungen Dresden / Bridgeman Images)

Plate section II: *The Gardens of the Villa Medici in Rome*, Velázquez (Museo Nacional del Prado Madrid / Bridgeman Images); *Melanconia*, Giorgio de Chirico (© DACS 2017); *Sleeping Pilgrim*, Markéta Luskačová (Arts Council Collection, Southbank Centre, London © Markéta Luskačová) • *Las Meninas*, Velázquez (Museo Nacional del Prado Madrid / Bridgeman Images); *The Spinners*, Velázquez (Museo Nacional del Prado Madrid / Bridgeman Images) • *The Rape of Europa*, Titian (Isabella Stewart Gardner Museum, Boston, MA, USA / Bridgeman Images); *Pallas and Arachne*, Rubens (Virginia Museum of Fine Arts, Adolph D. and Wilkins C. Williams Fund) • *Diana and Actaeon*, Titian (© The National Gallery, London); *Daedalus and the Minotaur*, Rubens (A Coruña Museum of Fine Arts © Ministerio de la Cultura) • *The Hunt in the Forest*, Uccello (© Ashmolean Museum, University of Oxford); *Minotaur, a Cup in the Hand, and Young Woman*, Picasso (Private Collection / Photo © Christie's Images / Bridgeman Images) • *Pardo Venus*, Titian (Louvre, Paris, France / Bridgeman Images); *Déjeuner sur l'herbe*, Manet (Musée d'Orsay, Paris, France / Bridgeman Images) • *Minotauromachie*, Picasso (Ashmolean Museum, University of Oxford, UK / Bridgeman Images); Picasso wearing a bull's head, Edward Quinn (© edwardquinn.com); Detail from an Attic black-figure amphora (Louvre, Paris, France) • *Bacchus and Ariadne*, Titian (National Gallery, London, UK / Bridgeman Images)

ACKNOWLEDGEMENTS

To the wonderful Jonathan Cape team: Dan Franklin, Bea Hemming, Michal Shavit, Clare Bullock, Suzanne Dean, Jane Selley.

To Peter Ward for the hardback book design.

To my agent Peter Straus.

To Katharine Viner, Jan Thompson, Jonathan Shainin, Jonathan Freedland and Randeep Ramesh at the *Guardian* for kindly making it possible for me to write this book.

To those who provided help, inspiration (sometimes unwittingly) or labyrinthine chat: Richard Baker, Nick Barley, Phyllida Barlow, Andy Beckett, Peter Benson Miller, Kate Bland, Fiona Bradley, Xan Brooks, James Davidson, Kyle deCamp, Susanna Eastburn, Adrian Fisher, Marie Fisher, Carlos Gamerro, Barbara Graziosi, Kai Green, La'shae Green, Laura Hassan, Alice Hewitt, Daisy Hewitt, Rupert Higgins, Stuart Kelly, Dan Kidner, Dawn Lawrence, Mark Leckey, Gareth Llŷr Evans, Alice Macfarlane, Richard Nelsson, Natalie Nougarède, Costas Panayotakis, Alberto Perez Cedillo, Elizabeth Price, Alison Roberts, Paul Roberts and colleagues at the Ashmolean, Anne Ryan, Joshua St Johnston, Charlotte Schepke, Clare Stevens and colleagues at Hereford Cathedral, Cynthia Smart, Hugo

Spiers, Rosie Toop, Michelle Ussher, Margot Waddell, Mark Wallinger.

To Sophie Hay for her beautiful photographs. To Sophie Harris for her skilful labyrinth illustrations.

To the staff, artists and scholars of the British School at Rome, February 2016; and of the American Academy in Rome, February 2017.

To the staff of the Rare Books & Music reading room at the British Library.

To Jon Day, Keith Miller and Tim Whitmarsh, who offered such perceptive comments on an early draft of the book; and to Barbara Marsh, who gave a poet's advice on the translation of *Peliaco quondam.* Imperfections and errors, of course, are my own.

It is impossible to imagine this book existing without the wisdom, encouragement and kindness of Matthew Fox.

Index